John Addington Symonds
Culture and the Demon Desire

Also by John Pemble

THE INVASION OF NEPAL
MISS FANE IN INDIA
THE RAJ AND THE KINGDOM OF OUDH
THE MEDITERRANEAN PASSION
VENICE REDISCOVERED

John Addington Symonds

Culture and the Demon Desire

Edited by
John Pemble

First published in Great Britain 2000 by
MACMILLAN PRESS LTD
Houndmills, Basingstoke, Hampshire RG21 6XS and London
Companies and representatives throughout the world

A catalogue record for this book is available from the British Library.

ISBN 0–333–77131–1

First published in the United States of America 2000 by
ST. MARTIN'S PRESS, INC.,
Scholarly and Reference Division,
175 Fifth Avenue, New York, N.Y. 10010

ISBN 0–312–22836–8

Library of Congress Cataloging-in-Publication Data
John Addington Symonds : culture and the demon desire / edited by John
Pemble.
p. cm.
Includes bibliographical references and index.
ISBN 0–312–22836–8 (cloth)
1. Symonds, John Addington, 1840–1893—Criticism and
interpretation. 2. Homosexuality and literature—England–
–History—19th century. I. Pemble, John.
PR5523.J65 1999
828'.809—dc21   99–42755
                                                        CIP

Selection, editorial matter and Chapter 1 © John Pemble 2000
Chapters 2–10 and Appendix © Macmillan Press Ltd 2000

This book is printed on paper suitable for recycling and made from fully managed and sustained
forest sources.

10 9 8 7 6 5 4 3 2 1
09 08 07 06 05 04 03 02 01 00

Printed and bound in Great Britain by
Antony Rowe Ltd, Chippenham, Wiltshire

Contents

List of Plates

Editor's Preface

Symonds's readers were born in the middle decades of the nineteenth century. Their loyalty kept his reputation alive and most of his books in print until the 1930s; but his prestige faded as they aged and died off. To the post-1870 generations he was a superseded *littérateur*; and some even of his admirers outgrew their initial enthusiasm. Edith Wharton (who was born in 1862) recalled Symonds and Pater as the authors of period-pieces on art that had gone out of date in the late 1890s. 'With the publication of Berenson's first volumes on Italian painting,' she wrote in her memoirs, 'lovers of Italy learned that aesthetic sensibility may be combined with the sternest scientific accuracy, and I began to feel almost guilty for having read Pater and even Symonds with such zest.' In Bloomsbury and modernist circles Symonds was remembered as a pathetic, pre-Freudian casualty from the homosexual penumbra. He had never fully established himself as a poet; now he forfeited his claim to be taken seriously either as a critic or as a historian. 'I feel Symonds too much of an amateur in art,' said Roger Fry. 'I like his history better; but then I'm only an amateur in history.' What he had published was no longer interesting, and what made him interesting remained unpublishable. So between the wars no-one wrote about him – no-one, that is, except his dedicated and impecunious friend and literary executor Horatio Brown, and his well-intentioned but anxious daughters Margaret Vaughan and Katherine Furse. And what they wrote was predictably evasive. Brown was obediently reticent on all matters of sex. Margaret fictionalized her father as an emasculated Platonist. Katherine depicted a student whose interests and problems with regard to sex were purely scientific.

In 1954, two years after Katherine Furse died, John Hale published *England and the Italian Renaissance*. This contained the first substantial discussion of Symonds in almost half a century. It also contained the first direct reference to 'the homosexual element in [his] nature'. However, the essay did little to extricate Symonds from Victorian discretion and post-Victorian disfavour. Hale read Symonds's work essentially as an index to his psychology, and suggested that it was an outlet for suppressed illicit longing. He suggested, in other words, that Symonds had not been a practising homosexual. And his verdict on the *oeuvre* was negative. He argued that latent homosexuality had impoverished rather than

enriched Symonds's vision and critical faculties, since it had subordinated his judgement to his feelings.

Shortly before the Second World War, Virginia Woolf had urged
Katherine Furse to 'let the cat out of the bag'. When the initiative was
finally taken, there was a new, transatlantic way of putting it. Cats no
longer came out of bags – gays came out of closets; and Symonds was
among the first rediscoveries of alternative America. He was a notable
recruit to its pantheon, because his kudos had in the United States
remained more or less intact. Van Wyck Brooks, in a critical study published in New York in 1914, had sanitized his image by dismissing
'certain crass misunderstandings' connected with his name; and the
academic community had continued to value his contribution to the
historiography of the Renaissance. From the 1910s until the 1950s
Symonds was to American students a venerated scholar who had
forsworn the flesh for the higher realms of learning. He figured, for
example, in Wallace K. Fergusson's *The Renaissance in Historical Thought*
(1948) as 'a frustrated and disease-ridden man of letters who had spent
most of his life in books'. The change of perception that came with the
reversals and re-evaluations of the 1960s was therefore dramatic. Reticence, not veracity, was now taboo, and Symonds was refloated by dis-
closures that twenty years before would have sunk him. In 1964 Phyllis
Grosskurth, a young Canadian scholar, published a Freudian biography
based on unpublished letters and the hitherto inaccessible memoirs.
There followed three substantial volumes of correspondence, edited
from Detroit by Herbert Schueller and Robert Peters; and then in 1984
the memoirs themselves finally appeared. The measure of distortion in
earlier accounts of Symonds was now made fully apparent. The man the
world had known as a neurasthenic aesthete, burning his incense at
the shrine of Beauty and confining his passions to literature, had in
fact been an active homosexual and a homosexual activist: part of a
Victorian subculture and a pioneer in the campaign for homosexual
emancipation. The uncensored record of his life – unique in the docu-
mentation of nineteenth-century sexual psychology – turned out to be
a rich mine of material for the new social and cultural history, focused
on issues such as gender, sexuality, and dissidence.

In the postmodern era Symonds has therefore been taken considerably further than where the post-Victorians left him. The political and
historical significance of his studies of sexual inversion has been analyzed
by Jeffrey Weeks, Wayne Koestenbaum, and others. Peter Allan Dale, in
a long and searching article published in *Clio* in 1988, brought his
Renaissance in Italy into the repertoire of 'metahistory', and revealed its

proto-Freudian discontent with the constraints of modern civilization. Much, however, remains to be said. In a sense, Symonds was rediscovered only to be re-marginalized. His critical writings have remained half buried, while those of Ruskin, Pater, and Wilde have been fully excavated from the Herculaneum of Victorian reputations. Furthermore, there has been no attempt to test the validity of Phyllis Grosskurth's summary verdict on his poetry ('execrable'). Perhaps recent critical interest has been carried clear of him by its radical drift. Despite his sexual dissidence, his notoriety as a pagan and immoralist, and his declared sympathy with the principle of democracy, Symonds resists identification with the transgressive, antinomian subtext that has been decoded from the work of his contemporaries – from the work of Oscar Wilde, especially. Wilde has been rehabilitated as an outsider and a militant, not just because he was a persecuted homosexual, but because he was Irish, and because he teased and destabilized his bourgeois audience. Wilde's work, it has now been suggested, contains postmodern repudiations of self and identity, and postcolonial deconstructions of masculinity. Symonds, on the other hand, adopted liberal, evangelizing methods. His strategy was not subversion, but conversion – and this can look like complicity in the light of Foucauldian theories about homosexuality as a 'construction' that legitimizes the power of medico-legal authority to 'cure', to punish, and to silence. Furthermore, he was a wealthy man who spent much of his life abroad – which means that he appears, *prima facie*, to belong with those privileged sexual tourists who spared the establishment embarrassment by exporting their homosexuality, by opting out instead of coming out. The contrast with Wilde, again, looks damning. Wilde confronted the establishment by choosing *not* to go abroad in the critical moment before his arrest.

Whatever the reason or reasons, there has been a tendency to overlook or underestimate the range and significance of Symonds's work, the sadness of his circumstances, and the depth of his commitment to the cause of reform. The essays that follow suggest that he was more the victim than the accomplice of a society that stigmatized and gagged its sexual heretics. But they suggest too that there was more to his private suffering than legal prohibitions and a Protestant conscience – just as there was more in his published work than the morbid responses of sexual repression. The knowledge that he suffered from a dangerous and infectious disease enhanced the guilt that attached to his homoerotic relationships; yet his homoerotic instincts enhanced the versatility of his vision, and enabled him to make fresh use of the humanistic, iconographic tradition in aesthetics. Symonds fully appreciated the hermeneutical value of myth and symbol, literature and history – especially the history of ideas.

It was this aspect of his writing that made it seem old-fashioned to Bloomsbury critics like Roger Fry and Clive Bell. For them the redeeming feature of his criticism was its formalistic component. Symonds's willingness to predicate 'pure art', and his discovery that the content of a picture could be recessive under certain conditions of colour, line, and mass, anticipated both Berenson's theories and their own. No doubt it was Symonds's acute sensitivity to what Fry called 'the expressive elements of design' that prompted Fry to admit – somewhat grudgingly – that Symonds's books had the root of the matter in them. Panofsky and his followers then made Berenson and Bloomsbury look old-fashioned, and revived interest in the 'Victorianism' of the Victorians. Bell's and Berenson's talk of 'significant form' and 'tactile values' has therefore dated. But Symonds's formalistic concerns, which like those of Ruskin and Pater were part of a more broadly holistic aesthetics, have remained in tune with contemporary approaches to art. They serve, what is more, as an important reminder that the Victorians were never exclusively preoccupied with the descriptive and ethical aspects of painting and sculpture. In fact, taken together, Ruskin, Pater, and Symonds – the three chief arbiters of Victorian taste – reinforce the suspicion that 'Victorianism' is itself a construction, contrived in order to make room for the living in critical territory pre-empted by the dead. *Tout est dit, et l'on vient trop tard.*

In their original form these essays were papers delivered at a symposium convened by the Department of the History of Art and the Department of Historical Studies, University of Bristol, in the spring of 1998. The supremely appropriate setting was Clifton Hill House, once Symonds's home and now a University hall of residence and conference centre. The organizing committee consisted of Michael Liversidge (dean of the Faculty of Arts and chairman), Annie Burnside (warden of Clifton Hill House), Joan Pickering, Ian Venables, and myself. Financial support came from the Alumni Foundation of the University of Bristol and from public funds administered by the British Academy. A generous donation from Andrew Milner made possible a recital of Ian Venables' song cycle of settings of poems by Symonds.

I extend warm thanks to my colleagues on the committee for advice, help, and encouragement received both while engaged on my own paper and while preparing the collection for publication, and to Michael Richardson of the Special Collections, University of Bristol, and Wim de Wit, of the Research Library at the Getty Research Institute, for ready co-operation in organizing the illustrations. I am grateful, too, to the Arts Faculty Research Fund of the University of Bristol for making provision for editorial assistance, and to Anne Merriman for expert secretarial support. Like everyone else involved with the symposium, I owe a special debt to Annie Burnside. It was her idea, and her dedication, determination, and hospitality were an inspiration.

Bristol, March 1999   *J. P.*

Note: In the reference notes at the end of each chapter, place of publication has been omitted where this is London.
The editor is responsible for translations that appear in footnotes.

Notes on Contributors

Stephen Bann is professor of modern cultural studies at the University of Kent. He has published *The Clothing of Clio* (1984), *Under the Sign* (1994), and *Paul Delaroche: History Painted* (1997). His essays have been collected in *The Inventions of History* (1990) and *Romanticism and the Rise of History* (1995).

Howard J. Booth teaches English at the University of Kent. He has published a number of articles on nineteenth- and twentieth-century literature, and is the co-editor of a special issue of the *D. H. Lawrence Review* ('Lawrence and the Psychoanalytic', 1998) and of *Modernism and Empire* (1999).

Whitney Davis is John Evans Professor of Art History at Northwestern University. His recent publications include *Drawing the Dream of the Wolves: Homosexuality, Interpretation, and Freud's 'Wolf Man'* (1995) and *Replications: Archaeology, Art History, Psychoanalysis* (1996).

Phyllis Grosskurth is emeritus professor of English at the University of Toronto. She has published biographies of John Addington Symonds (1964), Havelock Ellis (1980), Melanie Klein (1986), Margaret Mead (1988), and Lord Byron (1997), as well as a study of Freud's inner circle and the politics of psychoanalysis (*The Secret Ring*, 1992).

Peter J. Holliday is professor of the history of art and classical civilization at California State University, Long Beach. He edited and contributed to *Narrative and Event in Ancient Art* (1993), and has published articles in *The American Journal of Archaeology*, the *Art Bulletin*, and other journals.

Jonathan Kemp is a doctoral student at the University of Greenwich, researching into the genealogy of sexuality. He is also a playwright, and co-manager of the Planet Martha Theatre Company.

Rosella Mamoli Zorzi is professor of Anglo-American literature at the University of Venice, Ca' Foscari. Her publications include *Robert Browning a Venezia* (1989), and two editions of the Venetian letters of Henry

James – *Lettere a Miss Allen* (1993) and *Letters from the Palazzo Barbaro* (1998).

John Pemble is reader in history at the University of Bristol. His books include *The Mediterranean Passion: Victorians and Edwardians in the South* (1988) and *Venice Rediscovered* (1995).

Alex Potts is professor of the history of art at the University of Reading. He is the author of numerous articles on the visual arts and aesthetic theory in the eighteenth and nineteenth centuries, and of *Flesh and the Ideal: Winckelmann and the Origins of Art History* (1994).

Bart Schultz teaches in the Social Sciences Collegiate Division of the University of Chicago. He is the editor of *Essays on Henry Sidgwick* (1992) and of the electronic text *The Complete Works and Select Correspondence of Henry Sidgwick*. He has also contributed to *The Routledge Encyclopedia of Philosophy*, the new supplement to *The Macmillan Encyclopedia of Philosophy*, and the *Dictionnaire d'éthique et de philosophie*.

Ian Venables is a composer whose works have been performed at the Wigmore Hall, the Purcell Room, and the Three Choirs Festivals, by such artists as Ian Partridge, David Briggs, the Chilingirian Quartet and the Duke Quartet. He has set five of Symonds's poems as a song cycle.

Chronology

1834	Marriage of Dr John Addington Symonds and Harriet Sykes.
1840	Birth of John Addington Symonds on 5 October, at 7 Berkeley Square, Clifton, Bristol.
1844	Death of his mother.
1851	The Symonds family moves to Clifton Hill House.
1854–8	At Harrow School.
1858	Matriculates at Oxford (Balliol College).
1860	Newdigate Prize for English Verse.
1862	Graduates with first-class honours in *Literae Humaniores*. Elected to an Open Fellowship at Magdalen College.
1863	Chancellor's Prize for an English essay on 'The Renaissance'. Leaves Oxford following a nervous breakdown. Travels widely on the Continent.
1864	Moves to London to study law. Marries Catherine North.
1865	Birth of his first child, Janet.
1866	Abandons legal career on his father's advice. Travels in Italy and France.
1867	Birth of his second child, Charlotte (later Mrs Walter Leaf). Travels in France and Switzerland. Second breakdown at Cannes. Leaves London and moves into 7 Victoria Square, Clifton, Bristol. Friendship with Henry Sidgwick.
1869	Lectures on Greek literature at Clifton College. Birth of his third child, Margaret (later Mrs William Vaughan). Beginning of friendship with Norman Moor and Horatio Brown.
1870–1	Travel and literary work.
1871	Death of his father, aged 64. Moves with his family into Clifton Hill House. Marriage of his sister Charlotte to T. H. Green.
1872	Publishes *An Introduction to the Study of Dante*.
1873	Publishes *Studies of the Greek Poets, First Series*.
1874	Publishes travel journalism as *Sketches in Italy and Greece*.
1875	Publishes *The Age of the Despots* (first volume of *Renaissance in Italy*). Birth of his fourth child, Katherine (later Mrs Charles Furse).
1876	Publishes *Studies of the Greek Poets, Second Series*. Lectures at the Royal Institution on Florence and the Medici.

1877	Publishes *The Revival of Learning* and *The Fine Arts* (second and third volumes of *Renaissance in Italy*). Fails to be elected to the Professorship of Poetry at Oxford.
1877–8	Passes his first winter at Davos, as guest of the Greens.
1878	Publishes *Many Moods* (verse); *Shelley*; and a translation of the sonnets of Michelangelo.
1879	Publishes *Sketches and Studies in Italy*. Publication of Italian translation of *The Fine Arts*.
1880	Publishes *New and Old* (verse). Moves permanently to Davos.
1881	Publishes *Italian Literature, Part One* and *Italian Literature, Part Two* (fourth and fifth volumes of *Renaissance in Italy*). Begins relationship with Angelo Fusato, a Venetian gondolier.
1882	Publishes *Animi Figura* (verse). The Symonds family moves into Am Hof, their newly built house at Davos.
1883	Publishes *Italian Byways*. Completes and has privately printed *A Problem in Greek Ethics*.
1884	Publishes *Wine, Women, and Song* (verse translations of Goliardic songs); *Vagabunduli Libellus* (verse); and *Shakespeare's Predecessors in the English Drama*.
1886	Publishes *Sir Philip Sidney*; *The Catholic Reaction, Part One*, and *The Catholic Reaction, Part Two* (sixth and seventh volumes of *Renaissance in Italy*); and *Ben Jonson*.
1887	Publishes a translation of the memoirs of Benvenuto Cellini. His daughter Janet dies of consumption.
1889	Begins to write his memoirs.
1890	Publishes a translation of the memoirs of Count Carlo Gozzi, and *Essays Speculative and Suggestive*. Publication of the French translation of *An Introduction to the Study of Dante*.
1891	Writes and privately prints *A Problem in Modern Ethics*.
1892	Publishes (jointly with his daughter Margaret) *Our Life in the Swiss Highlands*. Collaborates with Havelock Ellis on a study of sexual inversion. Publishes *The Life of Michelangelo Buonarroti*.
1893	Publishes *In the Key of Blue and Other Essays*, and *Walt Whitman: A Study*. Publication of A. Pearson's abridgement of *Renaissance in Italy*.
1893	Death of Symonds in Rome, 19 April.
1895	Publication of *John Addington Symonds: A Biography*, by Horatio Brown.
1896	Publication in Leipzig of Symonds's and Ellis's *Das Konträre Geschlechtsgefühl* ('Sexual Inversion').

1897 Suppression by Catherine Symonds and Horatio Brown of the English edition of *Sexual Inversion*. The book was subsequently reissued under Ellis's name alone, but its sale was banned in Britain following a prosecution for obscenity, and publication was transferred to the United States.

1913 Death of Catherine Symonds.

1923 Publication of *The Letters and Papers of John Addington Symonds*, edited by Horatio Brown.

1925 Death of Margaret Symonds (Vaughan).

1926 Destruction of Symonds's diaries and personal papers, following the death of his literary executor, Horatio Brown. The memoirs alone were preserved, with an embargo against publication for 50 years.

1937 Death of Charlotte Symonds (Leaf).

1952 Death of Katherine Symonds (Furse).

1984 Publication of Symonds's *Memoirs*.

1
Art, Disease, and Mountains

John Pemble

Whoever looks for Symonds encounters the language of psychopathology. Even while he was alive, his poetry was being read as a signpost to madness;[1] and after his death there were further suggestions of mental disease. Tributes and reminiscences referred to the 'hysterical', 'neurotic', and 'pathological' aspects of his character. 'Some have wondered,' wrote Arthur Symons, 'whether Symonds was altogether sane'; and he wondered himself when he recalled 'the morbid, disquieting, nervous, contorted, painful expressions of his face: the abnormal, almost terrible fixity of his eyes'. The other Symonds, 'the brilliant talker, the genial companion' remembered by his friend and biographer Horatio Brown, could not obliterate the image of someone who was, in the words of the *Dictionary of National Biography*, 'disabled by physical and spiritual maladies'.[2]

Symonds's sanity was called into question because he was demonstrably degenerate. During most of his life the theory of racial degeneration dominated the aetiology of both physical and mental illness, and Symonds was a classic instance of degeneracy as the condition was professionally and popularly described.

According to one school of medical thought, degeneration was morbid deviation from a human prototype. According to another, it was regression to a primitive stage of human development. The leading deviationists were the French psychiatrists Bénédict Morel and Jean Moreau de Tours. The idea of regression, or psychopathic atavism, was associated chiefly with Cesare Lombroso, an Italian criminal psychologist.[3] Lombroso was especially well known in Britain. His works were translated and popularized; his theories were adopted by Henry Maudsley, the eminent neurologist;[4] and he probably provided the leading idea for Robert Louis Stevenson's famous story *The Strange Case of Dr Jekyll and Mr Hyde* (1886).[5] So the question 'What is degeneration?' led to differing answers; but the question 'Who are the degenerate?' admitted something like consensus. The degenerate included the chronically sick, the sexually aberrant, and the highly gifted. They were, in other words, people like Symonds – who was tubercular, homosexual, and deeply responsive to artistic and literary stimuli. And they were degenerate because their cognates were. Heredity explained the condition, and perpetuated the process whereby succeeding generations became less and less healthy, both mentally and physically. The medical history of Symonds's family was typical. There had been tuberculosis and madness on the maternal side; and of his mother's three children, two were still-born and a third died of acute hydrocephalus.[6]

Symonds suffered from the malady known as 'phthisis' or 'consumption' – terms once applied to any wasting illness, but by mid-Victorian times restricted to pulmonary tuberculosis. This disease is related to leprosy, and like leprosy it causes ulcers which develop into cavities, destroying tissue and blood vessels. As the lung disintegrates, haemorrhages of increasing severity ensue, and the patient finally dies of suffocation. The disease is called tuberculosis because it is characterized by the presence, in the periphery of the lung, of tubercles – nodules of cheesy colour and consistency. In Symonds's day the cure for this affliction was unknown, and it was widely doubted that cure was in fact possible.

Hitherto consumption had always been regarded as a feverish and in-flammatory sickness: as an unhealed ulceration of the lungs, with tubercles understood as a separate and secondary symptom. The treatment had therefore been the traditional 'lowering' therapy, involving phlebotomy (bleeding), purging, and sedation. However, when Symonds was diagnosed as phthisical, medical opinion was changing, and the theory of degen-eration was being applied to this as to other areas of pathology. Many doctors were adopting the view that phthisis was not a specific disease, but a diathesis – that is to say, a general condition of debility, a 'derangement of the nutritive functions'.[7] This diathesis was congenital, and it predisposed the patient to both somatic and psychic disorder. The somatic disorder was the tubercle – now understood as a quasi-malignant tumour which preceded ulceration in the lung. Ulceration, in other words, was now regarded as a secondary feature of phthisis, and treatment was deter-mined not by the inflammation, but by the debility.[8] A fortifying regimen was indicated, involving large doses of cod-liver oil, a dry tonic climate, and a discipline of exercise, abstinence, and wholesome diversion. The psychic disorder was a certain type of insanity – what Henry Maudsley called 'phthisical mania'. Maudsley, among others, noted that tubercu-losis of the lungs was more common among the insane than among the sane, and that the insane often had tubercular offspring. His deduction was that tubercle and insanity were collateral symptoms of degeneration.[9] By recognizing consumption as a degenerative condition, the medical profession was in effect classifying it as incurable. Science knew no such thing as a cure for degeneration in the individual, and degeneration in the race could be reversed only through the long-term effects of eugenics (control and manipulation by the state of human reproduction). The most that the suffering individual could hope for was remission, which was brought about by spontaneous calcification of the ulcers in the lungs. The morbid areas were sealed off by a natural defensive response of the body. However, the tuberculosis was thereby merely contained, not eliminated, and reactivation was possible at any time.[10]

Homosexuality, likewise, featured in the semiotics of degeneration. Medical science classified homosexuality as unnatural, and qualified it as either vicious or morbid.[11] The vicious variety was acquired, through responsible acts of choice. It was therefore punishable as crime when it proved resistant to treatment. Morbid homosexuality was congenital and involuntary. It was therefore neither punishable nor treatable. Rather, it required the compassion – and the constraint – that were reserved for incurable madness. Richard von Krafft-Ebing, the leading Austrian authority on sexual psychopathology, described it as 'a fundamental sign of degeneration and . . . a partial manifestation of a neuropsychopathic state, in most cases hereditary'.[12] It was generally defined as 'moral insanity' – that is to say, insanity involving disordered conduct, but not hallucination or delusion. Lombroso and Maudsley described it in this way because they understood it to be atavistic degeneration – a lapse into primitive behaviour that was classifiable as insanity in the present stage of evolution. 'Good moral feeling,' wrote Maudsley, 'is to be looked upon as an essential part of sound and rightly developed character in the present state of human evolution in civilised lands.'[13] Symonds, whose homosexuality was an open secret, and who acknowledged the congenital nature of his inversion, was therefore diagnosable as incurably insane according to criteria which were widely accepted in medical circles and which had been endorsed by his own father (in a work on criminal responsibility, published in 1869).

And the diagnosis was strengthened by his public role as aesthete, critic, and poet. In the judgement of late nineteenth-century medicine, no-one was more degenerate, and therefore more strongly predisposed to madness, than men and women of art and letters.

Psychiatry identified artistic creativity – literature especially – as something closely associated with mental disease. Moreau de Tours conjectured that genius was essentially a morbid condition akin to insanity[14] – an old idea that was now given new validation and greater extension by the cultural prominence of psychiatry in France. The leading lights of the French literary scene – Musset, Balzac, Baudelaire, Hugo, Flaubert, Saint-Simon, Comte, Zola – were all diagnosed as mad and classified according to the new nosology of degeneration. 'Névropathe' was one of the most common categories employed by French psychiatry in its dealings with art.[15] But not only genius was mad. Creative people in general – those defined as partial geniuses, and those possessing what Moreau called 'an excess of the artistic temperament' – often exhibited mania and delirium. Children of such parents were at high risk of mental disease, because it was among the classes in which eminent minds were most numerous that the incidence of insanity was highest.[16] In Italy, Lombroso invoked the creativity of the mad in order to prove the madness of the creative.[17] He defined genius as 'a true degenerative psychosis belonging to the group of moral insanity', and reduced almost the whole of European art and literature since the Renaissance to an inventory of madness and mental aberration. In *L'Uomo di genio* (1889) he claimed that he had 'found even in the sanest and most complete genius the incomplete and rudimentary forms of mania'; but the concept of sane genius disappeared from his later work,[18] and like the French psychiatrists he extended the circumference of madness to include the merely talented. The world of contemporary literature he perceived as full of 'mattoids' (*mattoidi*), who were gifted, scholarly, and semi-insane. Lombroso's most famous – or notorious – disciple was Max Nordau, whose *Entartung* was first published in Germany in 1892 and then widely translated. Dedicating the work to his Italian master, Nordau proclaimed: 'Degenerates are not always criminals, prostitutes, anarchists, and pronounced lunatics. They are often authors and artists.'[19] And in the present age so often was this the case that the exceptions merely proved the rule. Almost every expression of modern art and the modern mind incurred his feverish denunciation: the Oxford Movement, Pre-Raphaelitism, Wagnerism, the Parnassians, Symbolism, Mysticism, Decadence, Realism, Ibsenism, Nietzsche – the muster of hysteria and degeneracy was endless. Moreover, not only authors and artists, but their audiences too, were classified as psychopathic. Nordau made psychopathology virtually co-terminous with modern culture. His book was a baroque travesty of the theory of degeneration, and few medical professionals were prepared to go so far. But not even the most moderate dissented from the view that the incidence of insanity had increased as the level of civilization had risen.[20]

Symonds's reputation indicated quite clearly that he belonged with these cultural degenerates. Both during his lifetime and after his death he was regarded as one of the chief exponents of aestheticism, paganism, and immoralism. He was ranked with Pater as a rediscoverer and connoisseur of the artistic crime and criminal art of the Renaissance. Oscar Wilde numbered him among the writers who had divorced historiography from morals. The poet Edward Lefroy coupled 'Symonds-Sophistry' with 'Pater-Paganism' as a characteristic feature of pernicious 'Pseudo-Hellenism'; as 'Anglo-Byzantine for the worst passions and most carnal inclinations of humanity'. Henry James portrayed Symonds as an apostle of 'the gospel of art', whose writings expressed a view of life 'profane ... independent, and little likely to be thought edifying'. The French critic Paul Desjardins described him as 'foncièrement païen'. 'Il n'avait pas,' he explained, 'une conscience vive du mal qui cohabite avec nous, du péché.'* William Barry, in his study *Heralds of Revolt* (1904), grouped him with Nietzsche, Swinburne, and Pater as a 'latter-day pagan'. He was often linked with the Decadent movement in literature, which began in Paris in the 1880s and reached London in the early 1890s – and the anecdotal evidence tells us why. That 'Oxford perfume' and those 'strange oppositions and contradictions in his slightly faded and fatigued countenance' which were noticed by Henry James; those disconcerting shifts and jarring ambiguities in his talk, described by Robert Louis Stevenson; that 'portmanteau full of culture' which he was supposed to carry on all his travels; that predilection for late Latin lyrics; that early death from a wasting disease – all contributed to the image of a neo-Byzantine, of an over-refined product of an exhausted civilization.[21] Symonds, it seemed, was quintessentially Decadent, and his Decadence was one more proof of his degenerate, of his psychopathic, condition.

Yet Symonds never proclaimed himself a Decadent, and he never wished to be seen as one. He distanced himself from theorists of Decadence such as Gautier, Bourget, and Remy de Gourmont by rejecting artifice and declaring his allegiance to nature. He was uncomfortable with the slogan 'Art for Art's sake', and with the accretions of 'pedantry, affectation, and aesthetical priggishness' that had accumulated around 'culture'.[22] These were the legacy of Matthew Arnold, hierophant of the intellectual dandies. Symonds signified his aversion by arguing like one of Arnold's Hebraizing Philistines. 'A great and puissant nation,' he asserted, 'does not live by sensibility and knowledge, but by the formation of

---

*He had no vivid consciousness of the evil in us, of sin.

character, by the development of personal energy.'[23] Nor did he have
much time for Pater and Wilde, about whom he was very uncompliment-
ary.[24] His preference was for Walt Whitman and Pierre Loti, writers who
eschewed the arcane and esoteric effects of 'style'. Symonds disowned
'style' and linguistic experimentation. So if, as has been persuasively
argued, Decadence was essentially a matter of language, a strategy
designed to revitalize a written idiom classified by philology as dead[25] –
then no, Symonds was not Decadent. He made no claim to kinship with
the author of the 'poisonous book' that features in *The Picture of Dorian
Gray*. Its 'curious jewelled [prose], full of argot and archaism' was not
the prose he wrote. He once said that he aimed at 'the barest form of language',[26] but it would be more accurate to say that he took the language
as he found it, and wrote loosely, promiscuously, redundantly – 'like,'
said Disraeli, 'a newspaperman, with more vigour than taste'. Henry James,
with justice, complained of his 'repetition and feverish overproduction'.
The American critic Van Wyck Brooks described his work as 'rather the
product of energy than of power'.[27] 'Vigour', 'feverish overproduction',
'energy' – those are not the attributes of Pater and his imitators; and
Pater could hardly have exclaimed of Symonds, as he exclaimed of the
Euphuists in *Marius the Epicurean*: 'What care for style! What patience of
execution! What research for the significant tones of ancient idiom!'

Symonds, in fact, was dismayed by his own legend. He exhibits what
might be called anxious Counter-decadence. In his prolixity he was
trying to write himself free of his Decadent captivity – because he acqui-
esced in the medical thinking that linked literary Decadence with racial
degeneration. His life was overshadowed by insinuations of madness, and
much – perhaps most – of what he wrote was directed to persuading
the world and persuading himself that he was sane. Yet he aimed to
demolish his own myth without subverting the ideas that nurtured it.
The dutiful son of an eminent physician, he assented to the medicalization
of sexuality and art, and he argued within the boundaries of entrenched
assumptions about physical, mental, and moral health. Burdened with
a Protestant conscience, and swayed by current notions of sanity and
madness, he endorsed the verdict of the intellectual establishment
concerning phthisis, homosexuality, and art. He staked his claim to salvation
not on the errors of orthodoxy, but on the Calvinistic concept of an
élite. What he proposed was that *some* phthisis was curable; that *some*
homosexuality was natural; that *some* art was healthy: that there were,
among the tubercular, the sexually inverted, and the creative, companies of the elect – a few exceptions who proved the rule, sealed the fate of
the rest, and preserved intact the fabric of Victorian civilization.[28]

In Symonds's creed, healthy art was art which was 'the expression of man's delight in nature and in his sympathy with human joys and sufferings'. It was art whose cynosure was 'noble pleasure', and which acknowledged 'a special duty' to the moral qualities of truth, goodness, and service. 'Art cannot ignore morality,' he wrote. 'To claim unqualified independence for it would show a radical misconception of its nature.' So, although 'many things [were] beautiful in art which morality condemn[ed] and which [had] no practical utility', art was art in spite of, and not because of, such aberrations.[29] True art inhabited 'spiritual altitudes where the lust of the eye and the longings of the flesh [were] left behind'.[30] This ideal of health and sanity had been realized in the art of ancient Greece. It therefore became the abiding concern of Symonds's career to discover enduring Hellenism. Guided by Hegel, he perceived in Greece a symbiosis of art and religion;[31] and he sifted the legacy of the Italian Renaissance for evidence of an identical achievement in the modern world. Or, rather, he sifted the Renaissance art that he liked – because his aim was not to rehabilitate the Renaissance. It was to rehabilitate himself, by demonstrating the Hellenic pedigree of his own tastes and preferences. This explains why he showed little interest in Raphael, whose *a priori* claim to Hellenism was strong,[32] and directed his search to artists who were much more problematic – Signorelli, Cellini, and Michelangelo, most notably.

It was a futile search, and he recorded its failure in the third volume of *Renaissance in Italy*, published in 1877. He discovered that the artists who appealed to him most deeply merely reflected his own *dipsychia*. Instead of synthesis, in which art and religion enhanced each other, they revealed only 'the double mind of the Renaissance': an unresolved antagonism between Christianity and paganism. The Hegelian dialectic had faltered, leaving modern art stranded between two conflicting ideals, and imperfect by the standards of each. It was neither authentically pagan nor eminently Christian, but a monstrous hybrid – a Hermaphroditus.[33] Renaissance art at best was only impurely Greek. It had been hampered by Christianity, which was hostile to figurative art; yet without Christianity it had been no more than heathen sensuality, a 'soulless animalism' devoid of innocence and thought.[34]

The Renaissance figure who obsessed Symonds was Michelangelo, and it was to Michelangelo that he returned later in life, still in search of the redeeming Hellenic afflatus. But the substantial *Life of Michelangelo*, published in 1892, merely amplified the earlier note of disillusion.

The revisited Michelangelo remained an artist of gigantic stature, 'definite in solitary sublimity, like a supreme mountain seen from a vast distance, soaring over shadowy hills and misty plains into the clear ether of immortal fame'.[35] Moreover, he was a Platonist, nurtured on *Phaedrus* and on the *Symposium*, and matching the exalted Platonic ideal both in his life and in his art. These offered 'no single detail which [was] sensuous, seductive, enfeebling in moral principles'.[36] The figure of Adam on the Sistine ceiling, and the dying slave sculptured for the tomb of Julius II (see Plate 5b), ranked among the greatest creations of his genius, and signified the triumphant vitality of Greek intellectualism. 'It is impossible,' wrote Symonds, 'while gazing on this statue, not to hear a strain of intellectual music. Indeed, like melody, it tells no story, awakens no desire, but fills the soul with something beyond thought and passions, subtler and more penetrating than words.'[37] Yet even Michelangelo evinced the double mind, the *dipsychia*, of the Renaissance. He remained a hybrid, a spirit divided between Hellas and Christendom, whose work both honoured and betrayed the ancient example.[38]

His moral sanity was unimpeachable; yet there were unmistakable harbingers of degeneration, of deviation from Hellenic health, in his violence, his savagery, his penchant for menace and terror. And his insensitivity to nature, his 'unrelenting contempt for the many-formed and many-coloured stage on which we live and move',[39] was a clear anticipation of Decadence. Michelangelo's nudes inhabited a void: a lunar landscape lit by a 'clear grey twilight'. The wholeness and harmony of the Greek vision were absent. Here were only 'thought and naked flesh and posture . . . aridity of composition, isolation of plastic form, tyranny of anatomical science'.[40] Michelangelo's figures were not the figures of life. Their faces were masks, 'splendid commonplaces', redolent of the statues of latter-day Rome – those 'effigies of emperors . . . whose lineaments the craft of a declining civilisation has preserved for us in the forms which caricature the grace and strength of classic sculpture'.[41] And where, in Michelangelo, was the fortitude of the Greeks, their Stoicism? To Ruskin, Michelangelo's indifference to faces, obsession with dead anatomy, and violation of architectural truth had signified Satanic carnality and pride. To Symonds they signified neurosis: the suffering of a man 'discomforted and terrified, upon the point of losing heart'.[42]

So the best that Italy could offer remained much less than Symonds needed. He needed heroes who had attained to Goethe's formulation of the Greek ideal: *Im Ganzen, Guten, Wahren/ Resolut zu leben;** and he began to write about the Renaissance confident in the belief that they were characters in his story – the story of 'the first transcendent spring-

*To live steadfast / In the Whole, the Good, and the *True*

time of the modern world'. What he found as his work progressed were the spiritual casualties of a world that was falling apart. The land of the Renaissance therefore merely intensified his inner sense of crisis. 'Italy,' he once wrote, 'devours the body and the soul of me.'[43] In the realm of modern art Greece had not, after all, been reborn, and the way to rehabilitation lay elsewhere. It lay, he thought, in Switzerland, which was at the opposite pole to Italy on the mental map. 'Italy,' said the wisdom of the age, 'is human; Switzerland is divine. The lowlands are corrupt; the mountains are pure.' The Alps, innocent of art, history, and literature, confronted man not with culture but with nature, the handiwork of God.

Symonds had been led to Italy by Hegel. Hegel's lectures on the philosophy of history taught him that the way to freedom was opened by the conquests of reason and culture. He was led to Switzerland by Michelet, for whom the way to freedom was the way from culture to nature, illuminated by natural science. In *La Montagne* (1867), Michelet had expounded the Alpine pilgrimage as a release from the mortifying claims of humanism: 'Si j'avais suivi l'homme seul, la sauvage histoire de l'homme, j'aurais faibli de tristesse... Lorsque, dans l'étude humaine, l'haleine allait me manquer, je touchais Terra Mater, et reprenais mon essor.'* For Michelet, the geology of the Alps was enlightenment. It revealed the magnitude of Europe's debt to nature – to its power, to its wisdom, to its fecundity. Among the mountains the accessories of the imagination therefore seemed redundant:

Peu de livres, je vous prie... Tout livre humain est petit en présence de ce grand livre vivant... Les livres, même religieux, mystiques, ici sont de trop. Les religions spéciales ont la foix faible, souvent fausse, devant cette haute religion qui les domine, les embrasse. Dieux du monde, faites silence! Laissez-moi entendre Dieu!** [44]

That voice became Symonds's own. He made his home in Davos, far from libraries in a high, remote, and sparsely populated Alpine valley; and here, posing for the family Kodak amid 'the perpetuity of nature',[45]

*If I had followed man alone, nothing but the wild history of man, I should have faltered from sadness. Whenever, immersed in the humanities, my breath began to fail me, I would reach out to Terra Mater, and my impetus would be renewed.
**Only a few books, please! All human books are petty in the presence of this great living book... Even religious and mystical books are superfluous here. The voices of special religions are feeble, even false, before this great religion which dominates and embraces them. Worldly gods be quiet! Let me hear God.

he echoed what Michelet had written about 'libertés d'âme' and 'vierges de lumière qui...réjouissent...les yeux fatigués d'insomnie.' He was never a mountaineer, but he had memories of his father's mountaineering friends, and these stimulated his discovery of the outdoor athletic life. So the author of *Renaissance in Italy* and the *Life of Michelangelo* has his footnote in the history of Swiss winter sports, as the father of British tobogganing.[46] And that footnote explains, perhaps, the ambiguities, the self-contradictions, of those works. They are skewed by inner rifts and tensions, there is an antithetical pull beneath their polemic, because they were written by a man increasingly ill at ease in his role of culture-monger to the fashionable élite. 'I have never,' he wrote feelingly,

> been able to take literature very seriously. Life seems so much graver, more important, more permanently interesting than books...The world only expects culture of me. But in my heart of hearts I do not believe in culture, except as an adjunct of life.[47]

However, Michelet had taken Symonds to a Switzerland that was far from Rimbaud's Abyssinia. By now the Alps were culture's territory just as surely as Italy was. They were culture's antidote to its own despair; its cure for the *mal du siècle*. Mountains as a refuge from 'le bruit des arts, le fracas des plaisirs ostensibles, les cris de la haine, et les perpétuels gémissements de l'anxiété et des douleurs'* had been discovered by Senancour's Oberman,[48] rediscovered by George Sand's Lélia and Matthew Arnold's Empedocles, and consecrated by Ruskin and the scholar-mountaineers. Ruskin, in the fourth volume of *Modern Painters* (1856), had designated Mountain Gloom and Mountain Glory as God's revelations of His anger and His power; and it had been Ruskin's intention – never realized – to supplement *The Stones of Venice* (his tribute to culture) with *The Stones of Chamonix*, an apotheosis of nature. Symonds's Stoical utterances had been heard before. He was never more literary, more recognizably 'cultured', than in his pantheistic Alpine verse, and to read it is to be made aware of the self-deception in his act of renunciation. Culture was a one-way ticket. For a connoisseur of the Renaissance, there was no readmission to the company of innocents who knew nothing of Michelangelo.[49] It has rightly been said of Symonds that he was always and everywhere an exile; but his note of Epicurean regret is nowhere more

---

*the din of the arts, the fracas of ostensible pleasure, the screams of hatred, and the perpetual moaning of anxiety and pain

authentic than in his mountain poetry. The benediction of the Alps ('health and composure of the passionless mind') could not eclipse the sunlight of the South –

> the strong
> Light of the lands I love, the lands for which I long.

He could not resist the allure of Italy; yet neither could he overcome the sense of malediction and turpitude that Italy always aroused in him. For Michelet, periodic withdrawal from nature made for an 'heureuse alternance.' It meant salutary re-engagement with history and moral law. For Symonds, it meant descent into Sodom. He returned again and again to what he called 'the cities of the plain'; and when he died, in Rome, he was an exile still – a penitent who knew that he was not among the elect.[50]

In the world of sexual inversion, as in the world of art, Symonds looked for the survival of a Greek achievement. No custom or institution adopted by Greece in the golden age could qualify as degenerate. For Symonds, as for all educated Victorians, it was axiomatic that Hellas had witnessed 'one of the most brilliant periods of human culture ... in one of the most highly organized and nobly active nations'.[51] But Hellenism as he perceived it was different from the disembodied, sweetness-and-light version of Matthew Arnold. In Symonds's view, the Greeks had been remarkable for their tolerance and encouragement of sexual inversion. They had known that what was abnormal was not necessarily unnatural; that homosexuality could be 'masculine, military, chivalrous'. The continuing existence of Greek homosexuality would therefore prove that sexual deviance could still be sane. Unhappily it appeared to be the case that this natural, virile form of abnormality had not outlasted the miraculous moment of Periclean Athens. 'The nobler type of masculine love developed by the Greeks,' Symonds wrote, 'is almost unique in the history of the human race'; and, in discussing the subsequent history of inversion, he laid under contribution all the current vocabulary of pathology. Homosexuality in later Athens, in Corinth, Rome, Syria, and Egypt, had illustrated a process of degeneration and decay that culminated in 'lust', 'vice', 'grossness, effeminacy, and aesthetic prettiness'.[52] Symonds claimed, in *A Problem in Greek Ethics*, that he was 'approaching the subject from another point of view than that usually adopted by modern justice, psychiatrists, [and] writers on forensic medicine'; yet he withheld the freedom to choose a homosexual lifestyle, and he surrendered to public authority the right to judge and to punish wilful deviance. His plea for toleration was rigorously selective. As he defined it, the 'problem in modern ethics' was 'how to repress vice without acting unjustly towards the naturally abnormal, the unfortunate, and the irresponsible'[53] – and in his lexicon 'vice' was a very comprehensive term. It included homosexuality that was acquired rather than inherited, and it subsumed the 'effeminacy, brutalities, and gross sensualities that were characteristic of imperfectly civilised and luxuriously corrupt communities'.[54] The only homosexuality that earned his approval was that which qualified as 'Greek Love'; and Greek Love connoted a rare and perhaps lost epiphany. Symonds described it as 'a ladder for scaling the higher fortresses of intellectual truth, which it is now well-nigh impossible for us to realise as actual'.[55] His own transgressions confirmed its elusiveness. No-one aspired more ardently to match the Greek ideal, and no one reproached himself more bitterly for failing to do so. Homosexual encounters almost always left him feeling sordid, unworthy, criminal; and in his last years he began to doubt that Greek Love had ever in fact existed. 'Who shall say,' he wrote, 'whether the Platonic ideal evolved from the old Greek chivalry of masculine love was ever realised in actual existence?' And it seemed that, if it had ever been a reality, it had been so under conditions so exceptional and so evanescent as to make its survival a virtual impossibility.[56]

It was in Switzerland, the sanest and least degenerate of modern countries, that Symonds had a glimpse of what he was looking for – the Hellas that was missing, presumed dead. Among the peasants of the Graubünden he recognized – as Rousseau had done a hundred years before among the peasants of the Valais – an idyll of health and pastoral self-sufficiency. 'This free life,' he wrote, 'in common with open nature . . . has helped to form the Swiss character. It has implanted self-reliance and the love of liberty in stalwart bosoms, while it has no less certainly contributed to the nerve and fibre of manly limbs.'[57] His perception of the Swiss replicated his perception of the Hellenes, who had been distinguished from barbarians by 'love of political independence . . . contempt for Asiatic luxury . . . [and] gymnastic sports'.[58] In the company of Swiss athletes the analogy was compelling. Apollo, Achilles, Hermes, the Apoxyomenos came crowding to his mind when he attended the *Turnfest* in Geneva; and in the physical intimacy of these young men, in their fellowship, their abstinence, and their high-minded masculinity, there was a striking reminiscence of ancient Attic chivalry.[59]

Yet Symonds's rediscovery of Hellas in Helvetius provided no assurance of personal salvation. In his Alpine testimony, published in the volumes of verse *Animi Figura* and *New and Old*, redemption is abrogated

by a landscape of desolation, abandonment, and ruin, and by the ravages
of illicit yearning:

> I did but see thee and pass by,
> Gazing with half-averted eye
>   Lest Love should leap
> Upon my heart like winds that dash
> The rock-entwining mountain ash
>   Adown the deep.
>
> Yet as I looked and saw thee stand
> Twixt sun and shade with lifted hand
>   And bright eyes blue,
> With curving lips half-opened free,
> And hair that curled tempestuously,
>   And heightened hue;
>
> Receiving full on furtive eyes
> The magic of thy soft surprise,
>   The magic spell
> Of some sweet trouble in thy mind
> Scarce felt like tremblings undefined
>   On a clear well;
>
> Into my soul of souls a god
> With wild fire flew, and flaming trod
>   Her secret shrine...[60]

Symonds found in the mountains a refuge from the torments of
desire and guilt, only to fall again a prey to tortured longing. In
company with Senancour, he discovered that he existed 'pour [se]
consumer en désirs indomptables, pour [s]'abreuver de la séduction
d'un monde phantasmique, pour rester atterré de sa voluptueuse
erreur'.* In 1892 Symonds told his daughter Margaret: 'I love beauty
with a passion that burns the more as I grow old. I love beauty above
virtue.' Therein, as he saw it, lay his betrayal of the Greeks, his
'voluptueuse erreur'; and like George Sand's Lélia he endured the
martyrdom of those who appeal to the spirit and are answered by the

---

*to be consumed in unquenchable desire, to drink of the seductions of an illus-
ory world, to be overwhelmed by its voluptuous error

flesh. 'Depuis dix mille ans j'ai crié dans l'infini: *Vérité, vérité!* Depuis dix mille ans l'infini me respond: *Désir, désir!*'*[61]

So to the calm that he could not reach was added an ideal that he could not match, and Switzerland levied a toll of expiation and self-rebuke. One further promise remained. The Alps could still assist his claim to sanity, because they seemed to demonstrate that not all consumption was incurable. The mountain treatment was a deliverance for Symonds, both because it gave him a new lease of life and because it challenged the current understanding of his disease. Degeneration was by definition irreversible. So, if phthisis was curable, it could not be a degenerative condition.

In 1877 Symonds was told by his Bristol doctor John Beddoe that he was suffering from phthisis and that his left lung was already seriously damaged. Sir William Jenner, consulted in London, confirmed the diagnosis and warned him that he was in danger of rapid and fatal pulmonary collapse.[62] Symonds wrote that he arrived in Davos 'broken down in health, and with a poor prospect of being able to prolong [his] days upon this earth'.[63] His debility was such that he could not climb two flights of stairs without severe discomfort. At this time estimates of the duration of pulmonary tuberculosis varied from twelve months to five years at the most. Yet Symonds survived for another fifteen years. And these years were active, what is more. He was not a sick-room invalid. Medical science classified such improvements as remission, not cure; but they amounted to recovery by any reckoning, and they added to the evidence that was compelling the medical profession to revise its assumptions about the degenerative nature of the disease.

At the time when Symonds moved to Switzerland, the high-altitude treatment for phthisis was regarded by the orthodox not as quackery exactly, but rather as another far-fetched remedy in a long catalogue of desperate therapies. In fact high altitudes were regarded with scepticism even by the practitioners of nature cure and climatotherapy – of whom Jenner appears to have been one. He prescribed a Nile voyage for Symonds, but jibbed at the idea of a prolonged winter cure in the Swiss Alps. 'He replied,' Symonds recalled, 'that if I liked to leave my vile body to the Davos doctors, that was my affair; he had warned me.'[64] Physicians like Jenner saw the high incidence of cretinism and of goitre among the Swiss as evidence of the fundamental insalubrity of the

---

*For ten thousand years I have cried out to Infinity: *Truth, truth!* For ten thousand years Infinity has replied: *Desire, desire!*

Alpine valleys, and they reckoned that the rarefied atmosphere of the higher altitudes favoured haemorrhage and respiratory difficulties in cases of lung disease. To them, belief in the Swiss treatment for consumption looked like superstition, rooted not in science but in the magical and sacramental attributes of mountains as they featured in religious and imaginative literature.

However, orthodoxy soon caught up with Davos and with Symonds. By the 1880s, following the discoveries of Koch and Pasteur, the presiding idea in somatic pathology was no longer inheritance, but infection; and 20 years later some psychic disorders, likewise, were to be dissociated from heredity and linked to micro-organic infection – in this case, syphilis.[65] Dr Clifford Allbut, following Virchow and Niemayer, was arguing in the *Lancet* as early as 1877 that tubercles were not cancers, but abscesses, or inflammatory lesions, caused by bacteriological infection,[66] and his theory was verified in 1882, when Koch identified the tubercle bacillus. This was the discovery that confirmed what had long been doubted or denied[67] – that phthisis was a disease transmitted by contagion and inhalation. Antibiotics were as yet unknown; but antisepsis was by now a well-established principle, and the obvious way to treat consumption was by delivering antiseptics to the seat of infection in the lungs. Various treatments were devised to this end, including the inhalation of tar and carbolic-acid fumes; the ingestion of creosote capsules; intravenous injections, and injections directly into the lungs; the inhalation of sulphuretted hydrogen into the rectum; and even the introduction of caustic sponges into the larynx. All proved futile, despite many sensational claims, and real hope seemed to be offered only by naturally occurring antiseptic or aseptic atmosphere, in which the diseased pulmonary tissue would either be healed by medicinal air or, isolated from pathogens, heal itself. How the air of Davos worked no-one was quite sure. The local doctors believed – initially at least – in treatment *by* the air, and specified its fungicidal dryness as its principal healing property. Dr Friedrich Unger, a pioneer of the Davos cure, summed up his therapy as 'Luft, gemische Nahrung, viel milch aber nicht ausschliesslich, mässige Dosen Alcohol, Oel vielleicht aber nicht zu viel, und überall Luft'.*[68] British physicians and their patients put more emphasis on treatment *in* the air, and shifted much of the responsibility for his fate to the invalid himself. As they saw it, Davos provided no more than a favourable, germ-free environment. The cure

---

*Air; a varied diet, mainly but not exclusively milk; a moderate intake of alcohol; cod-liver oil perhaps, but not too much; and above all, air

itself consisted in a rigorous regimen of diet, exercise, and self-discipline, and only the morally fit could expect to recover. Symonds's promise of benefit was characteristically selective. He wrote of the 'stern and strict rule of health' that the consumptive must observe, and warned: 'He must be content to rise early in order to enjoy the first gleams of sunshine, and to retire to bed early in order to get the prescribed quantity of sleep. He must not shirk his daily exercise upon the same frost-hardened roads.' Only those would be saved who submitted to a regimen of penitential endurance:

> Many who do not have moral energy enough to live the ascetic life for several months together neutralise the good of the climate by lounging in cafés and billiard rooms, by smoking and drinking, by sitting up late at night, and by trading on the stimulus of the air to pass a lazy, good-for-nothing existence which leaves them where it found them.[69]

Much else was absent from Davos, besides germs. 'There are no statues or pictures,' wrote Symonds, 'no historical buildings; the libraries are scantily furnished, the theatre is inadequate, the music third-rate.'[70] And this cultural sterility was a condition of its success. Only those might live who abjured what made life worth living. For life, in its higher sense, was itself a hostile intruder, a bacillus, in the hygienic atmosphere of the Alps – and health was a form of death. 'Honnête peuple suisse!' wrote André Gide in 1902, 'se porter bien ne lui vaut rien. Sans crimes, sans histoire, sans littérature, sans arts, c'est un robuste rosier, sans épines ni fleurs.'* In Symonds's Alpine world, as in that of Gide's immoralist, entropy obtained, measuring health regained by life relinquished. When Switzerland finally redeemed its promise, and readmitted him to the company of the sane, it left him with an even greater sense of loss, of exile, of *l'amour de l'impossible*. His adopted country offered Attic chivalry and Whitmanesque democracy; but at the same time it decreed his own exclusion. It confirmed the survival of Greek friendship; but it confirmed too the contagiousness of his disease. Consequently the 'honest delight' for which he craved – 'the ... delight in hand-touch, meeting lips, hours of privacy, close personal contact'[71] – was strictly forbidden. Symonds knew that his daughter Janet, who died of tuberculosis in 1887, had contracted the disease through nursing him;

---

*The worthy Swiss! Their health avails them nothing. Without crime, without history, without literature, without art, they are a sturdy rosebush devoid of thorns and flowers.

and he must often have wondered how many others he had infected, or put at risk, through sexual intimacy. In the province of affection he was a trespasser. So in a sense those sceptical doctors had been right. It was all a matter of magic, of superstition, of the legend of the Holy Grail. That legend was about to receive one of its most elaborate re-tellings, in the work of Thomas Mann; and knowing about Symonds helps us to read Mann – to read, especially, *Tristan* (1902), *Death in Venice* (1912), and *The Magic Mountain* (1924). These stories are all satires on the perpetual human quest for Socratic happiness, for superhuman calm, for a promised land; and Mann's cultured protagonists re-enact what is essentially the Symonds scenario. Like Symonds, they learn that 'health and composure of the passionless mind' is an unsustainable illusion; that the supercivilized have no refuge from the art, passion, and catastrophe of the Cities of the Plain; and that benediction, if it is to be had at all, is to be had in the world, not above and beyond it.

Although Symonds endorsed the medicalization of sexuality and of art, and fought only a limited campaign for toleration, his attitude was much more complex than that of an uncritical accomplice of the medico-legal establishment. He remained a vocal opponent of moral censorship,[72] and had he survived he would almost certainly – in public if not in private – have supported Oscar Wilde at the time of his ordeal, the patent 'viciousness' of Wilde's transgression notwithstanding. Furthermore, Victorian medical opinion was never monolithic, and Symonds moved with the vanguard of the profession. If he had lived longer he would without a doubt have abandoned degeneration as an explanation for madness and neurosis. The theory of degeneration was already looking old-fashioned at the time he died, because the role of inheritance was being questioned in both somatic and psychic aetiology. By now it was coming to be acknowledged that heredity was too imperfectly understood to warrant sweeping assertions about racial degeneration,[73] and sickness was being explained in terms of infection and repression. Symonds suggested, in his treatise on modern ethics (privately printed in 1891, but never published in his lifetime), that neurosis resulted from the suppression of congenital instinct.[74] He suggested, in other words, that neurosis was not mental disease, but emotional disorder – which was a clear anticipation of the ideas of Charcot and Freud.[75] The new psychiatry of Paris and Vienna gave up referring to a universal human prototype. It referred instead to a hidden individual self – the perverse, the unconscious. Freud defined neurosis as the consequence of deviance, not as its cause, and he demolished the notion of moral insanity in words that Symonds might have written: 'All who wish to be more noble-minded than their constitution allows, fall victims to neurosis; they would have been more healthy if it could have been possible for them to be less good.'[76] Horatio Brown reckoned that Freud would have found a disciple in Symonds. 'Had he lived,' he told Symonds's daughter Margaret Vaughan in 1923, 'he would certainly have taken an interest in this new-fangled, fashionable Freudian psychology.'[77] This suggests that Symonds was doubly unfortunate in dying so young. During the 20 years that followed his death, homosexuality was not demedicalized; but it was destigmatized. In psychoanalytical theory it remained abnormal – but it was no longer sickness. It was misfortune still; but not calamity. Freud would therefore have disencumbered Symonds of a great weight of psychopathological baggage, and delivered him from those imputations of insanity that distorted his public image and darkened his private life. In the Freudian age, Symonds would no longer have been persecuted by his own myth. Whether he would have been any the less neurotic, any 'healthier' in Freud's sense of the term, is another question. The claims of 'duty, principle, right conduct'[78] had probably been too thoroughly learnt; the spasms of sexual disgust too keenly felt. Symonds was tormented not only by the demon of madness, but also by the demon of sin. The loss of Hellas was the loss of Eden: a catastrophic fall from grace. Like so many Victorian Protestants, Symonds found himself in a labyrinth of self-loathing and guilt – and the way out did not lie through Vienna. His was a need, perhaps, not only for the couch, but for the confessional too. So, even if he had not died in Rome, his journey, like that of Oscar Wilde, might nevertheless have ended there.

Notes

1 See Hall Caine's review of *Vagabunduli Libellus, The Academy*, xxvi (29 November 1884), 349–50.
2 Arthur Symons, *The Memoirs of Arthur Symons*, ed. Karl Beckson (1977), 115–21; Leon Edel, *Henry James: The Treacherous Years* (1969), 119; Van Wyck Brooks, *John Addington Symonds* (New York, 1914), 105; R. L. Stevenson, *Memories and Portraits (Complete Works*, ix) (1907), 102; John Pemble, *Venice Rediscovered* (Oxford, 1995), 56; *Dictionary of National Biography*.
3 W. F. Bynum, Roy Porter, Michael Shepherd (eds), *The Anatomy of Madness* (1985); Daniel Pick, *Faces of Degeneration: A European Disorder 1848–1914* (Cambridge, 1989); Milton Gold, 'The Early Psychiatrists on Degeneracy and Genius', *Psychoanalysis and the Psychoanalytic Review*, xlvii (1960–1), 37–55.
4 See, for example, Maudsley's *Heredity, Variation, and Genius* (1908), 25.

5 Stephen Heath, 'Psychopathia Sexualis: Stevenson's Strange Case', *Critical Quarterly*, xxviii (1986), 93–107.

6 John Addington Symonds, *Memoirs*, ed. Phyllis Grosskurth (New York, 1984), 64.

7 Barbara Gutman Rosenkrantz (ed.), *From Consumption to Tuberculosis* (New York, 1994), 123.

8 Michael Warboys, 'The Sanatorium Treatment of Consumption in Britain', in J. V. Pickstone (ed.), *Medical Innovations in Historical Perspective* (Basingstoke, 1992), 47–66.

9 Veda Skultans (ed.), *Madness and Morals: Ideas on Insanity in the Nineteenth Century* (1975), 62–3.

10 See Frank Ryan, *The Forgotten Plague* (Boston, 1993).

11 For example, R. von Krafft-Ebing, *Psychopathia Sexualis*, Eng. trans. (Philadelphia, 1894).

12 Ibid., 225.

13 Skultans, *op. cit.*, 197.

14 Ian Downbiggin, 'Degeneration and Hereditarianism in French Mental Medicine, 1840–90', in Bynum, Porter and Shepherd, *op. cit.*, 189–207.

15 Frédéric Gros, *Création et Folie: Une histoire du jugement psychiatrique* (Paris, 1997), 60–88.

16 Gold, *op. cit.*

17 See *The Man of Genius*, trans. Havelock Ellis (1891).

18 Gold, *op. cit.*; William Hirsch, *Genius and Degeneration* (1897).

19 Max Nordau, *Degeneration*, Eng. trans. (New York, 1895), Dedication.

20 Hirsch, *op. cit.*, 324–5.

21 Oscar Wilde, *Intentions*, new edn (1913), 90–1; J. A. Symonds, *In the Key of Blue* (1893), 93, 195; Paul Desjardins, 'John Addington Symonds', *Journal des Débats* (29 April 1893); W. F. Barry, *Heralds of Revolt* (1904), Ch. X (originally published in the *Quarterly Review* [July 1895], 31–58); Mario Praz, *The Romantic Agony*, new edn (Oxford, 1951), 422, 424; Henry James, *Letters*, ed. Leon Edel (Cambridge, MA, 1974–84), ii, 101. See also James's *The Author of Beltraffio* – the character of Marc Ambient is based on Symonds. Other examples of this view of Symonds can be gleaned from Carl Markgraf, 'John Addington Symonds: An Annotated Bibliography of Writings About Him', *English Literature in Transition*, xviii, 2 (1975), 79–138.

22 J. A. Symonds, *Essays Speculative and Suggestive* (1890), 128; *In the Key of Blue*, 196.

23 Symonds, *In the Key of Blue*, 196.

24 J. A. Symonds, *The Letters of John Addington Symonds*, ed. Robert Peters and Herbert Schueller (Detroit, 1967–9), iii, 477, 479; Van Wyck Brooks, *op. cit.*, 91.

25 Linda Dowling, *Language and Decadence in the Victorian Fin de Siècle* (Princeton, NJ, 1989).

26 Symonds, *Letters*, iii, 491.

27 Phyllis Grosskurth, *John Addington Symonds* (1964), 247; James, *Letters*, iii, 410; Van Wyck Brooks, *op. cit.*, 233.

28 André Gide (like Symonds, a Protestant) adopted a similar strategy of 'displaced abjection'. See Jonathan Dollimore, *Sexual Dissidence* (Oxford, 1991), 54. For Symonds's fears for his sanity see *Memoirs*, 183, 283.

29   Symonds, *Essays Speculative and Suggestive*, 154–67.
30   J. A. Symonds, *The Life of Michelangelo Buonarroti*, 2nd edn (1893), ii, 166.
31   J. A. Symonds, *Renaissance in Italy, III: The Fine Arts*, 2nd edn (1882), 29.
32   Ibid., 36.
33   Ibid., 35.
34   Ibid., 107, 122, 136, 170–1, 174–5.
35   Symonds, *Michelangelo*, ii, 372.
36   Ibid., ii, 166.
37   Ibid., ii, 87.
38   Ibid., ii, 385.
39   Ibid., i, 172.
40   Ibid., i, 172, 279.
41   Ibid., i, 264; J. A. Symonds and Margaret Symonds, *Our Life in the Swiss Highlands* (1892), 306.
42   Symonds, *Michelangelo*, ii, 67–8.
43   Symonds, *Letters*, iii, 53.
44   Jules Michelet, *Oeuvres complètes*, xx, ed. Paul Viallaneix (Paris, 1987), 107, 206, 209. For a survey of literary alpinism see Claire Elaine Engel, *La Littérature alpestre en France et en Angleterre* (Paris, 1930). In his article 'Beyond Humanism: J. A. Symonds and the Plotting of the Renaissance' (*Clio*, xvii, 2 [1988], 109–37), Peter Allan Dale argues that Symonds's interpretation of the Renaissance owes more to Michelet than to Hegel, since the 'story' it tells is that of the first stirrings of the scientific spirit and the emancipation of mankind through a return to nature. But Symonds's *Renaissance* is an ambiguous work, and the story it tells is not the same as the story it contains. Symonds was made profoundly uneasy by the excesses of Renaissance sensuality, and he recognized in them much that was pathological and unnatural.
45   Symonds, *Swiss Highlands*, 125.
46   Arnold Lunn, *Switzerland and the English* (1944), 178–9.
47   Symonds, *Swiss Highlands*, 284; *Memoirs*, 255.
48   Etienne Senancour, *Oberman*, new edn (Paris, 1965), 67.
49   Symonds, *Swiss Highlands*, 223.
50   J. A. Symonds, 'The Alps and Italy' and 'Farewell to Tuscany' (in *New and Old*, 1880); *Sketches and Studies in Italy and Greece, First Series*, new edn (1905), 127.
51   J. A. Symonds, *A Problem in Greek Ethics*, privately printed (1901), 1; *In the Key of Blue*, 66.
52   Symonds, *Greek Ethics*, 7, 15, 59–60.
53   J. A. Symonds, *Sexual Inversion*, new edn (New York, 1964), 158.
54   Symonds, *Greek Ethics*, 19.
55   Symonds, *In the Key of Blue*, 61.
56   Ibid., 83, 86.
57   Symonds, *Swiss Highlands*, 178.
58   Symonds, *Greek Ethics*, 51.
59   Symonds, *Swiss Highlands*, 225–35.
60   See the sequence 'L'Amour de l'Impossible' in *Animi Figura* (1882), and 'On the Alp', 'The Capuzzin', 'In February', 'Waiting', and 'Prometheus Dead' in *New and Old*.

61 Senancour, *op. cit.*, 288; Symonds, *Letters*, iii, 711; George Sand, *Lélia*, ed. Pierre Reboul (Paris, 1960), 541.
62 Symonds, *Memoirs*, 256.
63 J. A. Symonds, 'Davos in Winter', *Fortnightly Review* (July 1878), 74–87; *Swiss Highlands*, 282.
64 Symonds, *Swiss Highlands*, 283; *Memoirs*, 260.
65 Sander Gilman, 'The Madman as Artist: Medicine, History, and Degenerate Art', *Journal of Contemporary History*, xx (1985), 575–97.
66 Clifford Allbut, 'Davos as a Winter Resort', *The Lancet*, 20 and 27 October 1877.
67 'A diathesis cannot be contagious' – Dr Thomas Watson in 1857. Quoted in Rosenkrantz, *op. cit.*, 45.
68 Allbut, *op. cit.* See also W. H. Vorman (ed.), *Davos: Its Local, Physical, and Medical Aspects* (1882), 42–53.
69 Symonds, 'Davos in Winter', *loc. cit.*
70 Symonds, *Swiss Highlands*, 124–5.
71 Symonds, *Sexual Inversion*, 190.
72 In 1889, for example, he signed a petition for the release of the publisher Henry Vizetelly, imprisoned for selling the works of Zola in English translation. See E. A. Vizetelly, *Emile Zola, Novelist and Reformer* (1904), 297.
73 Maudsley, *op. cit.*, 54–6.
74 Symonds, *Sexual Inversion*, 191.
75 Gilman, *op. cit.*, 582.
76 Sigmund Freud, 'Civilized Sexual Morality and Modern Nervous Illness', *The Standard Edition of the Complete Psychological Works of Sigmund Freud* (1953–74), ix, 191.
77 Pemble, *op. cit.*, 65.
78 Symonds, *Letters*, iii, 711, 714.

2

Truth and its Consequences: The Friendship of Symonds and Henry Sidgwick

Bart Schultz

> Henry Sidgwick is here, & is dissecting my essays under my eyes. He is doing me the compliment of reading them & trying to get something useful out of them.
>
> Good Lord! in what different orbits human souls can move.
>
> He talks of sex, out of legal codes, & blue books. I talk of it, from human documents, myself, the people I have known, the adulterers & prostitutes of both Sexes I have dealt with over bottles of wine & confidences.
>
> Nothing comes of discussions between a born doctrinaire & a born Bohemian. We want you to moderate between us. And you are not enough. We want a cloud of witnesses.
>
> *John Addington Symonds to H. G. Dakyns, 19 July 1890*[1]

I

There is much to apologize for, in befriending Henry Sidgwick. John Addington Symonds knew that, just as he no doubt knew much else about Sidgwick that a century of subsequent scholarship has failed to reconstruct. But perhaps today they finally have their 'cloud of witnesses'.

Born in 1838, two years before Symonds, Sidgwick achieved fame in his lifetime as a philosopher, ethicist, parapsychologist, and reformer – especially an educational reformer – a bright light in the movement for women's higher education and the modernization of the University curriculum. Virtually a lifelong denizen of Cambridge, where he became Knightbridge Professor, Sidgwick established his reputation with his first book, *The Methods of Ethics* (1874). Addicted to academic life, he missed only one term at the University from the time he began teaching in 1859 until 1900, when he resigned because of the cancer that would soon end his life. He could be lured away, for the Lent term of 1883, only by the prospect of a trip to Rome, which he took duly armed with his friend Symonds's book on Renaissance art. This departure from his academic routine is perhaps suggestive of the rather uncanny force that Symonds and his concerns exercised on Sidgwick. Although Sidgwick achieved the intellectual stature and academic respectability that eluded Symonds, things were different face to face, at Clifton or at Davos, where Sidgwick was always a welcome guest.

My claim is that, of all the currents sweeping through Sidgwick's life and work, none was more important than Symonds. The Symonds effect was pervasive: philosophical, ethical, religious, aesthetic. This was the friend Sidgwick most respected, and the other he most feared, intellectually and emotionally. Whenever he was driven to test the very core of his identity, 'Johnnie' did the testing and contesting.

Perversely, admirers of Sidgwick and Symonds have long been divided into two camps, the friends of Sidgwick or the friends of Symonds, each commenting on the other as little as possible. Thus, J. B. Schneewind's authoritative *Sidgwick's Ethics and Victorian Moral Philosophy* reveals the depth of Sidgwick's philosophical despair by reference to his journal exchanges with Symonds, but never tries to explain what made Symonds important to Sidgwick.[2] Phyllis Grosskurth's celebrated *John Addington Symonds* details how Sidgwick played censor-in-chief when it came to the construction of his friend's reputation and the production of Horatio Brown's highly misleading Symonds biography. Yet her intimations that Sidgwick's protectiveness accorded with Symonds's own doubts about 'coming out' – he allowed that his 'best work' was his 'least presentable', and that he had 'given pledges to the future in the shape of my four growing girls' – never move her to explore the nature of this relationship or why Symonds, his family and friends so counted on Sidgwick in their efforts to avoid the scandal threatened by public awareness of the 'best work'.[3] That the Sidgwick–Symonds friendship was one of the most intimate confidence and gravest philosophical import has heretofore been suggested only by a cloud of hints.

II

Henry Sidgwick, A Memoir, the delicately edited biography by Sidgwick's widow and younger brother Arthur, makes note of Sidgwick's visit in London in 1867. It explains that, although 'he had met J. A. Symonds – already a friend of his brother Arthur and of H. G. Dakyns – before this, the visit here referred to was the beginning of the intimate friendship between them which lasted as long as Symonds lived'. The *Memoir* quotes Symonds on the 'inestimable value' of their friendship, and states that to 'Sidgwick, too, this friendship was one of the things he most valued in life'.[4]

That their fundamental orientations towards life differed in core respects was also plain; indeed, Symonds, in the lines used for the epigraph to this essay, probably brought as much insight to this matter as anyone. He would praise Sidgwick for the questionable virtue of being an excellent 'scientific thermometer', or for casting a dry, white light on his own instinctive fondness for life over philosophy. Still, longer perspective may help us see why their friendship was at once personal and philosophical – or personal as political. Both owed their philosophical births to their struggles with hypocrisy, issuing in a singular symbiosis.

My goal is not to detail the precise nature of Sidgwick's sexual practices, or to show how the Sidgwick *Memoir* follows in some ways the pattern of Brown's biography, robing sexual conflicts in religious garb. Plausibly, J. M. Keynes's famous outburst, upon reading the *Memoir*, that Sidgwick 'never did anything but wonder whether Christianity was true and prove that it wasn't and hope that it was' may have revealed his own incomprehension of his forefathers. Without questioning the genre of such memoirs, Keynes allowed: 'Oh, I suppose he was intimate but he didn't seem to have anything to be intimate about except his religious doubts.'[5]

That the *Memoir* was a carefully censored work is obvious: sexual matters were simply not addressed. Sidgwick's role in the Brown biography merits only the casual remark that he took 'a very great interest in the Memoir of J. A. Symonds, which Mr H. F. Brown was engaged in writing'.[6] If this bland glossing-over is hardly surprising, neither should be the speculation that Sidgwick's deeper tendencies, however religiously tinted, were somewhere between Urning and Uranodioning, as dipsychical as Symonds's.[7] Various sources have noted that he was impotent in his marriage (to Eleanor Mildred Balfour), that nearly all of his closest friends were gay or bisexual (Symonds, Dakyns, Roden Noel, Oscar Browning, F. W. Myers), that his closest brother, Arthur, was gay (he had actually joined the Symonds circle first), and that he invested an extraordinary amount of his time in what was effectively sexual counselling (not only with Symonds, but also with his brother Arthur and with Oscar Browning, especially during the Eton crisis). And, throughout all these confidences and counsellings, his overriding concern is less to condemn the identities at issue than to urge the dangers to self and society of 'coming out'. Furthermore, he was profoundly shaped by his membership in that most famous of secret Cambridge discussion groups, the Apostles, which even in the nineteenth century had a homogenic aura, most vividly expressed in its celebration of the Tennyson–Hallam relationship. His 'Diary', from the spring of 1860, leaves little doubt as to his homosocial longing for intimate friendship.[8] And he, too, became a worshipper of Clough, later of Whitman, following the lead of Symonds if not the openness of Carpenter. He covered his tracks well, but the pattern of a life is not so easily covered.

But my aim here is to bring out some of the ways in which Sidgwick's philosophical and religious struggles – in their way quite genuine – ironically produced an effective intellectual stance on coming out and, more generally, on the notion of the 'double' or 'multiple' self, which, though born of Romanticism, would eventually come to pervade works as disparate as James's *Psychology* and DuBois's *The Souls of Black Folk*. This notion figured importantly in the rethinking of utilitarianism witnessed in Mill and Sidgwick, with their emphasis on Romantic authenticity, character formation and the evolution of sympathy. In combination with Symonds, Sidgwick would translate these concerns into a strategy of the closet and beyond.

Consider first one of the most important recent glosses on the *Methods*, a crucial corrective to Schneewind's account. Bernard Williams, in *Ethics and the Limits of Philosophy*,[9] rightly observes that:

> Sidgwick offered a utilitarian account of many dispositions that are usually thought to have intrinsic or nonutilitarian value. The values of justice, truthtelling, spontaneous affection, loyalty to your friends, a special concern for your own children, and so forth, might seem to involve an outlook that the thoroughgoing utilitarian would not endorse. But, Sidgwick insisted, you must consider the utilitarian value of those values, in the sense of the value of the state of affairs in which people have those values. If you do that, the utilitarian justification will extend much further than had been supposed.

Indeed, as Williams continues: 'Critical thinking, itself utilitarian, can reach the conclusion, as Sidgwick did, that one does not maximize utility by thinking, most of the time, as a utilitarian.'[10] The implications of this recasting of utilitarianism in an indirect, unconscious, or two-level form turn out to be vast. As Williams notes, there is 'a deeply uneasy gap or dislocation in this type of theory, between the spirit of the theory itself and the spirit it supposedly justifies'. This gap is bridged by a troubling account of the distinction between theory and practice cast as a distinction between 'two classes of people, one of them a class of theorists who could responsibly handle the utilitarian justification of non-utilitarian dispositions, the other a class who unreflectively deployed those dispositions. This outlook, which accords well with the important colonialist connections of utilitarianism, may be called "Government House utilitarianism".'

Among the 'striking consequences' of this position is an obsession with the problem of 'how much should be divulged'. On Williams's exegesis, although 'enlightened utilitarians might be able to live by "refined and complicated" rules that admitted exceptions to everyday practice', others might not, 'and trying to introduce those rules might "do more harm by weakening current morality than good by improving its quality". So utilitarians must consider seriously how much publicity they should give to "either advice or example".' As Sidgwick put it, for the utilitarian 'it may be right to do and privately recommend, under certain circumstances, what it would not be right to advocate openly; it may be right to teach openly to one set of persons what it would be wrong to teach to others; it may be conceivably right to do, it if can be done with comparative secrecy, what it would be wrong to do in the face of the world'. If this might shock people, it is perhaps for the best that most people should be so shocked: 'The opinion that secrecy may render an action right which would not otherwise be so should itself be kept comparatively secret; and similarly it seems expedient that the doctrine that esoteric morality is expedient should itself be kept esoteric.'[11]

Now Williams was content to advance his critique at a purely philosophical level; he never considered whether Sidgwick was a Government House utilitarian in practice, whether his Liberal Unionism was imperialistic, or to what extent he shared the views of his brother-in-law and former student, Arthur Balfour. Nor did he address the issue of sexual politics in this connection. One would never guess, from his account, how Sidgwick actually applied this view, what content he gave to his 'esoteric' morality or what kinds of activity he expected the utilitarian élite to engage in – or how he thought the conditions calling for élites might change with societal progress and education.

Such are the hazards of reading the *Methods* either by way of tightly controlled contextualism or fatuously abstract textualism. Indeed, there is much in Sidgwick that ought to surprise those with the standard prejudices against utilitarianism, mostly a messy mix of Dickens, Marx, and Foucault. The hidden history of utilitarianism contains a narrative of vanguardist subversion ranging from Bentham's argument for the decriminalization of sodomy, through the feminist and socialist experimentation of John Stuart Mill and Harriet Taylor, through the Sidgwick–Symonds circle, on to Moore and Bloomsbury and certain elements of radical pragmatism. Sidgwick, for example, hoped that the evolution of society might be such that people's benevolent, sympathetic dispositions would grow increasingly stronger as their religious superstitions faded, allowing at least the possibility of ethical socialism, more co-operative economic arrangements, and a form of ethical life and sentiment that could support itself in a post-religious era, should that come to pass.[12] If, like Mill, he generally held that, under the circumstances, advancing and testing the human potential through experiments in living would largely be the work of high-minded and far-seeing intellectual élites, he none the less also struggled with the question of how such circumstances might be changed – a question with which Symonds increasingly confronted him, as the vision of Whitman grew upon him. This was a development that Symonds celebrated, and Sidgwick, with cautious apprehension, deemed promising – though such a breathtaking somersault, from a form of Platonist élitism to homosocial democratic comradeship (later celebrated in Carpenter's *The Intermediate Sex*) could not help but worry him. As he once rather characteristically complained: 'I think a hundred times of what the British public are ripe for, for once that I think of what I believe. Perhaps the conviction is growing on me that the Truth about the studies I've set my heart on (Theology & Moral Philosophy) will not be found out for a generation or two.'[13]

The upshot here is that it is not only Sidgwick's *Memoir* that needs to be interrogated from the perspective of the epistemology of the closet, as Eve Sedgwick would put it, but also his magnum opus in moral philosophy.[14] The *Methods* yields a largely utilitarian take on that epistemology (a more persuasive one than Allan Bloom's neo-perfectionism alternative). It is precisely the Sidgwickian challenge to the 'publicity' requirement of moral rules that has so often served as a – if not the – focal point for the critique of utilitarianism advanced by Kantians and neo-Kantians, as well as by figures such as Williams and others oblivious to the problematics of gay epistemology. Publicity is inextricably linked to the question of secrecy – a grave issue for gay epistemology, but one sadly and question-beggingly pre-empted in traditional Hebrew–Christian and Kantian systems.

To illustrate, consider how the ethical views expressed in the *Methods* were reached. In the autobiographical statement that Sidgwick dictated shortly before his death, he discussed his years of religious 'Storm and Stress' – that is, of his growing doubts about religion – that led him to follow the example of his hero Clough and resign his position at Cambridge because he could not in good conscience swear to the Thirty-nine Articles of the Church of England, as required. He explained that, after a longish foray into Arabic and Hebrew (the better to deal with the evidences for Christianity), he 'had been led back to philosophy by a quite different line of thought from a practical point of view – that is, by the question that seemed to me continually to press with more urgency for a definite answer – whether I had a right to keep my Fellowship. I did my very best to decide the question methodically on general principles, but I found it very difficult, and I may say that it was while struggling with the difficulty thence arising that I went through a good deal of the thought that was ultimately systematised in the *Methods of Ethics*.'[15]

This struggle led to the only direct contact between Sidgwick and his philosophical hero, Mill. In 1867, he makes bold to write to Mill, explaining that the 'subject is the position which liberals (speculatively I mean, "Aufgehlärte" of various shades) ought to take up with regard to the traditional (in England the established) religion of the country. I wish to solve this question on principles of pure ethics, without any reference to the truth or falsity of any particular religion ... also to solve it according to principles of objective, social ("utilitarian") morality.' His hope is to avoid futile appeals to 'conscience', and by approaching the issue 'methodically and candidly' to approximate more closely the line 'between expedient conformity and inexpedient hypocrisy'.[16]

There follows a finely discriminating account of the different grades of conformity as determined by social role – for example, the difference between what might be expected of clergy versus what might be expected of others taking religious tests, or educators in general, or lay members of a congregation. As becomes clear in the pamphlet that was to follow shortly, 'The Ethics of Conformity and Subscription', Sidgwick was extremely sensitive to the casuistical problem here. Hypocrisy in the religious realm is especially fatal: 'It seems to me impossible that a man can satisfactorily perform the functions of pastor if his opinions are not more or less in harmony with those of his flock.' But, 'it is intolerable that he should be chained down ... to perpetual agreement with the least progressive section of them. In a natural state of things, he ought to be the first to see distinctly, while others are only obscurely feeling, the incongruity between the prayers he has to read and the real beliefs of his generation; and when the time is ripe for the removal of this incongruity, he ought to take a prominent part in its removal.'[17] The time was ripe for clergy and even such figures as himself to take action – hence the resignation of his fellowship. As he explained to Mrs Clough:

I feel very strongly the importance of 'providing things honest in the sight of all men'. It is surely a great good that one's moral position should be one that simple-minded people can understand. I happen to care very little what men in general think of me individually: but I care very much about what they think of human nature. I dread doing anything to support the plausible suspicion that men in general, even those who profess lofty aspirations, are secretly swayed by material interests.[18]

With evident appreciation for the example set by his hero Clough on the question of conformity, he had earlier observed: 'Lax subscription to articles was the way of Clough's world . . . To do what others do till its unsatisfactoriness has been thoroughly proved, and then suddenly to refuse to do it any longer, is not exactly heroic, nor is it the way to make life pleasant; but as a *via media* between fanaticism and worldliness, it would naturally commend itself to a mind like Clough's.'[19] Or like Sidgwick's.

Sidgwick did resign, though the University contrived to keep him on. The tests were abolished, and his academic career worked out after all. Mill liked his pamphlet, and wrote back that the question of the utility of truth was one that almost everyone was afraid to touch, and that Sidgwick should write a book about this, pitched at this more general level, not merely about religious conformity. The *Methods* was the result, and thus Sidgwick's religious crisis of conscience was transmuted into philosophical fame.

But the point is that the *Methods* was born in just this way, out of a passionate personal concern with the ethics of hypocrisy and secrecy. It was this, rather than colonial administration, that moved Sidgwick to fashion the casuistry of 'Government House' utilitarianism. He was, in parallel to Symonds at this point, wholly absorbed in the Cloughian mentality, Clough being, in Jim McCue's words, the 'agnostic who couldn't have cared more', but for whom sexual meditations and religious doubts (or religious meditations and sexual doubts) formed the poles of his agonizing over the perplexing voice of conscience.[20] If Sidgwick had begun from a decidedly more orthodox stance than Symonds, he was nevertheless every bit as consumed by the problem of hypocrisy in this formative period. Moreover, he was consumed by it in the company of Symonds.

At the time Sidgwick was developing the ideas that went into the *Methods* he was not overly impressed by the moral capacities of the 'simple-minded people'. And in that signal year of 1867 he not only made contact with Mill but also established a real friendship with Symonds, the tone of which is neatly captured in the letter he wrote just after the aforementioned visit in London:

> My dearest friend I cannot tell you all I feel: I have drunk deep of happiness: I have said to the Augenblick, 'du bist so schön' – I am so glad you say I have done you good: I must have given you my best: my best never comes out except when I am played upon & stirred by affection and subtle sympathy combined: when I do not get this, I become lethargic. Among the 'dim' common populations I seem to change and become common. I am so glad you let me stay with you so long; I might have felt that what of strange, new, delicious, rich had come into my life might pass out of it like a dream. I feel now that you are 'not something to be retracted in a certain contingency'.[21]

For his part, Symonds would write to their mutual friend Dakyns that 'Henry Sidgwick has been with me a week. He is numbered among mine.'[22]

Symonds was the soul-mate whom Sidgwick had long sought, as his struggles in the 1860s wore on, as his old Apostolic friends moved on. At this crucial juncture, his mentor Mill gave him direction and his friend Symonds gave him support and set an example, and he took the most forthright action against hypocrisy that he would ever take – his resignation. Symonds, too, was at this point struggling to break the surface. Although he dated his 'true self' back to 10 April 1858, and his meeting with Willie Dyer, that self had undergone lengthy and painful submersion. He had gone through a period of trying to 'cure' himself, chiefly through marriage. But, when he built this friendship with Sidgwick, his 'wolf' had returned with a vengeance, and he had suffered the dark night in Cannes in 1868, when Sidgwick witnessed him practically destroyed by the torment. The only alternative was honest acceptance: hence, he wrote the poetry that was to all intents and purposes an effort at coming out – not to mention *A Problem in Greek Ethics*, also begun at this time. For all their differences, his casuistry and Sidgwick's were much the same, and hammered out at the same time, together: one could honestly confront and accept one's condition, explore the possibilities with the support of knowing friends, and avoid hypocrisy while also avoiding open confrontation (or scandal) unless it was clearly demanded by the signs of the times in conjunction with one's social role. When Sidgwick confronted the 'miserable semi-hypocrisy that is paralysing the intellectual religion of England', it was in this measured and guarded way, after the manner of Clough.[23] And Symonds could appreciate that.

Now once the indirect, esoteric utilitarianism of the *Methods* is read in this light, it fairly hits one in the face that Sidgwick had worked out, on various levels, a philosophical approach to the question of sexual orientation and to the problematic of coming out. Admittedly, he lived in the age of hypocrisy rather than the age of AIDS, though the affinities binding our ages, of resistance and sympathy, of weakness, wasting and death, are striking. Yet Sidgwick's was a philosophy so completely framed by the problem of hypocrisy and the double life that it fitted his personal situation as neatly as Stoicism did the slavery of Epictetus. It takes very little translation – the substitution of 'clerisy' for 'clergy', for example – to adapt his advice about when to come out on religious matters into advice about when to come out (or stay in) on sexual ones. The time was simply not ripe for Symonds's erotic poetry, or his work on sexual inversion. Hence conformity, experimentalizing of a type, was still expedient, while the knowing worked quietly for change. The good of 'providing things honest' could, as a matter of contingent social realities, be counterbalanced by the bad of 'providing things honest'. Symonds was largely persuaded: at least, he did lock up his more explicit poetry.

Again, Sidgwick's religious struggles were sincere, more so than Symonds's. Symonds confessed that his character had been 'strongly influenced' by the discovery while at Harrow of the relationship between Alfred Pretor and the headmaster, Dr Vaughan. The shock of this 'and the casuistical reflections it engendered, had the immediate effect of dissociating piety from morality in my view of the religious life. There existed no doubt that Dr Vaughan passed for an eminently pious man; and it was equally clear that he indulged habits in secret which he denounced as sins from the pulpit.' Consequently, in brooding over this, Symonds 'began to suspect human nature at large of hypocrisy and inconsistency', so much so that a 'scepticism, cynical and jaded rather than logical or aggressive, checked the further growth of faith; just as a frost may throw back budding vegetation', and he 'broke into dangerous paths of speculation, and questioned the ground principles of social ethics'.[24]

Sidgwick's first mentor, Edward White Benson, would go on to become both another Sidgwick brother-in-law and Archbishop of Canterbury, and his influence had guaranteed that Sidgwick's Christian self-laceration would be quite genuine. The point here is simply that he struggled with both God and sex, and his philosophy turned out to be surprisingly serviceable on both fronts, as his capacious deathbed self-description might suggest: 'My aim ... has been the solution, or contribution to the solution, of the deepest problems of human life. The peculiarity of my career has been that I have sought light on these problems, and that not casually but systematically and laboriously, from very various sources and by very diverse methods.'[25]

To be sure, the shape of these inquiries shifted and evolved. Sidgwick changed – like Symonds, he grew less Platonizing. From the Cambridge Apostles, he had moved to the esoteric inquiries of the Society for Psychical Research, in which Symonds also took an interest, appealing to depth psychology in his unceasing effort to ground his ethical views and come to terms with the practical problems that pressed upon him. Yet two of the nine essays in *Practical Ethics*, which appeared in 1898 and which was the last book that Sidgwick published during his lifetime, return to the casuistical problem of religious conformity, and many of the others also deal with the problem of truth-telling in one context or another.

Thus, however sensitive to the actual historical conditions under which one must act, Sidgwick was absorbed in the problem of veracity throughout his life. It re-emerged time and again, especially when he questioned his academic role – that is, whether it was ethical to teach ethics when he was so sceptical about the foundations of ethics and religion. Though, for example, the time was ripe for him to resign his Fellowship in 1869, at a later critical point, in the 1880s, he came to a different conclusion. Increasingly sceptical about being able to vindicate even a limited theism (with parapsychological evidence of an afterlife), and troubled by his inability to demonstrate the superiority of utilitarianism to rational egoism, he wondered whether he had any right to be teaching ethics and philosophy in an academic setting:

> Some fifteen years ago, when I was writing my book on Ethics, I was inclined to hold with Kant that we must *postulate* the continued existence of the soul, in order to effect that harmony of Duty with Happiness which seemed to me indispensable to rational moral life. At any rate I thought I might *provisionally* postulate it, while setting out on the serious search for empirical evidence. If I decide that this search is a failure, shall I finally and decisively make this postulate? Can I consistently with my whole view of truth and its attainment? And, if I answer 'no' to each of these questions, have I any ethical system at all? and, if not, can I continue to be Professor and absorb myself in the mere erudition of the subject?[26]

Again, Symonds was there: all this is agonized over in the journal to Symonds, which details his despair over having 'tried *all* methods in turn, only to find that all in turn have failed – revelational, rational, empirical methods – there is no proof in any of them.' The significance of Symonds to Sidgwick's struggles is evident:

I have been thinking much, sadly and solemnly, of J. A. S.'s answer to my January journal. In spite of sympathy of friendship, I feel by the limitations of my nature incapable of really comprehending the state of mind of one who does not *desire* the continuance of his personal being. All the activities in which I truly live seem to carry with them the same demand for the 'wages of going on'. They also carry with them concomitant pleasure: not perhaps now – aetat 49 – in a degree that excites enthusiasm, but quite sufficient to satisfy the instinctive claims of a man who has never been conscious of having a creditor account with the universe. Whether if this pleasure failed I could rely on myself to live from a pure sense of duty I do not really know; I hope so, but I cannot affirm.[27]

That answer had read:

I am alluding to the passage of your Diary, in which you announce your expectation of having to abandon in this life the hope of obtaining proof of the individual soul's existence as a consciousness beyond death. What this implies for yourself, in its bearings I mean, upon Moral Philosophy, and its bearing upon the sustained quest of twenty years, I am able to appreciate.

And I may add that it was for myself also a solemn moment, when I read that paragraph in the Diary, through the measured sentences of which a certain subdued glow of passion seemed to burn. I do not pretend that I had ever fixed my views of human conduct clearly or hopefully upon the proof of immortality to our ordinary experience. I do not deny that I never had any confidence in the method you were taking to obtain the proof. I will further confess that, had you gained the proof, this result would have enormously aggravated the troubles of my life, by cutting off the possibility of resumption into the personal-unconscious which our present incertitude leaves open to my sanguine hope.

Ethics, I feel, can take care of themselves – that is to say, human beings in social relations will always be able to form codes of conduct, profitable to the organism and coercive of the individual to the service of its uses. In humanity, as in nature, 'est Deus, quis Deus incertum'.

I have no apprehension for civil law and social and domestic institutions, even though the permanence of personal consciousness after this life remains undemonstrated. Those things are necessary for our race, of whose position in the universe we are at present mainly ignorant; and a sanction of some sort, appealing to imagination, emotion, unformulated onward impulses, will always be forthcoming. Man has only had about 6,000 years of memory upon this planet; and the most grudging of physicists accord him between ten and twenty millions to come. Dislocations of ethical systems, attended by much human misery, possibly also by retrograde epochs of civilisation, are likely to ensue. History, if it teaches anything in its little span of past time, prepares us to expect such phases in the incalculably longer future. But our faith lies in this: that God, in the world, and in humanity as a portion of the world, effectuates Himself, and cannot fail to do so. I do not see, therefore, why we should be downcast if we cannot base morality upon a conscious immortality of the individual.

But I do see that, until that immortality of the individual is irrefragably demonstrated, the sweet, the immeasurably precious hope of ending with this life the ache and languor of existence, remains open to burdened human personalities.

A sublime system of ethics seems to me capable of being based, in its turn, upon that hope of extinction. Demonstration, *ex argumento ipso* [by the argument itself], will not here be attained. But I am of opinion that the persuasion, if it comes to be reasonably entertained, of man's surcease from consciousness when this life closes, will afford quite as good a basis for submission to duty as any expectation of continuance in its double aspect of hope and fear has lately been.[28]

The philosophical glimmerings in this letter, partly reflections cast by the tragic death of Symonds's daughter Janet, are quite remarkable – a marriage of Hegel, Whitman, and Darwin that foreshadows James and Dewey while subtly tapping the more mystical tendencies of Carpenter.[29] It hints at the transition to a new religion, and expresses hope for an alternative between supernaturalism and egoism. And it comports not at all with the Foucauldian image of essentializing, bipolar Victorian discursive practices strangling the free play of sexuality.

Sidgwick struggles to emerge from his continuing crisis in the following journal entries, from 1888:

> I have been since I wrote to you in a state of mind so familiar to me that I ought to be proof against the illusions connected with it – and yet I am not proof – the state of knowing that before long I have to make a decision of fundamental importance, a decision that must profoundly influence my life and outlook on things in general one way or another, feeling that I have sufficiently examined all the *pros* and *cons* that my intellect can discover, and that the matter is therefore ripe for decision; feeling at the same time that my mind is not moved to a decision today, and that it must settle down into decidedness tomorrow or the day after: and that when this moment comes the existence I am leading in a kind of tunnel under the surface of ordinary human life will have come to an end: I shall emerge into the open air and experience a rush of the kind of clear ideas and emotions that one is prompted to communicate to one's friends.[30]

He explains that he has been in this state for two months, but since he also explains that it has to do with the 'tenability of my position here as a teacher of Ethics' – that is, precisely the concern voiced in his earlier journal entries, from 1887 – this must simply refer to an enhanced sense of urgency about the subject. The solution is at hand, however, for he goes on to write: 'What I intended to say is that I have [now] emerged from my tunnel by an act of will, and do not mean to let my mind turn on this hook any more for the present.' In the next entry, he explains how now he takes

> life more as it comes, and with more concern for small things. I aim at cheerfulness and I generally attain it. I have a stronger *instinctive* repugnance to cause pain or annoyance to any human being. In old times, when the old idea of judgment at which all would be known still hung about me, I was more concerned about being *in the right* in my human relations ... But now I have let this drop into the background, and, though I still feel what Carlyle calls the 'Infinity of Duty', it is only in great matters I feel it; as regards the petty worries of life, I feel that both the Universe and Duty *de minimis non curant*: or rather the one Infinite duty is to be serene. And serene I am – so far![31]

One can detect in this something of Symonds's liberating view that 'Ethics ... can take care of themselves', or the sentiment in his memoirs:

'I can now declare with sincerity that my abnormal inclinations, modified by Whitman's idealism and penetrated with his democratic enthusiasm, have brought me into close and profitable sympathy with human beings even while I sinned against law and conventional morality.'[32]

Ironically, Symonds's challenge to Sidgwickian despair seems to have helped Sidgwick maintain the double life he had long lived. As Sidgwick put it to an old school friend:

> Experience has convinced me that what contents me would not content others; and therefore for the last ten years – since in 1870 I gave up, to avoid hypocrisy, my Fellowship at Trinity – I have 'kept silence even from good words', and never voluntarily disclosed my views on religion to any one. But I have never thought it right to conceal them from any one who seriously wished to have them, and had any claim to be answered.[33]

Symonds helped Sidgwick continue this double life, in religious and ethical matters, and in friendships. But it was an attitude that Sidgwick himself had long perfected:

> Feeling that the deepest truth I have to tell is by no means 'good tiding', I naturally shrink from exercising on others the personal influence which would make men [resemble] me, as much as men more optimistic and prophetic naturally aim at exercising such influence. Hence as a teacher I naturally desire to limit my teaching to those whose bent or deliberate choice it is to search after ultimate truth; if such come to me, I try to tell them all I know; if others come with vaguer aims, I wish if possible to train their faculties without guiding their judgments. I would not if I could, and I could not if I would, say anything which would make philosophy – my philosophy – popular.[34]

In an 1881 letter to J. R. Mozley he claimed that destroying the hope for a happy immortality would 'seriously increase' the danger of the 'dissolution of the existing social order'.[35]

A different conclusion – but the same type of reasoning that had led to his resignation, and which illustrates again how Sidgwick was the complete strategist of the closet, the author of *The Methods of Ethics*. He might have added that, in the case of sexual orientation, very few had any claim to be answered, the effects of an increasingly homogenic culture were uncertain, and premature honesty could be disastrous (as the

Wilde case would show). Thus he counselled Browning against Eton, and Symonds against posterity. And yet, for all that, some did have such claims, some could see the way dimly ahead, some were bound to keep working for change. In sexuality, as in theology, there could be no turning back, and a heavy duty fell on the clerisy.

III

Thus, at two crucial periods of personal and philosophical crisis, Sidgwick turned to Symonds; not exclusively, but with an emotional and intellectual intensity and engagement that was unparalleled in his other relationships. And Symonds responded, though the support that he provided (and received) always carried a challenge as well, something 'other'.

Paradoxically, when Sidgwick worked out a resolution to his late-life crisis, grappling with that 'emotionally necessary' theism or fundamental faith in the moral structure of the universe that he feared he could not live without, he left some room for doubt whether Symonds was not the better representative of universal benevolence. At least, Symonds's education of desire, and 'hope of a new chivalry', seemed to mesh quite well with 'Government House' utilitarianism.

Quite possibly, Symonds's exasperation with Sidgwick's enthronement of philosophy and philosophers proved especially helpful; there is a positively weird self-importance in the way Sidgwick forever worried about the state of public morality as though its care and keeping were exclusively his responsibility. His effortless invitation to readers to consider matters 'from the point of view of the Universe' is odd not only because of the absurdity of supposing the Universe to have a point of view, but also because of the way he presumes that he has ready access to such a thing. His letters are forever revealing how he thinks that he is on the verge of discovering the 'secret of the Universe', some truth that will make everything hang together meaningfully. How different is Symonds's confession: 'To transcend, to circumvent, to transact with the law of the world, is impossible. To learn anything final about it is probably denied the human intellect.'[36] This was surely the better lesson to draw from Mill.

What really stirred Sidgwick about Symonds's response was the unerring way in which it went to the very heart of Sidgwick's worries about ethics, religion, and himself. Sidgwick was, in truth, haunted by fear of his own egoism. Unable to dispel this through theology or philosophical ethics – recall how the *Methods* ends up with the 'dualism of practical reason', utilitarianism and egoism in a draw, rationally speaking – his continuing quest was sharply exposed by Symonds as tainted by the very thing that he took himself to be battling against. Recall, too, his explanation of his resignation – that he cared very much about what the 'simple-minded' people thought of human nature, and that he dreaded 'doing anything to support the plausible suspicion that men in general, even those who profess lofty aspirations, are secretly swayed by material interests'. It was, for Sidgwick, an all too plausible suspicion, though he had never been able to confront its full reality in the manner of Symonds. The inevitable shadow of his efforts to render humanity more sympathetic and benevolent, more utilitarian in that sense, was his morbid (highly Nietzschean) fear that the trail of egoism covered all, even the 'moral order' of the universe that he sought so desperately to vindicate. As early as 1862, he had worried that 'Bain is the only thoroughly honest Utilitarian philosopher I know, and he allows self-sacrifice and [things connected with it] to constitute a "glorious paradox", whereas Comte and all practical Utilitarians exalt the same sentiments into the supreme Rule of life. These are the views I am trying to reconcile.'[37]

He never did reconcile them, at the level of philosophical theory, but Symonds helped him wonder, as did James, whether there might be more to experience than any such quest could assimilate, and whether the quest itself might be symptomatic of the problem to be overcome. He had, in a sense, condemned himself to a lifelong insistence that he be shown, by God or by reason, why his own interests should not come first. During this period of crisis, in the 1880s, he had explained to Myers, in reference to the work with mediums that they had been conducting, that he feared that 'this last effort to look beyond the grave would fail; that men would have to content themselves with an agnosticism growing yearly more hopeless – and had best turn to daily duties and forget the blackness of the end'.[38] Only the subtly subversive Symonds could plant in him the flicker of insight that the demand for proof itself betrayed his egoistic bent, and predetermined a hopeless conclusion. And that helped, personally and politically.

The fates were rather kind to Sidgwick, and as the 1890s wore on his hopes for psychical research revived – thanks to what he and other researchers regarded as important new evidence of communication from 'the Other Side'. His absorption in psychological enquiry, or personality theory, was the chief vehicle for his explorations of esoteric morality, though he always remained a true disciple of Mill. In effect, he assimilated both Mill's hopeful agnosticism about what friendship between the sexes might become and his call for the development of a new science about the sources of character formation, ethology, advanced partly by different experiments in living. Sidgwick carried these and other Millian concerns, such as the utility of truth and the need for a clerisy, into a much more detailed and developed confrontation with the possible defences of religion, orthodox and reformed, and common-sense morality – not to mention the cognate problems of what a transfigured society might look like, when it came to this crucial practice of the 'higher pleasures' of friendship. Although this search had led him and his collaborators to research into dream analysis, the significance of hallucinations, the levels of the unconscious, and other rich, depth-psychological inquiries that would have been quite beyond Mill, for Sidgwick there really was an enduring concern with the emotional necessity and explanation of a religious outlook, if only theistic, that was the heir of the Millian injunction to explore the utility of truth, religious belief, and the capacity for sympathy. In leading his double life, and conducting the various enquiries from which he hoped light would come, he made himself an experiment in living, a test of how far one might go in living without 'the wages of going on' – a self-analysis of his 'true self' that would tell much about the possibilities for society. Hence, the dread of his own egoism; hence, the utter fascination with Symonds.

The affinities between Sidgwick's self-experimentation and Symonds's are striking. In 'Is Prayer a Permanent Function of Humanity?', an early essay probably read to the Apostles, Sidgwick recast the question to ask 'will prayer be a universal function of the ideal humanity?' and challenged his religious sentiments with an appreciation of 'a rather rare and very admirable class of men: men that are in mind what the models of the Greek Statues were in body, healthy, finely moulded, well nerved, symmetrical'. He admits, rather arrogantly, that 'religion will always be beneficial and often of vital necessity on the one hand to natures where the emotional and passionate elements preponderate over the rational and active: and again to those whom constitution or fortune have depressed and saddened'. Thus, he will not 'speak of the sensual herd of whom Religion will ever be the only real elevator'. But the symmetrical people pose a tougher problem, since they

seem so really fitted for this world as it is. They live to the full, the natural life, and never seem to wish for more. They need no stern teaching to make them prefer the lower good to the higher: they carry off with an airy cheerful manliness the ills that flesh is heir to. It seems as if with them every moment, every thought, taken from the Present that they feel so real and devoted to the shadowy invisible, must be a loss.

Such a one might feel in reading history as if mankind had gone to sleep after the bright sunny days of Athenian life and were now just waking up again after the long nightmare of medieval superstition.

Sidgwick 'can just' find sympathy for such a view, but he feels 'the other side with much more force'. The other side, of course, holds that 'the virtue and happiness that religion has produced in the unsymmetrical and weak' could produce 'still greater effects of the same kind' in the 'symmetrical and strong'. Furthermore, 'there is one trial that may befall the most symmetrical – old age which is rarely borne as well as youth by the non-religious'. This is not to say that the world has not 'protest to make against the church'. Religion is 'not yet quite fitted to become the crown of glory of a symmetrical nature', but Sidgwick 'cannot believe the long elaboration of centuries to be in vain' and he looks 'forward to a type of man combining the highest pagan with highest medieval excellences' – that is, with a much greater capacity for sympathy and benevolence.[39] His 'true self' harboured a Theistic heart.

This was another topic of abiding import for Sidgwick; in fact, Myers recalled his addressing the issue at a meeting of the Synthetic Society, held on 25 May 1900, which is to say at his last such philosophical meeting. It was of enduring importance to him precisely as part of his evolving enquiry into the basic emotional fabric of human life, and the potential for coping with a post-theological age. He would consider the question posed by the 'symmetrical people' over and again, in a wide variety of contexts, and it was evidently connected with the entire problematic of hypocrisy, religious conformity, and esoteric morality. The symmetrical people were deeply suggestive of alternative ways in which such a morality had realized itself and might again do so, and perhaps, in due course, might lessen the need for esotericism. Which calls irresistibly to mind Symonds's hopes for a Whitmanesque age combining the Greek ideal with medieval chivalry, newly applied:

He [Whitman] expects Democracy, the new social and political medium, the new religious ideal of mankind, to develop and extend 'that fervid comradeship', and by its means to counterbalance and to spiritualise what is vulgar and materialistic in the modern world. . . . If this be not a dream, if he is right in believing that 'threads of manly friendship, fond and loving, pure and sweet, strong and life-long, carried to degrees hitherto unknown' will penetrate the organism of society, 'not only giving tone to individual character, and making it unprecedently emotional, muscular, heroic, and refined, but having deepest relations to general politics' – then are we perhaps not justified in foreseeing here the advent of an enthusiasm which shall rehabilitate those outcast instincts, by giving them a spiritual atmosphere, an environment of recognised and healthy emotions, wherein to expand at liberty and purge away the grossness and the madness of their pariahdom? . . . Eliminating classical associations of corruption, ignoring the perplexing questions of a guilty passion doomed by law and popular antipathy to failure, he begins anew with sound and primitive humanity.[40]

It is not far-fetched, given what Sidgwick owed to Symonds, to suggest that he regarded him in crucial respects as a fellow traveller in the quest to reconcile classical and medieval excellence, one who often touched the ideal of symmetry, a kind of symmetry of which Symonds's sexual orientation was but a further manifestation. For Symonds held, after all, that in 'practical rules of conduct' the only sin is the 'indulgence of any natural craving so as to injure the whole organism'.[41] For Sidgwick, the Uranians were fellow-explorers of future possibilities, sports of nature requiring careful veiling from present political realities. He even found in Symonds a modern, sympathetic striving to enter into the views of others, to listen and converse, across the lines of class and gender, at a pitch that he could not rival. Symonds, with Whitman and Carpenter, posed with some urgency the question of just what kind of moral psychology benevolence did demand.

On the other side, one hears the Sidgwickian note in Symonds's close to *A Problem in Modern Ethics*: 'The half, as the Greeks said, is more than the whole; and the time has not yet come to raise the question whether the love of man for man shall be elevated through a hitherto unapprehended chivalry to nobler powers, even as the barbarous love of man for woman once was. This question at the present moment is deficient in actuality. The world cannot be invited to entertain it.'[42]

And if death were the great test of the human viability of any ethic, any ethology – and it was so in many more senses than one, given the self-shedding heroics of gay sexuality – then Symonds was the one friend Sidgwick had found who challenged him to the core. Much could be made of Symonds's painful, semi-mystical struggles with his own identity. His *Memoirs* record that in his earlier years he would sometimes fall into a trance-like state:

It consisted in a gradual but swiftly progressive obliteration of space, time, sensation and the multitudinous factors of experience which seemed to qualify what we are pleased to call ourself. In proportion as these conditions of ordinary consciousness were subtracted, the sense of an underlying or essential consciousness acquired intensity. At last nothing remained but a pure, absolute, abstract self. The universe became without form and void of content. But self persisted, formidable in its vivid keenness, asking or rather feeling the most poignant doubt about reality, ready as it seemed to find existence break as breaks a bubble round about it. And what then? The apprehension of a coming dissolution, the grim conviction that this state was the last state of the conscious self, the sense that I had followed the last thread of being to the verge of the abyss and had arrived at demonstration of eternal *maya* or illusion, stirred or seemed to stir me up again.[43]

Such states, which he experienced with diminishing frequency until the age of 28, impressed upon Symonds 'the phantasmal unreality of all the circumstances which contribute to a merely phenomenal consciousness' and led him to ask, for the rest of his life, which was the unreality, 'the trance of fiery vacant apprehensive sceptical self from which I issue, or these surrounding phenomena and habits which veil that inner self and build a self of flesh-and-blood conventionality?' Still more disturbing: 'What would happen if the final stage of the trance were reached – if after the abduction of phenomenal conditions beyond recovery, the denuded sense of self should pass away in a paroxysm of doubt? Would it be absorption into the real life beyond phenomena? Could another garment of sensitive experience clothe again that germ of self, which recognised the unsubstantiality of all that seem to make it human?'

Sidgwick, for all his ghost-seeing agonizing over the question of personal survival, seems never truly to have felt – from the inside, as it were – this kind of doubt about the substantiality of his own existence, a fear of dissolution here and now, or potential for some form of ecstatic, oceanic merging with creation. Occasionally, he remarks on the distancing of retrospection, how 'one never really can sympathise completely with one's former self, and the sense of the incompleteness of sympathy produces a faint but deep discord in the innermost of one's nature'.[44] Yet his own shuddering, ontological insecurity has more to do with doubting his continued existence after death. It was only Symonds, suspended in an aura of doubt between the absoluteness of self and the utter dissolution of self, who could vivify and make real for him 'the deepest problems of human life'.

In a way, Symonds raised in connection with homogeneic identity the concern that the brilliant feminist Mona Caird raises in connection with feminism, when she makes Hadria, in *The Daughters of Danaus*, ask: 'Don't you think people grow egoistic through having to fight incessantly for existence – I mean for individual existence?...One has the choice between egoism and extinction.' But, like Whitman and Carpenter, he was attracted to another alternative. In Tennyson's words: 'All at once, as it were, out of the intensity of the consciousness of individuality, the individuality itself seemed to dissolve and fade away into boundless being, and this not a confused state, but the clearest of the clearest, the surest of the surest, utterly beyond words, where death was an almost laughable impossibility, the loss of personality – if so it were – seeming no extinction but the only true life.'[45] Little wonder that the self-conscious, self-important Sidgwick was entranced.

If all of this still sounds highly Apostolic, that is surely no coincidence: Sidgwick had, by his own reckoning, been profoundly moulded by that experience of élite comradely enquiry, Maurice-style Platonism, and self-discovery. But as he aged, much of his youthful arrogance fell away, and he was drawn more to the Whitmanesque (or pragmatist) belief that the experience of people in 'the thick and heat of the struggle of active life' was vital to moral progress. With Symonds, his Platonist predilections began to yield to an openness as to future societal possibilities. Strange as it sounds, the culmination of the classical utilitarian tradition was thus modulated into the vanguardism of gay liberation. One might be forgiven for concluding that, at that time and that place, real progress was being made.

Perhaps then, in the end, Sidgwick was a bit better than his academic reception has allowed, in its chilly neglect of his sympathetic reaching towards Symonds, and of the very possibility of utilitarian friendships coherently carrying this meaning. In an 1872 letter to Dakyns, which might just as well have been written to Symonds, 'the point of view of the Universe' broke down and confessed: 'I feel often as unrelated and unadapted to my universe as man can feel, except on the side of friendship; and there, in my deepest gloom, all seems strangely good, and you among the best...But "golden news" expect none, unless I light perchance on the secret of the Universe, in which case I will let you know.'[46]

Notes

1 J. A. Symonds, *The Letters of John Addington Symonds*, ed. Robert Peters and Herbert Schueller (Detroit, 1967–9), iii, 475–7.

2   J. B. Schneewind, *Sidgwick's Ethics and Victorian Moral Philosophy* (Oxford, 1977).

3   Phyllis Grosskurth, *John Addington Symonds: A Biography* (1964), 280–94, 318–19.

4   *Henry Sidgwick, A Memoir*, ed. A. Sidgwick and E. M. Sidgwick (1906), 166.

5   Quoted in R. Harrod, *The Life of John Maynard Keynes* (New York, 1951), 116–17. Works on Keynes and Bloomsbury generally have been singularly obtuse on this subject.

6   *Memoir*, 533.

7   The allusion is to Clough's *Dipsychus*, from the Greek *dipsychos* meaning 'twin-souled' and used to refer to the conflicts between the demands of the conscience and the demands of the world. A thoroughgoing absorption in Clough is another common bond between Symonds and Sidgwick.

8   This work is included in Henry Sidgwick, *The Complete Works and Selected Correspondence*, ed. B. Schultz (Charlottesville, VA, 1997).

9   Bernard Williams, *Ethics and the Limits of Philosophy* (Cambridge, MA, 1985).

10   Ibid., 107.

11   Ibid., 108–9.

12   See *Miscellaneous Essays and Addresses*, ed. A. Sidgwick and E. M. Sidgwick (1904), and *Complete Works*.

13   *Memoir*, 97.

14   See Eve Sedgwick, *Epistemology of the Closet* (Berkeley, CA, 1990); and George Chauncey, *Gay New York* (New York, 1994), 375, n9 (for some important qualifications to the metaphor of the 'closet').

15   *Memoir*, 38.

16   See 'Miscellaneous Letters', in *Complete Works*.

17   Henry Sidgwick, 'Conformity and Subscription', in *Complete Works*.

18   *Memoir*, 201.

19   H. Sidgwick, 'The Poems and Prose Remains of Arthur Hugh Clough', in *Miscellaneous Essays*, 68, n1. This essay is singularly revealing of Sidgwick's priorities; and of the selections from *Dipsychus* he pregnantly remarked that 'its utterances are at once individual and universal, revealing the author to the reader, and the same time the reader to himself'. Ironically, Symonds had aided in producing this still quite veiled selection of Clough's works.

20   Arthur Hugh Clough, *Selected Poems*, ed. Jim McCue (1991), Introduction.

21   This letter is printed for the first time in 'Letters to John Addington Symonds', in *Complete Works*.

22   Symonds, *Letters*, i, 742.

23   Sidgwick to Dakyns, 20 June 1862, in *Complete Works*, 2nd edn (1999).

24   J. A. Symonds, *Memoirs*, ed. Phyllis Grosskurth (1984), 243.

25   *Memoir*, 33–4.

26   Ibid., 467.

27   Ibid., 471.

28   Symonds, *Letters*, iii, 206–7.

29   Ibid., iii, 674–6.

30   *Memoir*, 484.

31   Ibid., 485–6.

32   Symonds, *Memoirs*, 189.

33   *Memoir*, 346.

34   Ibid., 396.
35   Ibid., 357.
36   Symonds, *Memoirs*, 249.
37   *Memoir*, 78.
38   Quoted in A. Gauld, *The Founders of Psychical Research* (New York, 1968), 322.
39   This essay is printed for the first time in *Complete Works*.
40   J. A. Symonds, *Studies in Sexual Inversion*, new edn (New York, 1975), 93–4.
41   Symonds, *Memoirs*, 250.
42   Symonds, *Sexual Inversion*, 193.
43   Symonds, *Memoirs*, 57–8.
44   *Memoir*, 330.
45   Quoted in Edward Carpenter, *Towards Democracy*, new edn (1985), 412, n1.
46   *Memoir*, 259.

3

A Problem in Gay Heroics: Symonds and *l'Amour de l'impossible*

Jonathan Kemp

In his *Memoirs*, Symonds refers to homosexuality as 'the love of the impossible'. If we assume that by 'love' he meant desire – or sex – then what was so impossible about it? It certainly went on, so in that sense it wasn't impossible. We may therefore legitimately ask: how did the discourse that emerged around homosexuality at the end of the nineteenth century foreclose the possibility of love – or desire, or sex – between men?

At a time when it was generally perceived as effeminate, Symonds attempted to 'masculinize' homosexual love, and I shall explore the ways in which he tried to do this by synthesizing his own position as a homosexual writer with the position of medical men such as Havelock Ellis. With Symonds, who is cited as the first person to use the word 'homosexual' in an English publication, the homosexual discourse was characterized from its very inception by anxieties around issues of private/public, knowledge/ignorance, subjectivity/objectivity.

Like Edward Carpenter, Symonds is seen as a pioneer of the health model of homosexuality, and as someone who, through his essays *A Problem in Greek Ethics* and *A Problem in Modern Ethics*, instigated a move towards greater social tolerance. Yet his *Memoirs* express the conviction that he was suffering from an incurable sickness, a 'congenital aberration of the passions' which had been 'the poison of [his] life'. Between these two statements, where can we locate the 'truth' of homosexuality and its emergence into discourse? How did the initial discursive appearance of a homosexual *type* relate not only to a medical model but also to actual lived experience? Moreover, how can we make sense of this apparent contradiction between the private and the public self?

The *Memoirs* of John Addington Symonds, when finally published in 1984, were given the curious subtitle: *The Secret Homosexual Life of a Leading Nineteenth Century Man of Letters.* Anyone familiar with the figure of Symonds and his role in homosexual history (see, for example, Jeffrey Weeks's *Coming Out*) will find it odd that Symonds's homosexuality could be referred to as a secret. True, it would have been foolish publicly to parade one's homosexuality in light of the Labouchere Amendment of 1885, which criminalized 'acts of gross indecency' between men with a sentence of up to two years' hard labour; but Symonds has earned a place in gay history as a pioneer, not a man with a 'secret' homosexual life. His writing alluded to it, his close friends were aware of it, and, so far as it was possible at the time to live openly as a gay man, Symonds did: so where's the secret? The word 'secret' functions here as an attitude of critics and writers on Symonds much more than it reflects Symonds's own position, which seems to have been fairly open. In *Effeminate England* (1995), Joseph Bristow refers to the 'open secret' of Symonds's homosexuality within his circle of friends. His homosexuality was a secret that everyone knew but no-one talked about, a characteristic of homosexual discourse.

In *The Novel and the Police* (1988), D. A. Miller writes that secrecy can function as 'the subjective practice in which the oppositions of private/public, inside/outside, subject/object are established, and the sanctity of their first term kept inviolate'. And he argues that 'the phenomenon of the "open secret" does not, as one might think, bring about the collapse of those binarisms and their ideological effects, but rather attests to their fantasmatic recovery'. For Symonds, as for lesbians and gay men today, the disclosure of one's sexuality is a constantly negotiable event. By shifting the responsibility for the fate of his memoirs on to his literary executor, Symonds avoided such a negotiation. The *real* secret, for students of gay history, is the revelation of Symonds's true feelings about his homosexual desire, which he describes in the memoirs as an 'inexorable and incurable disease'. In public, he was perceived as a progressive man of letters, poet, intellectual, free-thinker. In private, he regarded his homosexual desire to be an innate sickness from which his abilities as a writer and thinker suffered immeasurably. The ideological effects of the private/public divide are thus fantasmatically recovered, and what Eve Sedgwick calls the 'crisis of definition' is anxiously aroused.

Symonds was acutely aware of the assumed objectivity of science and the so-called subjectivity of literature. When he was scouting for someone with whom he could write a book on inversion, he admitted in a letter to Edward Carpenter: 'I need somebody of medical importance to collaborate with. Alone, I could make but little effect – the effect of an eccentric.' The man he approached for this collaboration was Havelock Ellis, a young heterosexual doctor just then making a name for himself in the field of sexology. The pair never met, but the collaborative result of their correspondence was *Sexual Inversion*, published in 1897, one of the first works on homosexuality to appear in English (although it was originally published in German due to Ellis's fear of legal repercussions). Symonds avoided accusations of indecency by specifying his readership: men interested in scientific phenomena. In Symonds's *Memoirs*, the chapter dealing with his homosexuality is entitled: 'Containing material which none but students of psychology and ethics need peruse'. The message is clear: everyone else should move on to the next chapter to avoid offence or confusion – this is esoteric stuff.

Symonds is adopting the highbrow tones of the doctor, and for under-standable reasons. As Wayne Koestenbaum has explained in *Double Talk* (1989), sexology 'promised to be a forgiving branch of an implacably homophobic culture'; and Symonds 'longed to blend his voice with the impeccable tones of the doctor', to avoid accusations of prurience or, worse, partisanship. The guise of a doctor replaces subjectivity with objectivity, and the homosexual's own voice becomes subordinate to the authoritative voice of medicine. What Foucault calls the reverse dis-course – whereby the homosexual begins to speak on his own behalf, using the same categories and terms by which he is medically disquali-fied – was not allowed to function independently; it was contingent on theories and vocabulary and protocol set down by the medical discourse. Like a colonized race learning the master language before being able to articulate dissent, Symonds and others like him had at their disposal only the language of science with which to work towards legitimacy.

The latter half of the nineteenth century saw the emergence of a dialectic between the medical and the literary that is extremely interesting. The roots of this dialectic can be traced to that period of taxonomic frenzy by which the invert/Uranian/homosexual was constructed within European discursive practices, with the consequential paradigmatic shift from sin to sickness that still prevails in Western thought. As Weeks has written, these '"scientific" theories ... formed the boundaries within which homosexuals had to begin to define themselves'. Weeks suggests that the widespread adoption of neologisms, such as 'Uranian' and 'invert', during this period 'marks as crucial a turning-point in attitudes to homo-sexuality, as the adoption of "gay" as a self-description of homosexuals in the 1970s'.[1] But it was homosexual men of letters such as Symonds and Carpenter who took up the gauntlet and responded to the medical-ization with a view to emancipation. Homosexual doctors, if there were any, kept quiet. This immediately set up a discourse around subjectivity/ objectivity, knowledge/ignorance, and private/public.

Symonds's death in 1893 meant not only that he missed the Wilde trials and their horrific impact on the lives of English homosexuals; it meant also that he did not see the project with Ellis through to completion and publication. After his death, his writings on homosexuality were suppressed by his literary executor, Horatio Brown, and his role in the writing of *Sexual Inversion* was effectively erased. However, the nature of discourse clearly works in the face of such erasure, as evidenced by the anonymity of the case histories which constituted the foundation of medical observation. These authorless narratives supply the experiential data upon which medical 'truth' was based.

Symonds both resists the medical insistence on sickness whilst *at the same time* articulating it to explain and defend his sense of same-sex desire as somehow at the very core of his being; combining, as Rudi Bleys puts it, 'a fierce rejection of the physician's pathological etiology' *and* an 'acceptance of it as a scientific alibi for his profile of himself having a distinct, inescapable identity'.[2] In his correspondence with Ellis, Symonds expresses great concern that collaborating with a doctor will present homosexuality in the wrong light, whilst also offering the only valid mode of objective representation.

In a letter to Horatio Brown, Symonds refers to the *Memoirs* as having a unique value in their 'disclosure of a type of man who has *not yet been classified*', a curious comment when one considers that by the time Symonds wrote the autobiography he was well aware of the medical profession's zealous taxonomy of inverts. Indeed, he could be said to have contributed to such classification by his collaboration with Ellis.

Was he, perhaps, referring to the *self*-classification rather than the taxonomic tagging from above, explicitly foregrounding the reversal of discourse which Foucault was later to theorize? Perhaps this hitherto unclassified type was the non-effeminate homosexual, which type Symonds seems to have been, and which medical science ignored in favour of those examples which supported the third-sex/inversion trope because it was more in line with their theories of perversion and degeneration. In the *Memoirs* Symonds describes himself both within *and* against Ulrichs's taxonomics:

> With regard to Ulrichs, in his peculiar phraseology, I should certainly be tabulated as a *Mittel Urning*, holding a mean between the *Mannling* and the *Weibling*; that is to say, one whose emotions are directed to the male sex during the period of adolescence and early manhood; who

is not marked either by an effeminate passion for robust adults or by a predilection for young boys; in other words, one whose comradely instincts are tinged with a distinct sexual partiality. But in this sufficiently accurate description of my attitude, I do not recognise anything which justifies the theory of a female soul. Morally and intellectually, in character and taste and habits, I am more masculine than many men I know who adore women. I have no feminine feeling for the males who rouse my desire.

In Ulrichs's taxonomy a *Mannling* is a masculine homosexual, a *Weibling* an effeminate one. Between these two poles, Symonds strings his flag. Symonds explicitly challenges the medical association of 'feminine feeling' with a desire for males, and yet his desire for 'sound and vigorous young men of a lower rank' suggests an idealization of working-class masculinity which contrasts with his own class position and personal ill-health. Like Carpenter and Forster, he never chose male lovers from his own class. Describing a pick-up with a grenadier, Symonds contrasts himself – 'a slight nervous man of fashion in [his] dress clothes' – with this 'strapping fellow in a scarlet uniform'; Symonds was 'strongly attracted by his physical magnetism'. A lifetime of illness would seem to have led Symonds to associate his own homosexual desire with sickness, and the objects of his desire with health. Therefore, while health equalled masculinity, sickness equalled femininity. Although Symonds contests the notion of 'feminine feeling', he would seem to associate his sickness (both his tuberculosis and his homosexuality) with a lack of masculinity and virility.

Regarding the *Memoirs*, Symonds was torn between being 'anxious . . . that this document should not perish', and desiring that it be not 'injurious to my family'. He wrote: 'I have to think of the world's verdict – since I have given pledges to the future in the shape of my four growing girls.' Unsure how to solve the problem, Symonds left it to Brown, his executor, to decide. Brown published a biography of Symonds two years after his death composed almost entirely of extracts from the *Memoirs*, but with all references to his homosexuality excised, thus negating the book's very *raison d'être*. On Brown's death in 1926, the manuscript went to the London Library with a 50-year ban on publication.

Symonds complained towards the end of his life that he had never properly spoken out on homosexuality. Yet the *Memoirs*, whilst affording him the vehicle to do so privately, are less than explicit. Even the anonymous case-study of himself included in *Sexual Inversion* is reticent about what he actually did with other men, and is more concerned with the aetiology and development of his homosexual desire. But, like the above passage from the *Memoirs*, the case history presented in *Sexual Inversion* refutes any effeminacy: 'He is certainly not simply passive and shows no signs of *effeminatio*. He likes sound and vigorous young men of a lower rank from the age of 20 to 25. I gather from his conversation that the mode of pleasure is indifferent to his tastes.'

Like Carpenter's case history in *Sexual Inversion*, Symonds denies any indulgence in sodomy ('certainly not simply passive'). The message is clear in both case histories: sodomy is for sissies. The association of being 'simply passive' with *effeminatio* bears witness to the problematics of homosexual discourse (social acceptance versus sexual honesty, deconstruction of stereotypes versus internalized homophobia), and points to the constant anxiety, not only around sodomy as feminizing, but also effeminacy as the sure sign of sexual passivity.

This tension between the private and public selves is amply exemplified by the subtle yet poignant differences between one scene in the case history and its corresponding description in the *Memoirs*: namely, Symonds's erotic daydreams of naked sailors. In the *Memoirs* he writes:

> Among my earliest recollections I must record certain visions, half-dream, half-reverie, which were certainly erotic in their nature, and which recurred frequently just before sleeping. I used to fancy myself crouched upon the floor amid a company of naked adult men: sailors, such as I had seen about the streets of Bristol. The contact of their bodies afforded me a vivid and mysterious pleasure.

In the case-history:

> About the age of 8, if not before, he became subject to singular half-waking dreams. He fancied himself seated on the floor among several adult and naked sailors, whose genitals and buttocks he contemplated and handled with relish. He called himself the 'dirty pig' of these men, and felt that they were in some way his masters, ordering him to do uncleanly services to their bodies.

The case history omits any reference to Bristol, yet the anonymity allows for more sexual explicitness. The egality of the first scene gives way to a scenario of sexual subservience in the second, 'A' (the pseudonym chosen by Symonds)[3] submitting to the self-appellation of 'dirty pig' and obeying orders from a crouched position between the sailors' thighs. The more detailed account was possible, Koestenbaum concludes, only when Symonds had given up his signature. Moreover, both his extreme youth and his low position suggest that this is a fantasy about being a 'bottom', which conflicts with Symonds's claim to be 'not simply passive'. This conflict epitomizes the dilemma: 'Can a male be homosexual, combine with another male, without a loss of virility?'[4] The ever-present spectre of feminization haunts relations between men.

In her introduction to the *Memoirs*, Phyllis Grosskurth comments on the book's 'curious admixture of candour and evasiveness', calling it 'a hybrid, falling somewhere between literature and a psychological case-history', and wondering why, if he was writing primarily for himself – or for posterity – could he not be entirely frank? She highlights the contradiction between Symonds's repeated insistence that the initial impetus for the *Memoirs* was a desire 'to help others as unfortunate as himself' and her own observation that 'the frequency with which he uses the words "abnormal", "morbid", "unwholesome" suggests a growing suspicion that he might be some kind of monster'.

Symonds himself talks of 'the strain of this attraction and repulsion – the intolerable desire and the repudiation of mere fleshly satisfaction', the war between 'a beauteous angel' and 'a devil abhorred'. In this text, as in the man himself, the afflictions of a homophobic culture wrestle with the exalted sentiments of homosexual love.[5] Likewise, in his poem *Phallus Impudicus*, included in the *Memoirs*, the image of a phallic mushroom – 'poisonous and loathsome ... spawn of hell' – is contrasted with the romantic vision of his sleeping lover's genitals as 'the firm rondure of love's root of joy'; 'unhallowed, foul desire/Dry lust that revels in the fleshly mire' shockingly counterpointed by the image of male beauty as 'a deathless fire', the desire for it 'a divine, undying thirst', a joy which is 'Soul-born soul-nourished'. The war between such polarized images was a war which raged not only within Symonds, but within the homosexual discourse itself.

Although he recognized his desire for other men at an early age, Symonds repressed those feelings and tried to live a 'normal' life according to Victorian morals and social mores.[6] This – of course – involved marriage, at the age of 24, when he was, he claims, 'still unconscious' of the sensuality of his desires for other men, although he was capable of romanticizing about them quite easily. His marriage, he hoped, would 'satisfy the side of [his] nature which thrilled so strangely when [he] touched a boy'. Yet within 15 months of marriage his desires, still unsatisfied, threatened the tranquillity he sought.

Symonds recounts from this period a graffito which profoundly troubled him: 'an emphatic diagram of phallic meeting'. This imagery was of 'so *penetrative* a character ... that it pierced the very marrow' (my emphasis) of his soul. It became for him a defining moment in the discovery of his sexuality, a recognition, however crudely represented, of what he most desired: 'That obscene graffito was the sign and symbol of a paramount and permanent craving of my physical and psychical nature.' This sign and symbol pornographically condenses the distress of a desire hegemonically invalidated.

In the *Memoirs*, this revelation is succeeded by the birth of his first daughter, an event which foregrounds the sterility of the male–male union, to render that graffito a cipher, a zero. This sterility is further illustrated by the fact that at that time Symonds was only mentally investing in homosexual imagery and not physically acting on those impulses; a behaviour which, in the light of his procreative signifier – that is, a child – would define his identity as heterosexual, not homosexual: his homosexual identity would appear to amount to zero. Which begs the question: Where does an identity come into being? Is it on the psychological or the physical plane? Is it constituted *by* desires or the acting out *of* those desires? Moreover, does the physical have less bearing on discursive reality than the psychical, the material less than the enunciative?

Foucault's analysis of sexuality focuses on the discursive impulse to distil every facet of human personality down to the existence of a true, essential, and *pre*discursive sexuality, with the result that, for the homosexual,

> nothing that went into his total composition was unaffected by his sexuality. It was everywhere present in him: at the root of all his actions because it was their insidious and indefinitely active principle; written immodestly on his face and body because it was a secret that always gave itself away.[7]

An 'open secret', no less.

In *A Problem in Modern Ethics* Symonds criticizes the physiognomy argument – which saw in the body of the homosexual unmistakable signs of his deviant desires. In the *Memoirs*, however, he colludes with it, confirming Foucault's argument by believing that his entire personality and ability to function as a writer and thinker were detrimentally affected by his homosexual desires: 'It cannot be doubted that the congenital aberration of the passions which I have described has been the poison of my life.' He refers to the time and energy wasted on expressing it, how it has 'interfered with the pursuit of study', how his marriage 'has been spoiled by it'. Symonds believes he carries within him 'the seeds of what I know to be an incurable malady', a 'deeply rooted perversion of the sexual instincts (uncontrollable, ineradicable, amounting to monomania)to expose which in its relation to my *whole nature* has been the principal object of these memoirs' (my emphasis). He calls this 'uncontrollable' sexual instinct 'the wolf', and describes it as 'that undefined craving coloured with a vague but poignant hankering after males'. Upon viewing the phallic graffito, Symonds was assaulted by this hankering, this wolf. He writes: 'The wolf leapt out: my malaise of the moment was connected into a clairvoyant and tyrannical appetite for the thing which I had rejected five months earlier in the alley by the barracks' (i.e. sex with a grenadier). With this realization comes a clearer definition of that 'vague but poignant hankering after males'. Yet that vague hankering is experienced as 'a *precise* hunger after sensual pleasure, whereof I had not dreamed before save in repulsive visions of the night' (my emphasis). As with Freud's Wolf Man,[8] a 'deviant' sexuality is here linked with a wolf, a wild and predatory carnivore, an animal closely linked in folklore with unimaginable and unconscious fears. Symonds lycanthropizes his homosexual desire as brutal and savage, something which preys tyrannically on the precariously maintained stability of his heterosexual marriage. Symonds's 'civilized' self is at the mercy of a primitive and untamed sexual self which lies in waiting, ready to leap out in moments of weakness to 'wreck [his] happiness and disturb [his] studious habits'. Grosskurth quotes a letter written by Edmund Gosse to Symonds in 1890 which describes his own struggle with homosexual feelings, and in which a similar lycanthropy occurs:

> I know all that you speak of – the solitude, the rebellion, the despair
> . . . years ago, I wanted to write to you about all this, and withdrew
> through cowardice. I have had a very fortunate life, but there has
> been this obstinate twist in it. I have reached a quieter time – some
> beginnings of that Sophoclean period when the wild beast dies. He is
> not dead, but tamer; I understand him and the trick of his claws.

Like Symonds, Gosse sees his desire as something separate from and in conflict with the civilized self, a 'wild beast' in need of restraint, and at whose mercy he is. It is the homosexual's life mission to 'understand him and the trick of his claws'.

The wolf would appear to be a potent and popular image in connection with homosexual desire. Proust, for example, when discussing the futility of a Sodomitic movement, or a city of Sodom (futile because no one would be seen dead in it), reasons that 'they [homosexuals] would repair to Sodom only on days of supreme necessity, when their own town was empty, at those seasons when hunger drives *the wolf* from the

woods' (my emphasis). In these scenarios, homosexual desire is a force
to be reckoned with. When it craves fulfilment, there's no denying it.
Symonds commits himself strongly to the belief that his desire for
males is instinctual and innate, and affirms that his attempt at redirect-
ing his desire towards his wife forced his 'true' instincts to reassert
themselves all the more violently. He presents the image of a man at
the mercy of a brutal force:

> God help me! I cried. I felt humiliated, frightened, gripped in the clutch
> of doom. Nothing remained but to parry, palliate, procrastinate. There
> was no hope of escape. And all the while the demon ravished my
> imagination with 'the love of the impossible'... From this decisive
> moment forward to the end, my life had to fly on a broken wing, and
> my main ambition has been to constitute a working compromise.

For Symonds, desire is a demon with fangs and claws with which one
must compromise in order to survive, the cause of great anxiety: a rather
postmodern concept of sexuality as something threatening to one's sense
of self. An intelligent, civilized man is reduced to blind panic – 'gripped
in the clutch of doom' – at the merest whiff of that demon, desire, the
almost gothic signifier of 'the love of the impossible', of a 'love that
dare not speak its name', from fear of being ravaged by the 'wolf' no less
than by punitive legislation.

This is wildly at odds with Symonds's liberationist position in *Modern
Ethics*, where it becomes simply a question of liberating the homosexual
from the social and legal constraints on his true self. If he had not been
forced – by fear of vilification and imprisonment – to hide his desire,
the homosexual, Symonds argued, would be a noble and socially valu-
able person. He claimed that the public perception of homosexuals as
suspicious and delinquent people is merely the inevitable result of their
position in a culture that refuses to allow them to express themselves. If
only society would get off our backs we would all be happy: this is a
supposition which ignores the often disturbing, unsettling, and threatening ways in which sexual desire – especially *dissident* desire – is experienced in terms of its destabilizing effect on our sense of coherence and
equilibrium. In *Modern Ethics* Symonds argues that social education is
the answer to oppression – a popular myth of modern sexual-liberationist
discourse (what Foucault calls 'the repressive hypothesis').

The image of a man in torment would seem to contradict the more
popular portrait of Symonds as a sexual pioneer at ease with his sexuality
and fighting for greater social tolerance. Is the best a homosexual can

hope for 'a working compromise' with a demonic, voracious sexual appetite over which he has no control? At best, a life flown 'on a broken
wing'? Symonds was clearly caught between wanting to emphasize the
pain experienced by homosexuals in a culture which oppressed them
and wanting to expound a theory of homosexual desire as an innate,
healthy, and natural phenomenon. Although not necessarily mutually
exclusive positions, the dilemma this created in Symonds resulted in a
concept of identity as precariously contingent on oppression and the
medicalization of teleologically conceived sex behaviour. Without the
torture, the oppression, from which to struggle and forge a sense of self,
could one attain the status of a coherent identity? Liberationist gay
movements also claim that gay identity is heroically wrested from an
oppressive and life-denying discourse and maintained in the face of complete adversity, an opinion Foucault criticizes by seeing sexuality as the
product of a discourse *contingent on* such notions. In her biography of
Symonds, Grosskurth presents 'the problem' of Symonds's homosexuality as not only 'the overwhelming obsession of Symonds's life' but also
the 'central fact about the man', thus exemplifying Foucault's theory of
the prediscursive claims of sexuality.

   As Symonds's tortured self-oppression indicates, the construction of this
discursive belief in a central, true sexuality acted as a powerful means of
self-surveillance, policing every gesture, every thought, every appetite.
This rigorous examination of oneself for signs of inversion found its
apotheosis in Xavier Mayne's *The Intersexes* (1908), which contained a
questionnaire for readers keen to discover whether they were 'at all an
Uranian'. But, as Koestenbaum points out, 'the book's secret purpose
was to stimulate them to self-knowledge', what Foucault calls a discursive reversal. Symonds's *Memoirs* – which were, in Bristow's words,
'a polemic about the specific identity that attended his sexual habits' –
could have played a central part in these private recognition scenes,
with their dramatization of one individual's sexual development and
emphasis on a teleological and tragic will to truth. Unfortunately, his
rather vague instructions to Brown to put his (Symonds's) family first in
all matters concerning his publications, meant the manuscript did not
see the light of day for nearly a hundred years.

   Unlike the *Memoirs*, however, Symonds's privately printed essay, *A Problem in Modern Ethics* (1891), which both Grosskurth and Weeks see as a
counterpart to the *Memoirs*, circulated within the homosexual under-
ground of the early 1890s, and it was undoubtedly a signal text in the
emergence of a coherent sense of the 'homosexual' as a particular type
of person/personality. Only 50 copies of the book were printed and,

despite the appearance on the title page of the disclaimer 'Addressed especially to medical psychologists and jurists', it appears to have been sent out mainly to fellow-inverts.

Grosskurth testifies that Symonds received hundreds of letters from men who identified with *A Problem in Modern Ethics*, who saw within its pages a mirror-image of their own feelings; men whose lives were characterized by constant conflict and furtiveness. For the first time, men whose sexual interest was predominantly – if not exclusively – in other men could read about themselves in a way that did not classify their desires as the product of sin or sickness. The margins of *Modern Ethics* were wide in order that recipients could return their copies with written comments, thus reversing the discourse and giving homosexuals a vehicle to speak out via this pseudo-scientific text, or, as Koestenbaum argues, making the readers collaborators. In this way, Symonds hoped to open up the debate to include inverts.

A tension was thus created between this desire to include the voice of inverts and Symonds's desire to collaborate with a man of science to lend authority to his own voice. As stated earlier, it was left to literary men to wrest from medical discourse the authority with which to speak out. But that voice must constantly refer back to medical authority: 'the specter of a homosexual doctor . . . dissolves contraries' (Koestenbaum). Subjectivity, oddly enough, is not seen as an authority. Medical 'objectivity' is the only discourse allowed a legitimate voice. As Gosse's words testify: 'The position of a young person so tormented is really that of a man buried alive and conscious, but *deprived of speech*' (my emphasis). This tension was one way through which a homosexual discourse was created, producing the concept of a 'gay identity' as something negotiated between medical prescription and free self-inscription – a battle between the subject and a society concerned with objectifying him. The medical categorization made identification possible, but it supplied a rigid and narrow paradigm in which such identification could occur. Science was the only position from which one could speak with impunity and without imputation.[9] All religions require articles of faith and bearers of authority, and medical science, rapidly becoming a new religion in the dying years of the nineteenth century, was to be no exception.

Yet by 'describing homosexuality from a position within the subject, and then denying that one has entered the subject and made it one's own', imputation constantly threatens to cast a shadow over the speaker, resulting in what Koestenbaum calls 'duplicitous double talk'. Medical authority on such an anxious subject is thus constantly threatened by the accusation that too much knowledge hints at personal experience. In short, it takes one to know one.

In *Modern Ethics*, Symonds dismantles various medical theories – Moreau, Krafft-Ebing, and Lombroso – and argues that medicine's focus on 'morbidity' (or pathology) as a cause or condition of homosexuality is wide of the mark. Symonds argues that morbidity is, rather, the *result* of living in a society which legislates and culturally prohibits homosexuality:

> The grain of truth contained in this vulgar error is that, under the prevalent laws and hostilities of modern society, the inverted passion has to be indulged furtively, spasmodically, hysterically; that the repression of it through fear and shame frequently leads to habits of self-abuse; and that its unconquerable solicitations sometimes convert it from a healthy outlet of the sexual nature into a morbid monomania.

Although we may find it easy to criticize this in the light of recent work such as that of Foucault, Symonds was, with such an approach, positing homosexual desire as a perfectly natural drive, not as the debauched behaviour of bored libertines or frustrated prisoners. For Symonds, homosexual desire is inborn and therefore natural, and 'there is no proof that they are the subjects of disease', which contradicts his claim in the *Memoirs* to be the victim of this disease.

Symonds's main concern in *Modern Ethics*, then, was to disassociate homosexuality from the morbidity/pathology model. By using the theories of Karl Heinrich Ulrichs, for whom homosexuals, or Urnings, possessed a woman's soul within a man's body, Symonds was able to root a discussion on homosexuality within a scientific paradigm without recourse to contemporary theories of morbidity, or degeneration. Ulrichs himself was not a doctor but a jurist, whose ideas greatly influenced the sexological discourse, and who therefore throws into doubt immediately the objective claims of science, and throws into relief the contours of this discourse and its dialectical nature. Unfortunately, the appropriation of Ulrichs's formula for arguing the biological naturalism of same-sex desire imported at the same time a theory of homosexuality which was based, first and foremost, on *gender-inversion*. 'The homosexual' as constructed within medical discourse was thereby violently at odds with traditional masculinity. In this way, sexual transgression became gender-transgression (and *vice versa*).

By corresponding regularly with Ulrichs, who now lived in Italy, and by his inclusion of Ulrichs's theories in *Modern Ethics*, Symonds acted as the portal through which the inversion trope passed into the consciousness of homosexual Britons. Along with the *Memoirs* and his earlier pamphlet, *A Problem in Greek Ethics*, it can, as Bristow says, be counted 'among the first modern documents to emphasize how human identity must primarily be understood in terms of sexual preference'. At the same time, Wilde's *The Picture of Dorian Gray*[10] was establishing a literary mirror in which many homosexuals recognized a way of being which refuted traditional masculinity and presented one conduit – arguably, the only visible and culturally permissible identity at that time – through which male–male love could be articulated. In the absence of a visible alternative, the inversion trope became the central trope for homosexuality.

Like many homosexual men of letters at that time, and like André Gide and Edward Carpenter after him, Symonds relied on the Greek model of pederasty in his defence of homosexuality. At the same time, however, it was denied that the Greek model rested on sodomy. Did this play no part in the lives of Victorian homosexuals? Hardly likely, if one looks at the few examples of homosexual pornography from the period. Was its absence in apologies such as those of Symonds and Carpenter, then, a deliberate avoidance of a delicate subject? Or was it, rather, a minority taste? And what do the answers to these questions tell us about the symbolic and cultural role of the orifice that dared not speak its name?

In *Modern Ethics* Symonds wrote:

> It is the common belief that one, and only one, unmentionable act is what the lovers seek as the source of their unnatural gratification, and that this produces spinal disease, epilepsy, consumption, dropsy, and the like. Nothing can be more mistaken, as the scientifically reported cases of avowed and adult sinners amply demonstrate. Neither do they invariably or even usually prefer the *aversa Venus*; nor, when this happens, do they exhibit peculiar signs of suffering in health.

In the process of denying this 'unmentionable act', Symonds finds himself paradoxically defending it as not detrimental to individual health. His position is further complicated when, discussing Mantegazza's theory of 'anomalous passions', he writes: 'That an intimate connection exists between the nerves of the reproductive organs and the nerves of the rectum is known to anatomists and is felt by everybody.' That 'felt by everybody' cunningly universalizes rectal pleasure and shifts the topic away from homosexuality. Given the stringent anti-buggery laws in place at the time, it is hardly surprising that the majority of case-studies in *Sexual Inversion*, for example, make no mention of it. As Ellis commented:

> It will be observed that in the preceding ten cases little reference is made to the practice of *paedicatio* or *immissio penis in anum*. It is probable that in none of these cases... has it been practised. In the two following cases it has occasionally been practised, but only with repugnance and not as the satisfaction of an instinct.

Sodomy is clearly considered not to be instinctual to the homosexual. If ventured, it inspires repugnance, not pleasure. Furthermore, Symonds's most potent symbol for male–male love establishes the sameness of male–male eroticism in purely phallic terms. By foregrounding the phallus and rejecting sodomy as the behaviour of effeminate degenerates, Symonds maintains a strong link between sodomy and effeminacy. Masculinity and passive sodomy thus become mutually exclusive phenomena, and effeminacy becomes the 'natural' and inevitable attribute of the latter. To be receptive inevitably emasculates within a dimorphic gender-system.

Recalling the Wolf-Man's primal scene, which for Freud was his witnessing his parents performing *coitus a tergo*, Symonds's 'fear of the wolf' can be read as a fear of sodomy. Just as the Wolf Man fears the castration which would be the inevitable outcome of allowing the father to penetrate him – a 'truth' confirmed by seeing his mother's lack of a phallus – so Symonds too fears the lycanthropic bestiality of sodomy and its concomitant emasculation and effeminization. This becomes the true *amour de l'impossible*, the thing that terrifies because it threatens one's manhood, to the point that sex itself becomes something to avoid. Symonds claims to want no more than 'the blameless proximity of [a] pure person'.[11] Sexual intercourse between men is an impossibility for Symonds, torn as he is between Hellenistic ideals and hellish desires.

Notes

1 Jeffrey Weeks, 'Discourse, Desire, and Sexual Deviance: Some Problems in a History of Homosexuality', in Kenneth Plummer (ed.), *The Making of the Modern Homosexual* (1981).

2 Rudi Bleys (ed.), *The Geography of Perversion: Male-to-Male Sexual Behaviour outside the West and the Ethnographic Imagination, 1750–1918* (1997), 209.

3 After Symonds's death, Ellis used the symbol 'Z' for Symonds's contributions to *Sexual Inversion*, thus demoting him from the beginning of the alphabet to the end. For a detailed account of their collaboration, see Wayne Koestenbaum, *Double Talk: The Erotics of Male Literary Collaboration* (1989), 43–67.

4 John Fletcher, 'Forster's Self-Erasure: Maurice and the Scene of Masculine Love', in J. Bristow (ed.), *Sexual Sameness* (1992), 74.

5 Indeed, the two positions seem to characterize homosexual discourse: Carpenter's perverse ruins and beautiful flowers, Proust's belief in the 'sometimes beautiful, often hideous' accursed race; and Gide's debauched sodomites versus honourable pederasts.

6 For a historical context, see Jeffrey Weeks, *Sex, Politics and Society: The Regulation of Sexuality since 1800* (1981), ch. 2.

7 Michel Foucault, *The History of Sexuality, Volume One: An Introduction* (Harmondsworth, 1979), 43.

8 See M. Gardiner, *The Wolf-Man and Sigmund Freud* (Harmondsworth, 1973); Whitney Davis, *Drawing the Dream of the Wolves: Homosexuality, Interpretation, and Freud's 'Wolf-Man'* (Bloomington, IN, 1995).

9 Ellis's concerns about writing on homosexuality were alleviated by a lecturer on insanity at the Westminster Hospital, who wrote: 'So long as you confine your appeal to the jurist, the alienist, and the scientific reader, no shadow of imputation ought to rest upon you.' Quoted in Havelock Ellis, *A Note on the Bedborough Trial*, privately printed (Watford, 1898).

10 After reading *The Picture of Dorian Gray*, Symonds wrote to a friend that he thought the novel 'odd and very audacious', 'unwholesome in tone', but nonetheless 'artistically and psychologically interesting', supporting the view that a dialectic existed between medical and literary discourses. Quoted in H. M. Hyde, *Oscar Wilde* (1976), 185.

11 John Addington Symonds, *Memoirs*, ed. Phyllis Grosskurth (1984), 266.

4
Symonds and Visual Impressionability

Whitney Davis

In a text apparently written in the late 1880s when he was in his late forties, John Addington Symonds recorded a disturbing dream. He finds himself the owner of a vast estate. Uneasily he wanders its walks and parks:

> My feeling was that for a time I had been forgetting the main factor of my life and being, and that the things upon which I had innocently been priding myself were as nothing in relation to that. Just then two figures on horseback appeared... [O]ne was my youngest daughter riding a spirited little Turkish horse. The other was a groom, stalwart but supple, mounted on a noble bright bay hunter. The girl, as she approached, waved her hand. The groom touched his hat, and looked me in the eyes with one of those faces, like a Greek athlete's, which comely English peasants sometimes have. Then, like a stabbing flash of forked lightning, the truth of my misfortune pierced sense and brain, and clove the marrow of my soul. Involuntarily, I plunged my hand through coat and shirt to the flesh above my heart, and found and recognised the devil's brand, the black broad-arrow of insanity – unmentionable, unconquerable – the misery that levels and makes prisoners of all men who are marked by it.[1]

That the handsome groom's glance provokes the dreamer to realize his own unspeakable 'misfortune' suggests that the 'devil's brand' must be his homosexuality; and he is overwhelmed by knowledge of its 'insanity'. At the time Symonds recorded this dream, the concept of *Homosexualität* which he encountered in Continental writings, like those of the jurist Karl Heinrich Ulrichs, did indeed present it as a diminished responsibility, in order to help absolve defendants accused of sodomy.[2] But since the mid-1860s Symonds had explored the social institutions of the past and of modern political theory – Greek pederasty, knightly chivalry, modern 'democracy' – in which homosexual bonding or at least altruistic fraternity was a normal, even an ideal, condition of social intercourse, rational and healthy.[3] Therefore the dream makes him fear the worst, building on even older anxieties – namely that, whatever one might say about past or ideal homoeroticism, his own life had been lived on the edge of perceptual and bodily health and sanity. Long before he encountered the emerging psychopathological theory of a 'hereditary neuroticism predisposing its subject to sexual inversion', an idea he partly accepted and partly rejected, he often associated what he called his own 'high degree of nervous sensibility' with his homoerotic yearning.[4] It was this relation, in fact, which he accepted as what the dream called the 'main factor of his life'. He gave it both the earliest date, attributing it to his later childhood if not before, and the latest ratification, offering it in his mature recollections as his best explanation of his own past history. Specifically, his 'inversion' had evolved – in his own subjective experience of himself – as an attenuation of visible and visual reality. In this chapter I want to look at early – childhood, adolescent, and undergraduate – stages and contexts of this self-understanding: that is, in the period of the 1840s, 1850s, and early 1860s.

Symonds's later views, developed in his studies of historical homoeroticisms published in the late 1860s, in his aesthetic and art-critical writings of the 1870s, and in his sexological and ethical reflections of the 1880s and 1890s – matters I shall not take up here – were rooted in this earlier period, well preceding his contact with emancipationist and psychiatric writings and instead reflecting other philosophies, notably Kantian idealism, Hegelian historicism, and the 'scepticism' devolving from Humean psychology. Though Symonds was a neo-Kantian critic, wrote neo-Hegelian history, and sometimes described himself as a sceptic, the role of these systems in the emergence of late nineteenth-century homoerotic culture has not really been worked out. Broadly, we should see Symonds as a crucial historical link in the transformation of Enlightenment into early twentieth-century psychologies of erotic meaning, mediating between the era of Winckelmann or Goethe and the era of Wittgenstein and Freud. In order to trace this intellectual genealogy between 1800 and 1900, we need not only to focus on Symonds himself at mid-century but also to recall the formative influence on him in this youthful period – namely, that of his father, born in 1807.

Dr John Addington Symonds had a well-developed interest in mental disturbance and the medical–juridical definition of insanity. Through the 1860s until his death in 1871, his son constantly turned to him for medical advice and counsel in intimate matters. Echoes of the doctor's opinions resonated in his son's thought long after their substance had been superseded by more contemporary psychology and even when Symonds himself had studied its literatures. Dr Symonds graduated in 1828 from Edinburgh, a centre for innovative medical psychology in the first half of the century, where he adopted the ideas of James Cowles Prichard, an Edinburgh graduate of 1809.[5] Prichard's delineation of 'moral insanity' extended Philippe Pinel's identification, in 1791, of a mania 'confined to the moral feelings and the emotions, just as in other cases the perceptive and reasoning powers are the sole subjects of disorder'.[6] For Prichard and Symonds, the 'perversions' of 'moral insanity' included inexplicable marital jealousy, uncontrolled temper, financial recklessness, and excessive fascination with sexual matters. They recommended that the affected person separate himself totally – or be forcibly separated – from the objects towards which the disordered feelings were directed. For example, when Dr Symonds discovered in 1859 that the headmaster of Harrow, Charles Vaughan, had had an affair with one of Symonds's schoolmates, he helped enforce Vaughan's resignation. He soon learned that his own son was prone to affections similar to Vaughan's, and Symonds describes in his *Memoirs* how his father advised him totally to avoid a young chorister at Bristol Cathedral, Willie Dyer, though Symonds kept the affair going in secret. Dr Symonds probably did not think that Vaughan or his son were 'morally insane' in his strongest sense. But, to use the criteria offered in his essay on criminal responsibility, because the headmaster had strayed so far from the 'ordinary standard' and 'with reference to what was [his] former temper and character', he was suffering a diminishment of responsibility at least bordering on a perversion of moral feeling.[7] Thus he should not be prosecuted, as his relatives feared would happen, but someone – Dr Symonds himself – would have to assume temporary control of him on his behalf. In this respect, the liberalized approach of Prichard and Dr Symonds stood midway between the long-established canonical and juridical condemnation of sodomy and other heteroclite affections, and the later medical–psychiatric therapy of 'homosexuality' and other supposed sexual anomalies.

The younger Symonds absorbed this long-term transformation in conceptions of non-conventional personal agency, often reverting to his father's language. To understand certain – but not all – homoerotic life stories, he would invoke moral insanity. He did not necessarily think that a person ought totally to avoid homoerotic feeling, to 'repress' or 'sublimate' it – to use later language. So, for example, on the one hand he regarded the 'ghastliness' of Walter Pater – whose sanitized Platonism sat uneasily with his affected persona – as a kind of living death. And on the other, he regarded some of his own homoerotic friends, such as Henry Sidgwick, as better persons than himself; they did not have the excesses of feeling displayed in the moral insanities.[8]

By contrast, however, the homosexual sentiments of his friend Lord Ronald Gower, the sculptor, dismayed him, even though he enjoyed London and Rome with him: Gower, he said, 'knows everybody, from the cabbies corporals & carabinieri up to the painters princes & plenipotentiary envoys', but he 'saturate[s] one's spirit in Urningthum of the rankest most diabolical kind'.[9] Symonds's worry was not so much that Gower pursued homosexual affiliations; indeed, it was Gower who was mildly impressed by Symonds's boldness in bringing along his Venetian gondolier Angelo Fusato to aristocratic country weekends in England.[10] But, unlike Symonds, Gower had become homoeroticized in almost all domains of his life. Everything from his great collection of memorabilia of Marie Antoinette to his daring exaggeration of the phallus of Prince Hal, the allegory of 'History' on his most famous sculpture, the Shakespeare Memorial at Stratford-upon-Avon, was a token of an organizing desire: as Symonds put it, everything was 'saturated' in a single sentiment or system of ideas. Symonds was unable fully to understand this culture as anything other than moral insanity. Instead of functioning as a *particular* feeling, organized along with other, equally important sentiments, such as Sidgwick's faith or Pater's celibacy, with Gower it had become as it were the very person himself. German medical psychology was soon to elaborate this very distinction between *Empfindung* or *Gefühl*, feeling or sentiment, however 'contrary', and *Interesse* or *Instinkt*, psychological orientation or instinct. While Richard von Krafft-Ebing's 1886 *Psychopathia sexualis* – taking up Heinrich Kaan's work of the same title of 1844 – studied *Empfindung*, Freud's 1895 *Project for a Scientific Psychology* began from *Interesse*. Unfortunately, the term *Homosexualität* – preferred by emancipationists like Ulrichs – could be applied in both domains, creating the misunderstandings that Freud tried to clarify in 1905 in his first essay on the theory of sexuality.[11]

In evaluating Gower's form of life, Symonds differed from his father's tradition in regarding it to be 'insane' not simply because of its unrelieved persistence and pervasiveness. Equally important, the mania tended towards delusion, towards incorrect thought, because it seemingly accepted an unreality, an image of what could not possibly be – shading subtly into actual perceptual and cognitive disturbance. But he could not readily document any such condition in friends like Gower, despite their moral laxity. His evidence was his own history.

In his father's collection of scientific books, young Symonds, about 10 years old, found 'a series of articles on spectral illusions'. As he later recalled, these 'took hold of my imagination' (*Memoirs*, 41). Dr Symonds, writing on apparitions, thought that ideas or images 'stored up in the memory might find their way to the organs of sense, and impress them; thus the idea of a deceased individual might reach the optic nerve, and produce spectres'.[12] Ghosts, then, originate in the beholder's mind; they are his own ideas – whether realistic or not – made visible. As Dr Symonds explained: 'Ideas may attain the same intensity as sensible impressions' when the beholder falls into a kind of half sleep or 'reverie'. In this con-dition, 'surrounding [real] objects assume a shadowy indistinct outline' and 'mental shadows or phantasms' can become confused with them if the underlying object-associations are, as he put it, 'unnaturally excited'.[13] For Dr Symonds, intense reveries and resulting apparitions manifest what his generation called *dipsychia* or 'double consciousness', the very term later applied by his son to his own erotic life (*Memoirs*, 96): a dividing of realistic and unrealistic sensory ideas, the latter marked by a persisting hallucinatory image of impossible states of affairs. Throughout his life, the younger Symonds felt himself to have an unusual visual impres-sionability; 'forms, colours, aspects of nature, faces, buildings, statues, pictures . . . leave keen and durable impressions on my sensibility' (*Mem-oirs*, 216–17). He did not suppose that he had simply been endowed with this sensibility. Instead, he saw it as the product of interaction between innate susceptibility to sensation – conceived, however, as we shall see, as *also* active, as an interested 'curiosity' or even 'craving' – erotic and sexual fantasies, aesthetic intuitions, and actual encounters both with people and with art. He explored this history with retrospect-ive self-consciousness in his *Memoirs*; we can say, in fact, that this his-tory is the central subject of the autobiographical study.

When he was about five to eight years old, Symonds would walk with his grandfather and cousins over the Clifton downs. As he recalled, on these walks he would 'pass from the sense of a tangible presence into a dream', a 'very definite phase of experience, approaching hypnotism in its character' (*Memoirs*, 56–7). Possibly he was simply exhausted. But we should not discount emotions of anticipation and fear: he was going to his grandfather's villa, where the old man, portrayed as a strict and gloomy Puritan, tried to teach him arithmetic and Latin grammar. Over the years, these separations became more pronounced and their affect-ive tone more differentiated. The trance would come on, for example, when the family went to worship at the local Blind Asylum, where in its ugly, depressing chapel Symonds later believed he must have 'developed a morbid sense of sin' by 'listening to the dismal sermons' (*Memoirs*, 39). Dr Symonds moved to Clifton Hill House in 1851, when his son was 11 years old, and was finally able to surround his family with books, art, and elegant furnishings. At this point Symonds's dreamy states – as he describes them in the remarkable essay 'Clifton and A Lad's Love' – became highly pleasurable reveries at his window overlooking the city, and particularly the Cathedral cloisters, where he was beginning to identify his sense of self-separation and aspiration with the persons of the choirboys.[14]

In his autobiography Symonds asserts that the trance was fundamentally a 'doubt about reality', 'an initiation into the mysteries of scepticism' or the possibility that, if differently rooted and linked, the chain of sensory ideas might provide or prove an entirely different world from the one we are in (*Memoirs*, 58–9). (I use Humean terms because Symonds's 'scepticism' is sometimes misunderstood merely as a doubt about the existence of God.) 'Often I have asked myself with anguish, on awakening from that formless state of denuded keenly sentient being, which is the unreality: the trance of fiery vacant apprehensive sceptical self from which I issue, or these surrounding phenomena and habits which veil that inner self and build a self of flesh-and-blood conventionality?' (*Memoirs*, 58). The trance itself, 'formless', 'denuded', did not actually provide a vision of what might lie on the other side of his break with the world. But beginning in his seventh year or so, Symonds also experienced the kind of 'waking dream' that Dr Symonds had studied in his work on apparitions – what we shall have to consider as the *re*connection, however 'unrealistic', of sensory impressions:

> Among my earliest recollections I must record certain visions, half-dream, half-reverie, which were certainly erotic in their nature, and which recurred frequently just before sleeping. I used to fancy myself crouched upon the floor amid a company of naked adult men: sailors, such as I had seen about the streets of Bristol. The contact of their bodies afforded me a vivid and mysterious pleasure. Singular as it may appear that a mere child could have formed such fancies, and unable as I am to account for their origin, I am positive regarding the truth of this fact. The reverie was so often repeated, so habitual, that there is no doubt about its psychical importance. (*Memoirs*, 62)

Symonds emphasized this vision again when he provided his case history for *Sexual Inversion*, co-authored with Havelock Ellis, where he was more explicit about its sexual dimension:

> He fancied himself seated on the floor among several adult and naked sailors, whose genitals and buttocks he contemplated and handled with relish. He called himself the 'dirty pig' of these men, and felt that they were in some way his masters, ordering him to do uncleanly services to their bodies. He cannot remember ever having seen a naked man at that time, and nothing in his memory explains why the men of his dreams were supposed to be sailors.[15]

We must be careful, of course, with these recollections. By the time he prepared these texts in the late 1880s and early 1890s Symonds had become a devotee, like many other homoerotically inclined readers, of Pierre Loti's novel *My Brother Yves* (1883), in which the educated narrator befriends an illiterate sailor, Yves, and sometimes describes him in erotically provocative situations – such as an episode set in the ship's prison.[16] But it is not likely that Symonds entirely projected such cultural representations back into his own boyhood, a case of what Carl Jung, in criticizing Freud's stress on infantile fantasy, would later call *Zurückphantasieren*;[17] as Symonds says, he had really seen sailors in Bristol, probably distinguished readily from other passers-by by their dress and their more free public behaviour. When he says retrospectively that he is 'unable to account for their origin' he means their origin as objects of a 'reverie' in which an unknown possibility, an empirical unreality, was envisioned – namely, the sailors' sexualized nakedness and his pleasure in contact with it. To use Dr Symonds's terms, in hypnagogic reverie the real world fades out and an apparition synthesizes previous sensory impressions coloured with 'unnaturally excited ideas' to produce an impossible world perceived and felt to be more 'real' than the by-now 'shadowy indistinct outline' of the empirical world. In other words, some association enabled Symonds to hallucinate handling the buttocks and genitals of the sailors without ever having seen a naked man – let alone having interpreted Loti's novelistic fantasy of the ship's 'Black Hole'.

One empirical rooting of the associative chain probably did lie in the sailors' own speech and gesture, which might have included homosexual allusions, ridicule, and jests; the little boy could well have heard them calling one another 'dirty pig' or similar epithets. In *My Brother Yves*, Loti replaced the more direct expressions among the sailors he knew with epithets like 'darling' and 'brother'. But we know a good deal about the colourful homoerotic labelling and camaraderie common among seamen since the seventeenth century. For example, in Edwin M. Land's semi-clandestine novel *Sailors Don't Care*, privately published in Paris in 1929, the sailors of the multinational merchant marine openly indulge in homosexuality and flaunt their phallic prowess. The hero, a middle-class New England youth, college-bound, becomes a cabin-boy, mascot of the crew, and potential bitch.[18] Symonds's sailor-fantasy evidently placed him at least partly as a being constructed *by* the sailors, a middle-class but potential boy-companion, perhaps girlish in their eyes; their female nicknaming and slang for sexual subservience was probably adopted partly as a means of managing the hierarchy enforced by their masters. They therefore directed it at a being they could regard as a source, or at least a symbol, of their own servitude. At any rate, it would appear that the sailors' homoerotic culture – whatever its own particular cultural and economic determinations might have been – effectively became a differentiating and orienting criterion in the development of Symonds's own feeling. As I have already noted, however, 'feeling' – *Empfindung* – is not basic orientation, *Interesse*. The sailors did not cause Symonds to develop a homosexuality he would not otherwise have possessed, as the psychopathologists of acquired homosexual vice wanted to have it. Symonds's retrospective motivation for giving such attention to the fantasy – in which he insists on the *un*reality of the scene, whatever its empirical stimulation – included the fact that by the late 1880s the theory of a real homosexual seduction was promoted by a psychotherapeutics determined to deny the emancipationists' narratives of an originary difference.[19] Therefore Symonds's description of the sailor-fantasy as 'reverie' relays his understanding that the sailors' real-world actions were interpreted by a dividing consciousness that *already* dimly grasped its difference and organized new worlds suggested by passing impressions. As we have seen, the reverie – perhaps linked to a 'seduction' or at least to a homosexuality directed *at* the subject *from* others and accepted *by* him – complements the trance, the sceptical relocation of the 'I'; and both spring from an obscure yet founding difference. In *Sexual Inversion* Symonds did not place the sailor-fantasy at the very origin of his homoeroticism. There he enumerates it as the *second* main factor in his childhood eroticism – the *first* being his even earlier 'curiosity', in a virtually all-female household, about the male sex:

> In early childhood, and up to the age of 13 he had frequent opportunities of closely inspecting the genital organs of both boys and girls, his playfellows. The smell of the female parts affected him disagreeably.

The sight of the male organ did not arouse any particular sensation. He is, however, of the opinion that, living with sisters, he felt more curious about his own sex as being more remote from him.[20]

This 'interest', however it is to be described, was carried through, and beyond, the sailors' empirical being to hallucinate the sexualized male nakedness he had never actually seen. (At this point it would be usual to refer to Freud's concept of archaic or infantile homosexuality as a primal – associatively unsecured and hence categorical – belief in one's own [male] sex. Freud's doctrine is, however, no explanation of Symonds's history of consciousness. In his doctrines of archaic homosexuality Freud responded to such case histories as that of Symonds himself, which he encountered by way of Krafft-Ebing's, Schrenck-Notzing's, and Ellis's compilations among others; to patients who had already absorbed homoeroticist narratives of *Bildung*, the most famous of whom, the Wolf-Man, wrote notes and essays on Baudelaire, Aubrey Beardsley, Proust, and Wittgenstein;[21] and to a handful of child cases, like 'Little Hans', brought by adult friends of psychoanalysis.)

Within a few years of its beginning, the sailor reverie gave way to others. Before Symonds was 10 he read Shakespeare's *Venus and Adonis*. As he later recalled:

It gave form, ideality and beauty to my previous erotic visions. Those adult males, the shaggy and brawny sailors, without entirely disappearing, began to be superseded in my fancy by an adolescent Adonis. The emotion [the sailors] symbolised blent with a new kind of feeling . . . [The poem] stimulated while it etherealised my inborn craving after persons of my own sex. (*Memoirs*, 62–3)

After the family moved to Clifton Hill House in 1851, Symonds had a tutor with whom he read widely in Greek and Latin literature. This enabled him to add the person of Hermes in the *Iliad* to his daydreams of Adonis. '"Like a young prince with the first down upon his lip, the time when youth is the most charming": [Homer's] phrase had all Greek sculpture in it; and all my dim forebodings of the charm of males were here idealised' (*Memoirs*, 73–4). We should again be wary of retrospective effects in these recollections, which in identifying the most archaic 'origin' of the boy's interests have subtly moved from 'curiosity about the male sex' to 'inborn craving' – anachronistically anchoring the teleology the autobiography hopes to demonstrate. But there is no reason to doubt Symonds's story of pre-pubescent daydreams about various boys in ancient,

Elizabethan, and modern literature. (The case history for *Sexual Inversion* adds that he was curious about the character Anzoleto in George Sand's novel *Consuelo* and about the boys in the seraglios of the Roman emperors, probably as he had read about them in Suetonius and Tacitus.) They too were integrated in an apparition. At Clifton Hill House he walked in his sleep until his father tied him to his bed, at which point a 'recurrent dream', replacing that of the sailors, started up: 'the beautiful face of a young man, with large blue eyes and waving yellow hair which emitted a halo of misty light... bent down, gazing earnestly and tenderly, until his lips touched my forehead'. As he put it later, '[t]his vision of ideal beauty... prepared me to receive many impressions of art and literature' (*Memoirs*, 77) – for example, the pictures of Simeon Solomon, which he viewed enthusiastically in the 1870s and 1880s.[22] Here too we should be alert to retrospection. By the time Symonds wrote his autobiography, a tale of the way 'homosexual' desires – such as those expressed in the sailor fantasy – were reorganized in ideal, aestheticized interests had become central to homoeroticist self-understanding and its cultural creation and criticism. When expressed by certain patients it helped suggest Freud's theory of the supposed artistic 'sublimation' of homosexuality, Leonardo da Vinci being his historical example.[23] But it had been Symonds's own aesthetic and critical essays of the 1870s and 1880s, along with works like Walter Pater's *Studies in the History of the Renaissance* (1873) or his *Marius the Epicurean* (1885), with its depiction of the boy-god Aesculapius appearing to young Marius at night to kiss and heal him,[24] that had allegorized this self-understanding in the first place. Therefore we must note that what 'prepared' Symonds for actual homoerotic works of art was not exactly the sexualized sailor fantasy. Rather it was an intervening stage of *its* hallucinatory idealization in the reveries of Adonis and Hermes: the spectre with blue eyes and yellow hair was not directly an aestheticization of sexual fantasy but instead, itself, a hallucinatory idealization of aesthetic visualizations – of Adonis, Hermes, and other figures from literature – in which the sailor fantasy had already been 'blent', as Symonds says, 'with a new kind of feeling'.

This new *Empfindung* was, it seems, the boy's absorption of the doctrine of artistic idealization precisely as a separation from and refinement of the world: as the charm (as in Hermes prefiguring the 'charm of males') or even the form (as in Adonis giving 'form, ideality, and beauty' to the sailors) introduced into the world not by sexual fantasy but by aesthetic intuition. Aesthetics would be studied by Symonds when he went to university; in its academic neo-Kantian versions it remained prestigious through the end of the century, despite many criticisms. (Benedetto Croce's

Aesthetics of 1902 remains the best source for the distinctively neo-Kantian theory of the non-empirical unreality – that is, the autonomous ideality – of art, what Croce would call its non-'existential' basis.)[25] We need not assume that Symonds was familiar with the details of any one of the several neo-Kantian aesthetic systems; their general common outlook had been widely disseminated. In the early 1850s, Symonds encountered it in the language with which his father and his friends – including Alfred Tennyson, whose *In Memoriam* had appeared in 1847 – discussed their art and poetry.[26]

To take one instance, Symonds tells us that Homer's Hermes had 'all Greek sculpture in it'. At Clifton Hill House in the early 1850s, his knowledge of Greek art was partly derived from the Eros attributed to Praxiteles, the 'Genius of the Vatican', represented in a photograph displayed by his father:

> I used to pore for hours over the divine loveliness, while my father read poetry aloud to us in the evenings. He did not quite approve, and asked me why I would not choose some other statue, a nymph or Hebe . . . [T]his photograph strengthened the ideal I was gradually forming of adolescent beauty. It prepared me to receive the *Apoxyomenos* and Marlowe's Leander, the young men of Plato and much else besides. (*Memoirs*, 78)

Despite his unease, Dr Symonds might well be credited with his son's fascination with the Eros, for he himself had written a poem about it, probably included among those he read aloud in the evenings. It is virtually a doggerel representation of the consciousness we can plausibly suppose he helped cause in his son:

> Ah! just like thee Love doth seem,
> Living in his long day-dream,
> Gathering from what's earthly real,
> Enough to deck his soul's ideal . . .
> Ever sleeping, waking ever,
> Such the fancy's bright endeavour,
> Such the sculptor's shaping skill –
> Thou lovely, lasting miracle![27]

Conventional among Victorian versifiers, such sentiments were fossilized in English Neoclassical and early Victorian sculpture. But they would, of course, have been novel to the boy. Despite his interests, however, he does not seem to have responded immediately to the homoerotic materials that he could have found in his father's collection, such as Richard Payne Knight's essay on the 'symbolical language' of ancient art, which made clear that the *kalos*-names on many Greek vases denoted the young men pursued by the male patrons of the vases themselves.[28] And in fact, when Symonds saw actual homosexual activity at Harrow, which he entered in 1854 at the age of 14, he was repelled: 'There was no refinement, no sentiment, no passion; nothing but animal lust in these occurrences. They filled me with disgust and loathing' (*Memoirs*, 94).

One schoolfellow, for example, was 'dirty in his dress and person, filthy in his talk, and shamelessly priapic in his conduct'; another was 'like a good-natured ape, gibbering on his perch and playing ostentatiously with a prodigiously developed phallus'; a third was a 'red-faced strumpet with flabby cheeks' (*Memoirs*, 94–5). Evidently the idealizations of Symonds's Clifton aesthetics had totally reorganized his sexual fantasy of the 1840s – his own dream of being the sailors' unclean slave, their 'dirty pig'. At Harrow he seems instead to have adopted a prissy, sentimental culture, displaying reproductions of various Madonnas and of Raphael's and Mücke's paintings of St Catherine, the latter probably cut from Mrs Jameson's recent handbook for ritualism in the visual domain.[29]

During his undergraduate years at Oxford, 'the quest of ideal beauty, incarnated in breathing male beings, or eternalized in everduring works of art, was leading me to a precipice' (*Memoirs*, 121). In 1861 a Bristol choirboy, Alfred Brooke, became his 'chief preoccupation', though they met only a few times. 'It was a sustained conflict between desire and conscience, in which the will exercised a steady empire over action, while dreams and visions inflamed the fancy and irritated the whole nervous constitution...with burning memories, feverish reveries, brain-thrilling songs, the tempting of the inner voice: "Stretch forth thy hand and pluck and eat!"' (*Memoirs*, 122–3). Alfred made it plain that he wanted sex. In the early summer of 1862 Symonds encountered him on the downs, but though the youth beckoned Symonds did not respond. Three years later he prepared a lengthy description of this encounter, apparently intending it to be a free-standing text; and then, many years after, he transcribed it into his autobiography:

> I saw him go: that white face offered to my mouth for kisses, the red lips paling with passion, the splendid eyes and throat, athletic and magnificent curve of broad square shoulders, and imperial poise of sinewy trunk upon well-knitted hips and thighs.

His dress concealed him not. With my soul's eyes I grasped his body in all its parts. He knew this; and therefore he smiled, beckoned, invited, promised, wooed. For he too was lascivious; my soul was not more lascivious than he; and he had many lovers. Still I suffered him to pass. Wherefore? O Soul, thou canst tell. Thou knowest, O my soul, when with faithful and infallible eye thou didst search the secrets of his flesh, that even then thy cry was one of bitterest disappointment. The flesh could not content thee, nor assuage the hunger which it stirred. In the moment of longing and lust, in that gaze of devouring curiosity and desire, thou didst perceive that he could only yield thee shame and want and hunger reborn after short satiety. (*Memoirs*, 126)

In this presentation, Alfred is almost a perfect match for the ideal form; he seems like a living, breathing statue. And in fact Symonds's ekphrasis was written under the shadow of his ecstatic study of the Apoxyomenos, the standing 'Athlete' in the Vatican attributed to Lysippos, seen a few months earlier. From Rome, Symonds had sent an ekphrasis of the statue to Dakyns:

As you change your posture, its *Sehnsucht*, (for all immortal statues breathe a melancholy beauty that betrays the soul of *Sehnsucht*), changes from deep passion to the lightest flow of half sarcastic mirth. At one time you hang upon the godlike lips & murmur that their bloom so soon must pass away. At another the bold chest & hardened arms awake a thrill of heroic daring. You see the stuff the gods were made of. Then again the passion changes when the soft curves of the hips & thighs tell tales of love. And lastly should your glance alight upon those level eyes & short crisp locks, all Hellas moves before you with a sound of tragic pipe & festal sonorous verse & rapt oration in the porches of the gods.[30]

For reasons to be pursued shortly, it is noteworthy that Symonds recounts (or imagines) himself moving around the statue, his changing angle of view and focus of interest animating it with seeming moods and attitudes; in itself the statue is still and comparatively expressionless. Clearly it had been visualized with Alfred partly in mind already; a poem of 1861 dedicated to him had heard the 'full floods of music' exhaled between his parted lips ('These statues of the Vatican breathe music,' he told Dakyns)[31] and the actual meetings of 1861–2 had revolved around Alfred's poses and glances, both seductive and commanding. A week after contemplating the Apoxyomenos in the Vatican, he found that the young men of Sorrento 'look like Athletes with deep ardent eyes',[32] and within a very few years practically every highly desirable male beauty resembled the Athlete – such as young Cecil Boyle, Dakyns's friend at Clifton College, whose 'magnificent shoulders, veins, & legs &... head of breeding & of beauty & of goodness' were such that Lysippos would not have 'refused an order for his portrait'.[33] But even if Alfred, and others, seem to replicate the Athlete, Symonds's 'faithful and infallible eye' can still tell the difference. Scrutinizing Alfred's body 'in all its parts' for the slightest recognition, a barely perceptible tumescence, any other stirring gives 'bitterest disappointment'. In the space of form and the time of art, Alfred can be erotically fascinating because he seems to be an infusion into the real world (his real body) of aesthetically desirable unrealities (his sculptural aspect). But this relation is utterly intransitive. His sculptural aspect is not to be contaminated by the motions or expressions of his real body – or if it is, it becomes less, rather than more, desirable.

In June 1862, shortly after the unconsummated meeting with Alfred, Symonds read an essay at Oxford on Greek sculpture, which I believe is the text 'The Ideal of Beauty in Greek Sculpture' published by Peter Holliday.[34] Cautiously Symonds indicated that Greek art depended on commemorating beautiful youths; as he put it, 'the *kalos* – a word almost untranslatable to less aesthetic minds [or to one who had not studied his Payne Knight] – coloured their morality instead of Duty'.[35] In general argument as well as in specific phrases and examples, 'The Ideal of Beauty' follows his father's monograph *The Principles of Beauty*, written in the later 1850s.[36] Symonds is less sure than his father that 'a Science of Abstract Harmony applicable to all Art' shows that 'the proportions of lines, angles, sounds & colours are all correlative & reducible to one human measure'.[37] This view was presented in Dr Symonds's chief sources, such as Hay's *Natural Principles of Beauty*: a beautiful figure should be constructed in the intersection of fundamental angles (like the angle from the navel to the tips of the arms hanging at rest, framing the genitals) resolving into a series of ellipses – especially in the female figure, perhaps a 'nymph or Hebe' such as Dr Symonds wanted his son to pore over instead of Eros.[38] But, like his father, Symonds was convinced that the human brain innately prefers proportional and harmonic order. Thus the Greeks must have had, he says, an 'innate love of proportion'.[39] In turn, then, logically speaking, the homoeroticism of Greek society must itself have been founded on it: love of proportion made the Greeks love boys. Not surprisingly, in *Studies of the Greek Poets*

Symonds's examples of the fundamental artistic 'ellipse' are images of young men swimming, riding, or sculling and their poetic–musical analogues, such as the dithyrambs sung by Athenian boys in the harpers' schools;[40] and in more technical art-critical study later in life he looked for just this formal feature in works of art.[41]

In the end, then, homoeroticism and aesthetic idealization can be fully mapped on to one another *logically* only by claiming that an 'innate love of proportion' (the aesthetic judgment) prefers the male body because it is intrinsically better proportioned (the homoerotic judgment). In various versions this argument can be found both in Winckelmann and Symonds, and throughout homoeroticist aesthetics. It was, however, flagrantly incompatible with the claim of empirical aestheticians like Dr Symonds that 'the ellipse rules the female figure' (as he paraphrased the painter Benjamin Haydon).[42] Because a purely *aesthetic* judgment must admit male and female bodies equally, ordinarily the ideality of the female figure, at least as depicted in art, will be acknowledged. But that judgment might be synthesized with homoerotic judgment if, following Croce, the aesthetic intuition or image was bonded to a category such as reality or quality or if, following Freud, the quality of aesthetic interest became identical with *Interesse*, basic orientation, itself – with the primal pleasurabilities and unpleasurabilities of the organism that are the very criterion of its sexual differentiation. And such judgment must reject the female body *on* aesthetic grounds and *as* 'unpleasant', to be described in terms of disgust and aversion. Though impressions of female ugliness are always complemented empirically by impressions of male ugliness, female monstrosity needs to be retrospectively centred in an alleged primal hallucination warranting the later pattern of asymmetric aesthetic idealization. This history of outlines, impressions, and shadows reciprocally animates the history of homoerotic idealizations we have already reviewed. In turn, such legends of the visual-aesthetic field of early life would be narrated by homo-sexually cultivated patients to late nineteenth-century psychotherapists and psychoanalysts – shaping their theory of homosexuality as the result of a supposed castration anxiety and masculine protest (expressing aesthetic disgust for the female) and supposed narcissism (expressing aesthetic preference for the male/self). But to avoid a deep anachronism, we should not use such concepts to interpret mid-nineteenth-century or earlier homoerotic cultures. We must avoid reduction of the homo-erotic or homosexual to the aesthetic, for in this logic it must always turn out that homoerotic culture manifests a perverse – a misogynistic and narcissistic – *aesthetic* judgment, even if its homoeroticism, as such, seems to be tolerated; it will always be as if homoerotic culture, though not sexually or 'morally' insane, is *aesthetically* so.

Symonds noted that, although Greek art established beauty in ideal proportion, it 'incurred the danger of monotony & restricted the manifestation of expression'[43] – for strong expression allegedly moves settled features or postures out of the positions in which ideal proportions are naturally manifested. But Symonds knew perfectly well that an active, expressive body can be no less harmonious in its proportions – though differently so – than the body in repose; he even cites examples such as Myron's Diskoboulos. In other words, Symonds preferred the ideal proportions of the still, expressionless figure, however 'monotonous', on grounds that had little or nothing to do with Greek artistic practices. Obviously he was in part echoing the aesthetics of Winckelmann. But as we have also seen, it was the real Alfred's slight movement and expression – the parting of his lips, the signal of his hand, the stirring in his trousers – that bitterly disappointed the fantasist, showing the real Alfred to be different from the ideal image that he seems to be in his statuesque pose and proportions. Thus Greek art is preferred when, and because, it resembles the still, statuesque Alfred; and Alfred is preferred when, and because, he resembles the still, statuesque Greek figure. Neither of these desirable objects is preferred over the other; both are required for the other; each has ramified rooting in the history of visual impressionability; and each motivates a coherent criticism of any images produced by the other. For this reason Symonds's homoerotic aesthetics understood as a whole form of life cannot be reduced to either pole, homoerotic *or* aesthetic: his approach to Alfred and other beloveds was not simply a function, however intricate, of his preferences in art; and his preferences in art were not simply a function, however intricate, of his homoerotic attractions. Rather it is the cumulatively intertwined and reciprocally inflected nature of the relation between homoerotic and aesthetic impressions that retrospectively constitutes, for the subject, the history of his consciousness.

Notes

1 'In Dreamland', *Miscellanies* (typescript c. 1885–9, Houghton Library, Harvard University), fol. 62–3. The whole composition, fol. 52–74, includes other dream reports as well.
2 See especially Hubert Kennedy, *Ulrichs: The Life and Work of Karl Heinrich Ulrichs, Pioneer of the Modern Gay Movement* (Boston, 1988).
3 See, for example, 'The Character of Achilles' (1866), in *Studies of the Greek Poets, First Series* (1873), 76–107.

4   J. A. Symonds, *The Memoirs of John Addington Symonds*, ed. Phyllis Grosskurth (New York, 1984), 64. Henceforth page references to this text will be provided in the main body of the text.

5   J. A. Symonds Sr, *Miscellanies by John Addington Symonds, M.D., Selected and Edited, With an Introductory Memoir, by his Son* (1871), 116–44. Prichard's ideas were presented succinctly in 'Insanity', in John Forbes, Alexander Tweedie, and John Conolly (eds), *Cyclopaedia of Practical Medicine* (1835), ii, 13–21; 'Soundness and Unsoundness of Mind', ibid., iv, 48–55; and *On the Different Forms of Insanity in Relation to Jurisprudence* (1842). See further Daniel Hack Tuke, *Prichard and Symonds in Especial Relation to Mental Science with Chapters on Moral Insanity* (1891).

6   J. A. Symonds Sr, *Miscellanies*, 136–7.

7   Ibid., 325–35. This lecture was given ten years after the Vaughan affair and makes no reference to it or to other individual cases which may have been personally known to Dr Symonds. But clearly it reflects his experiences and convictions.

8   For Symonds's views of Pater, see *The Letters of John Addington Symonds*, ed. Herbert Schueller and Robert Peters (Detroit, 1967–9), ii, 273, 336; iii, 41–2.

9   Ibid., iii, 606–7, 650. For Gower, see George C. Williamson, *The Lord Ronald Sutherland Gower: A Memorial Tribute* (1916).

10 Ronald Sutherland Gower, *Old Diaries 1881–1901* (1902), 157, 175.

11 For details on these developments, see Whitney Davis, *Drawing the Dream of the Wolves: Homosexuality, Interpretation, and Freud's 'Wolf-Man'* (Bloomington, IN, 1995), 115–40.

12 J. A. Symonds Sr, *Miscellanies*, 209–64 (quote from p. 230).

13 Ibid., 244.

14 Symonds,'Clifton and a Lad's Love', *In the Key of Blue* (1893).

15 Havelock Ellis, *Sexual Inversion* (1897), Case XVII.

16 See Symonds, *Letters*, ii, 929, 932–5; iii, 475–6.

17 See Davis, *Drawing the Dream*, 142–7.

18 Edwin M. Land, *Sailors Don't Care* (1929). Although Land stereotypes some of the sodomitical seamen as especially gross and aggressive, he does not indulge the generic homophobic fantasy that young Ned is homosexually innocent and the sexual victim of the sailors. Instead Ned is understood to desire and to accept – though not always to enjoy – the seamen's advances and ultimately he is paired off with a lover, a stowaway escaping a male brothel.

19 See, for example, and perhaps most influentially, Albert von Schrenck-Notzing, *Therapeutic Suggestion in Psychopathia Sexualis (Pathological Manifestations of the Sexual Sense), with Especial Reference to Contrary Sexual Instinct* (1894), trans. Charles Gilbert Craddock (Philadelphia, 1895).

20 Ellis, *Sexual Inversion*, Case XVIII.

21 See Davis, *Drawing the Dream*.

22 See Whitney Davis, 'The Image in the Middle: John Addington Symonds and Homoerotic Art Criticism', in Elizabeth Prettejohn (ed.), *Philistine and Aesthete in Victorian Britain* (Manchester, forthcoming).

23 See Whitney Davis, 'Freuds Leonardo und die Kultur der Homosexualität', *Texte zur Kunst*, v, 17 (1995), 56–73.

24 Walter Pater, *Marius the Epicurean: His Sensations and Ideas* (1885), i, 27–42.

1 John Addington Symonds.

2 The Laocoön, prior to twentieth-century restoration of right arm.

3 Wrestlers.

4b The Apollo Belvedere.

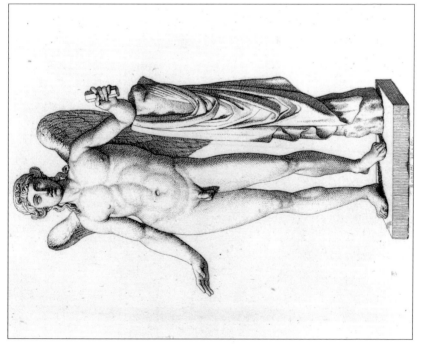

4a The Borghese Genius or Cupid.

5a The Ildefonso Group.

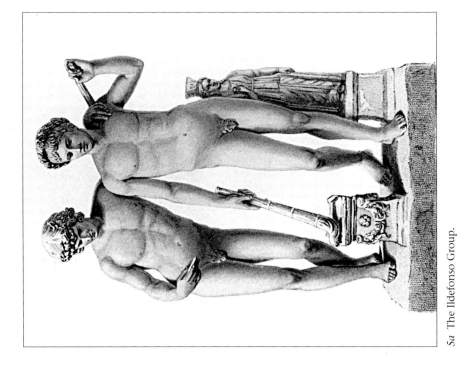

5b Michelangelo, Dying Slave.

6a Michelangelo, Day.

6b Michelangelo, Night.

7 Michelangelo, Four Ignudi.

8 Giambattista, Communion of St Lucy.

25 Benedetto Croce, *The Aesthetic as the Science of Expression and of the Linguistic in General*, trans. Colin Lyas (Cambridge, 1990). For aesthetic philosophy in the second half of the nineteenth century, see especially Bernard Bosanquet, *A History of Aesthetic*, 2nd edn (1904), 363–441.

26 For a full account of his father's tastes, literary and cultural circle, and so forth, as recalled and reconstructed by his son, see Symonds's introductory 'Memoir' in *Miscellanies*.

27 'To An Antique', *Verses by John Addington Symonds, M.D., F.R.S.Ed., &c., &c.* (Bristol, 1871), 43–4. In this privately printed memorial volume Symonds collected examples of his father's verse.

28 Richard Payne Knight, *An Inquiry into the Symbolical Language of Ancient Art and Mythology* (1818). This text was reprinted by the Society of Dilettanti and bound in with the second volume of *Specimens of Ancient Sculpture* (1835), which is one of the other books (more exactly, collections of images) that Symonds specifically tells us he used to pore over in his father's library (*Memoirs*, 78).

29 Anna Brownell Jameson, *Sacred and Legendary Art*, 2nd edn (1850).

30 Symonds, *Letters*, i, 436–7.

31 Symonds tells us that two poems about Alfred were written on 7 October 1861, after Alfred had passed beneath his window – inviting him with 'wondering wide blue eye/That said, "I wait! why will you not reply?".' These compositions were published as 'Renunciation I' and 'Renunciation II' in *Vagabunduli Libellus* (1884), 136–7, though the gender of the beloved was changed from male to female.

32 Symonds, *Letters*, i, 439–41.

33 Ibid., ii, 189.

34 Peter J. Holliday, 'John Addington Symonds and the Ideal of Beauty in Greek Sculpture', *Journal of Pre-Raphaelite and Aesthetic Studies*, ii, 1 (1989), 89–105. See Symonds, *Letters*, i, 354, where the essay is said to be on 'the ideal in Gk art'. Holliday suggests that the text was 'probably written' in the early 1870s for the Clifton College boys or for the students at a women's college in Bristol where Symonds lectured at that time. But internal evidence – as well as the correspondence noted above – suggests an earlier date for the manuscript and it is probably a draft of the Oxford discourse.

35 Ibid., 101.

36 Dr John Addington Symonds, *The Principles of Beauty* (1857); also in *Miscellanies*, 1–48.

37 Holliday, 'Ideal of Beauty', *loc. cit.*, 100.

38 See David Ramsay Hay, *The Natural Principles of Beauty as Developed in the Human Figure* (Edinburgh, 1852).

39 Ibid.

40 Symonds, *Greek Poets, First Series*, 398–423.

41 This seems to be the burden of the photographic experiments in which Symonds investigated the structure of well-known works, such as Hippolyte Flandrin's *Jeune homme assis sur un rocher* in the Louvre, in order to determine their underlying geometry (*Letters*, ii, plates following p. 64).

42 *Principles of Beauty*, 32; see 'Ideal of Beauty', 99. Needless to say, as Dr Symonds's illustrations suggest, empirical aesthetics found some part of its own rationale in heterosexual prurience. At the same time, it avoided prettifying the

male form by finding 'female' curves and ellipses in it and enquired instead, as Dr Symonds put it, into the aesthetics of its 'masculine power' (*Principles of Beauty*, 14).

43   Holliday, 'Ideal of Beauty', *loc. cit.*, 102.

5
Symonds and the Model of Ancient Greece*

Peter J. Holliday

John Addington Symonds was born into a privileged position in Victorian society, and both his life and his work reflect the values and restrictions of that position and that society. He was a pre-eminent interpreter for the Victorians of Renaissance history, Mediterranean travel, and – especially – classical Antiquity. Late nineteenth-century attitudes towards these subjects, as well as enlightened attitudes towards homosexuality, owed more to Symonds than to any other writer in English.[1] This chapter will consider the significance that Greece held for Symonds, establish in what ways his criticism – especially of Greek art – stands out from inherited views, and determine how his classical studies affected both his aesthetic deliberations and his calls for social reform.

From the mid-1700s until the early 1900s, ancient Greece and Rome provided the basic cultural reference points for educated Europeans. Rome had always been popular, but Winckelmann's aesthetics brought ancient Greece back into fashion, and in Britain ancient Greece became almost an obsession for many Victorians. The search for the remains of classical Greece was a great preoccupation of the eighteenth and nineteenth centuries, and archaeological digs excited scholars, the public, and tourists. The study of classical languages and literature provided the foundation of education in Britain's élite schools; *Literae humaniores*, or 'Greats', with Plato at its core, was the most venerable of Oxford curricula. Critics judged subsequent cultural achievements against the exemplars of classical poetry, philosophy, and art. Classical motifs appeared in painting, sculpture, architecture, and even in the design of household furniture and china.

*I should like to thank Christopher Baswell, Whitney Davis, Claire Lyons, Richard Meyer, and Patrick Sinclair for their thoughtful criticisms of this chapter.

The primary problem for Victorian critics was to determine what Greek civilization meant to the contemporary world. Europeans first became interested in Greek antiquity in the second half of the eighteenth century, when the values, ideas, and institutions inherited from Rome and Christianity became problematic for progressive thinkers. The age of enlightenment and revolution stimulated a search for new cultural roots and alternative cultural patterns. For agnostics and atheists, Hellas was the supreme example of a non-Christian society that had reached the highest degree of humane civilization; for radicals, Athens was the state that had come closest to political perfection. Thomas Paine saw 'more to admire, and less to condemn, in that great ... people, than in anything which history affords'.[2]

The major advantage of using Greece in one's arguments was that it could represent almost any value or outlook that a writer wished to ascribe to it. As W. H. Auden put it:

> The historical discontinuity between Greek culture and our own, the disappearance for so many centuries of any direct influence, made it all the easier, when it was rediscovered, for each nation to fashion a classical Greece in its own image.[3]

'We are all Greeks,' Shelley said, and this sentiment was to be echoed again and again throughout the century.[4] Swinburne called Greece the 'mother-country of thought and art and action'.[5] Symonds declared that all civilized nations were 'colonies of Hellas'.[6]

Symonds, although of a pre-Freudian era, was singular in his awareness of the importance of formative experiences, and in his *Memoirs* he laboured to reinvoke memories of his childhood.[7] 'According to my conception of such a work,' he wrote, 'the years of growth are the most important, and need the most elaborate analysis.'[8] Symonds had only the faintest memory of his mother, who died when he was 4; but the formidable figure of his father, a physician and reformer, dominated the first 30 years of his son's life. Competent, self-assured, in vigorous health, his father seemed to be everything the sickly boy could never be. As he grew older, the ideal conception of his father also incorporated the role of moral censor. It was only after his father's death that Symonds began to twist his way out of the tight coils of conventional pressures that had been choking him for over half his life. (Significantly, in his subsequent relations with young men Symonds treated them with a distinctly fatherly attitude.) The younger Symonds always felt overwhelmed by the figure of his stern and distant father: he found it difficult to live up to the example of his father's intellectual and political achievements. The elder Symonds had even exhibited a concern for aesthetic enquiry that foreshadowed his son's interests. In his *The Principles of Beauty* (1857) Dr Symonds developed a theory in mathematical terms to demonstrate the existence of an intrinsic beauty, inherent in the art-object and independent of the emotion it might arouse in the spectator. Like most mid-Victorian works, his argument was grounded in empirical philosophy tempered by Christian doctrine.

The younger Symonds was heir to a visual and literary language – a particular iconography and vocabulary for the expression of homo-sexual desire – learned from books and art; the model of ancient Greece was fundamental to this language. He and others testify how the books they read and the paintings and sculptures they admired awakened their sexual yearnings. Their first sexual 'experience', their initiation, was artistic and literary, and through the media of writing, painting, sculpture and, later, photography they passed on their cultural and erotic impressions to later generations. One of the first instances of sexual curiosity and closely connected budding aesthetic interests in the young Symonds found expression through Greek art. He discovered a print of a Praxitelean Cupid (see Plate 4a) that he would gaze at longingly while his father read poetry aloud in the evenings to the assembled family. This fixation disturbed Dr Symonds, who suggested that some other statue such as a nymph or Hebe might be more suitable.[9]

Symonds began to give some tentative expression to his sexual long-ings during late adolescence. He went up to Oxford in 1858 after having 'devoured Greek literature and fed upon the reproductions of Greek plastic art' during his revelatory last term at Harrow.[10] He studied Greek under the university reformer Benjamin Jowett, who established in the systematic study of the classics 'a ground of transcendent value altern-ative to Christian theology – the metaphysical underpinning of Oxford from the Middle Ages through the Tractarian movement'.[11] Hellenism thereby became a vehicle for channelling modern progressive thought into the Victorian civic élite.[12] Yet Greek studies were always potentially subversive. In *Maurice*, E. M. Forster describes how Clive Durham came to accept his sexual inversion while reading Plato at school: 'The boy had always been a scholar, awake to the printed word, and the horrors that the Bible evoked for him were to be laid to rest by Plato. Never could he forget his emotion at first reading the *Phaedrus*.' The conver-sion of Durham is not as precocious as it may seem to modern readers. In March 1858 Symonds spent a weekend in London in the Regent's Park home of a Mrs Bain. Upon returning late one evening from the theatre, he casually picked up a copy of Cary's crib of Plato, which they were reading in the Sixth Form, and turned by chance to the *Phaedrus*. He was spellbound. He read the dialogue right through, and then the *Symposium*. When he finally put the book down, dawn had already broken; he had not slept, and yet he seemed to be awakening to a new world. Symonds always remembered this night as a turning point in his life. In his *Memoirs* he wrote: 'Here in the *Phaedrus* and the *Symposium* – in the myth of the Soul and the speeches of Pausanias, Agathon and Diotima – I discovered the true *liber amoris* at last, the revelation I had been waiting for, the consecration of a long-cherished idealism.'[13] He concluded: 'My soul was lodged in Hellas.'[14]

Although the stories have striking parallels – the intelligent schoolboys, the homosexuality, the *Phaedrus* – Forster could not have known about Symonds's experience. The two incidents are both products of Victorian conditions.[15] Among the late Victorians, homosexual apologists used Hellenism to develop a counterdiscourse justifying male love in ideal or transcendental terms. Plato glorified the love of one man for another, but he also preached perfect chastity. Many Victorian inverts shared the high-mindedness of the age, and the philosopher's temperance chimed in harmony with their own beliefs. If Plato set them free, he also imposed a demanding standard for them to realize. Under the influence of Plato, Clive and Maurice do not consummate their love.

After discovering the *Phaedrus*, Symonds plunged into a romantic friendship with a choirboy.[16] Their emotions were passionate; in obedience to Plato, however, for more than a year they did no more than hold hands. In 1866 Symonds considered a friend's liaison with a schoolboy, posing the problem in the form of a dialectic: 'Is this Eros Greek? No. Is it what Plato would allow? No. What is the source of Arthur's love? Is it intellectual sympathy? No. Is it moral good? No. Is it chiefly aesthetical enjoyment and the pleasure of sensuousness? Yes. Are these likely to produce moral and intellectual strengths? No.'[17] Intellectual sympathy and moral good are Plato's criteria; Symonds condemns the affair simply because it is not, in the strict sense of the word, Platonic.

As a protégé of Jowett, Symonds showed true promise as a classical scholar. However, a jealous and embittered rival threatened to expose him with several youthfully exuberant and fulsome letters that Symonds had written earlier. Symonds found his academic career dashed before it began. He left Oxford, tried to pursue a heterosexual life, married, and fathered four daughters. Nevertheless, the male form remained the focus of his sexual and aesthetic fascination, and Greek studies provided a forum for his deliberations.

History originally meant nothing more than 'enquiry', and the early Greek historians freely mixed topography, ethnography, and travellers' tales. Herodotus began the discipline of history by directing these diverse elements towards the service of a unified and dramatic narrative: a process completed by the immensely tough intellect of Thucydides, who ruthlessly excised the decorative features of history and concentrated upon an account of events, chronologically arranged and keenly analysed. In the eighteenth century, however, historians once again began to investigate such things as climate, commerce, religion, and social habits. Symonds's writings conform to this tendency, returning to the infancy of the historian's art.

Symonds's literary endeavours exhibit all the complex anxieties of a modern temperament. Like many of his more progressive contemporaries, he believed that false social values, inhibiting aesthetic rules, and a puritanical Christian morality negatively affected modern culture. The main subjects of Symonds's scholarly research – the Elizabethans, the Italians of the Renaissance, and especially the ancient Greeks – reflect his search for prescriptive values appropriate for nineteenth-century life. Symonds undoubtedly wrote about those cultures because he found them aesthetically stimulating; however, he also adopted the contemporary conventional mode and saw in them men who were able to express themselves freely, unhampered by Victorian taboos. On one level his work was a means of sublimating his homosexual impulses and the anxiety they provoked; but what is more important, in such enterprises as the two volumes of *Studies of the Greek Poets* (1873, 1876), he endeavoured implicitly to make the case for homosexual legitimation to the general public in a moment of cultural liberalization.[18]

From the time he first started to write, Symonds was bitter because he could not speak freely of the overriding concern of his life. To write blatantly about homosexuality in his works on history and literature would have been both intellectually renegade and politically risky. As a consequence, when he felt compelled to speak, he usually used an oblique approach in which he cunningly allied ingenuousness and craft. (Symonds rarely used the word 'homosexual'; he preferred 'comradeship' or various generic terms derived from Ulrichs's coinage, 'Urning'.)[19] Reading carefully, his audience might none the less discern his sexual interests. For Symonds, the Greeks came to represent freedom of the spirit and intellectual integrity. Like other Victorians, he felt Greek art represented a mode of timelessness, of universal beauty at its best. The sculpture of the Greeks exemplified a school in which artists followed rules of *decorum*, rules that led to works produced in accordance with both good taste and high morality.[20] The German Hellenists, especially Johann Joachim Winckelmann, heavily influenced Symonds's writing (as was true of most British commentaries on Greek art).[21] Winckelmann introduced into the study of art the concept of historical cycles within which a civilization's creative powers, like a living organism, went through a process of growth and decay. He divided the art of antiquity into four periods: the archaic; the sublime or grand age of Pheidias; the beautiful; and the imitative.[22] Even after early nineteenth-century discoveries of original Greek sculpture in Greece and Asia Minor put the study of early Greek art on a new empirical basis, scholars tended to accept the basic logic of Winckelmann's model of artistic rise and decline. K. O. Müller's *Handbuch der Archäologie der Kunst* (1835), for example, retained Winckelmann's periodization of Greek and Roman art, which the author's inductive analysis of the available visual evidence failed to contradict.[23] When Carl Justi published his monograph on Winckelmann in 1867–72, this schema had become so self-evidently true that Justi no longer perceived Winckelmann as having invented it.[24]

The origins of Winckelmann's schema could be found in the ancient texts, and his reiteration of this model (which they could research for themselves in the classical sources) convinced the Victorians of its validity.[25] Symonds therefore neatly adopted Winckelmann's account: 'Greek sculpture,' he wrote, 'passes from the austere, through the perfect, to the simply elegant.'[26] Like other critics, Symonds retained the evolutionary construct postulated by Winckelmann, and simply used different examples to reconcile that development with recent finds in archaeology. By our standards, Winckelmann made a strange choice in the *Gedanken* (1755) when he cited the Laocoön (see Plate 2) as the paradigm of Greek art; yet his choice may seem justified when we recall that Pliny had called the group 'superior to all products of the arts of painting and sculpture'. It is perhaps even more perplexing that for Winckelmann this late Hellenistic *tour de force* of agonized expressionism exemplified *edel Einfalt und stille Grösse*, noble simplicity and calm grandeur.[27] Symonds, on the other hand, wrote of the Laocoön: 'It is only in the decadence of art that such disturbance of perfect harmony as we observe in the Laocoön was tolerated. There the physical agony of the father and the vain struggle of his two sons in the folds of the hideous serpents remind us of the Roman arena rather than the Greek studio.'[28] Significantly, both critics frame their arguments to support a central tenet of academic tradition: the demand for *decorum* under all circumstances. Like other Victorian critics, then, Symonds transferred a moral outlook originating in eighteenth-century criticism to the art of Greece. In turn, he upheld the Greek past as a source of wisdom for current ethical and cultural conduct. The dominant moral tone of the mid-Victorian period has not been abandoned, but it finds a new expression.

Winckelmann had further revolutionized the history of art by treating it organically, as a part of the growth of the human spirit; for him classical artistic achievement was inseparable from the material circumstances in which it was generated – Greece's superlative climate, beneficial social conditions, and liberal cultural environment.[29] In the nineteenth century the beauty of climate and natural scenery was more highly prized than ever before, and it was agreeable to think that it might have shaped the destinies of nations. Such views exercised a powerful hold upon the literary imagination.[30] Symonds adopted Winckelmann's anthropo-geographical ideas when he argued that the climate and scenery of Greece predisposed its inhabitants 'for developing a taste for beauty and the power of producing it'. He held that Athens was predestined to be the mother of reason 'by virtue of scenery and situation'; the radiance of the Athenian landscape had 'all the clearness . . . of the Attic intellect'.[31] That compelling polarity between North and South intensified a belief in the importance of climate; according to Symonds, the Greeks lived amid 'perpetual sunshine and perpetual ease – no work . . . that might degrade the body . . . no dread of hell, no yearning after heaven.'[32] (North-erners who travelled to Greece often let fantasy overcome experience. One has only to read Hesiod to learn that labour can be heavy in Medi-terranean lands, winters bitter, and food scarce.) Symonds accentuates the contrast: 'Of . . . this conscience, whole and pure and reconciled to nature, what survives among us now? . . . The blear-eyed mechanic, stifled in a hovel of our sombre northern towns . . . could scarcely be taught even to envy the pure clear life of art . . . which was the pride of Hellas.'[33]

For Symonds not only did the climate and landscape predispose the ancient Greeks to their creative genius, but the austerity of their environ-ment redeemed the nudity of Greek statues from the Victorian taint of sin. In his discussion of Theocritus and the Idyllists in the *Studies*, Symonds wrote: 'Straight from the sea-beach rise mountains of distinguished form, not capped with snow or clothed with pines, but carved of naked rock. We must accept their beauty as it is, nude, well defined, and unadorned, nor look in vain for the picturesqueness of the Alps.'[34] We might interpret this passage as an expression of sublimation, yet to Symonds it represented another call in his campaign against Victorian prudery.

Symonds also followed Winckelmann when he claimed that the polit-ical independence and religious organization of the Greek *polis* during the classical period helped nurture artistic excellence and allowed it to flourish; both writers argued that the passing of that liberty accounted for the perceived decline in Greek art. For the most part Winckelmann seems to allude to political liberty; he chafed at restrictive mores and rejected authoritarian governments, such as the German regimes of his own day.[35] Symonds also believed that freedom was the essential state in which humanity could develop and prosper, but he demanded that freedom encompass personal – including presumably sexual – as well as political liberty. 'The ideal of Greek life imposed no commonplace conformity to one fixed standard on individuals,' he declares, 'but each man was encouraged to compete and realise the type of himself to the utmost.'[36]

Most importantly, in Winckelmann's judgment Greek sculpture embodied ideal beauty. This was embedded in the context of Greek life, the sensual and philosophical nature of which Winckelmann thought uniquely fertile for the production of a masterpiece such as the Apollo Belvedere (see Plate 4b). Winckelmann's manifesto emerges in the opening pages of the *Gedanken*: 'Good taste... had its origins under the skies of Greece... The taste which the Greeks exhibited in their works of art was unique... The only way for us to become great or, if this be possible, inimitable, is to imitate the ancients.'[37] Greek sculpture and painting were the perfect representations of ideal beauty; a higher standard could not be achieved, and the moderns must therefore not just study Greek art, but try to copy it. This idea formed the basis of Winckelmann's art appreciation and criticism, and it was to serve as the foundation for contemporary aesthetics and the programme of modern pedagogy.

Symonds echoes both Winckelmann and his own father when he, too, postulates that Greek art embodies an absolute beauty. In Symonds's analysis, the ideal in classical sculpture was based first on the Greeks' innate love of exact and harmonious proportion. However, the Greeks balanced proportion with expression, the second basis for their ideal. Whereas proportion alone could lead to monotony, Symonds argues that an excess of expression could lead to an overzealous desire for effect, resulting in the excesses exhibited by the Laocoön.[38] The aim of great art, he argues, is to combine these two ingredients.[39]

Symonds presents his most comprehensive critique on the subject in a lecture, 'The Ideal of Beauty in Greek Sculpture'.[40] Here he postulates a third element in the Greek conception of ideal beauty: the depiction of youth, also seen by Winckelmann as essential to the Greek ideal. Although the modern assessment of classical art also recognizes a youthful or ageless quality as an important aspect of idealization,[41] Symonds's discussion takes on a partisan tone in arguing for the recognition of a specifically male beauty. Indeed, his metaphor for the Greek genius is unabashedly homoerotic:

> Like a young man newly come from the wrestling-ground, anointed, chapleted, and very calm, the Genius of the Greeks appears before us . . . The pride and strength of adolescence are his – audacity and endurance, swift passions and exquisite sensibilities, the alternations of sublime repose and boyish noise, grace, pliancy, and stubbornness and power, love of all fair things and splendours of the world, the frank enjoyment of the open air, free merriment, and melancholy well beloved.[42]

This genius is all boyish virility, although Symonds also echoes earlier Victorian writers who used youth as a metaphor for their contention that the Greeks represented the 'childhood' of Western civilization; such critics equated the Greeks with a people exemplifying human virtues and normal healthy impulses that an evangelical Christian culture had repressed.[43] Symonds later wrote that he was obliged 'to describe their genius as adolescent; for adolescence has a strength, and sorrow, and reflection so much only as is compatible with beauty'.[44]

Many of the later nineteenth-century aesthetes liked the metaphor of youth because it allowed them to allude to the 'cult of handsome young men'.[45] In the *Studies* Symonds, too, expressed the desire to 'seek some living echo of this melody' by visiting

> the water-meadows where boys bathe in early morning, or the playgrounds of our public schools in summer, or the banks of the Isis when the eights are on the water, or the riding schools of young soldiers. We cannot reconstitute the elements of Greek life; but here and there we may gain hints for adding breath and pulse and movement to Greek sculpture.[46]

However, unlike the aesthetes, Symonds was not content to dote passively on the beauty of male youth. Rather, he sought to understand the source of its beauty, and thereby perhaps rationalize his erotic impulses and justify his homosexuality to society.

Goethe became acutely aware of the connection between sexual emotion and the enjoyment of sculpture in Rome, where he spent his days among classical authors, his nights with his mistress. 'Do I not instruct myself,' he wrote, 'by studying the forms of her lovely bosom,

and running my hands down over her hips? Not till then do I understand marble rightly . . . I see with an eye that feels and feel with a hand
that sees.'[47] When this theme appears in English literature, it is usually
with a striking difference. Goethe had perceived that the imagination
might intertwine life and art, each enhancing the other; the Victorians,
more *angstvoll* than the great German, treated the tactile qualities of
sculpture as a substitute for dangerous delights.[48] The smoothly undu-
lating contours of an image functioned as a site for the simultaneous
avowal and disavowal of the potentially unmanageable anxieties elicited
by a 'real' body.[49] In academic theory, those ideal contours functioned
to fuse the apprehension of the overall form of the body and that of its
individual parts, negotiating a potentially disruptive disjunction.[50] As
Winckelmann wrote: 'The more unity there is in the connection between
forms, and in the flowing of the one into the other, the greater is the
beauty of the whole . . . A beautiful youthful figure is fashioned from
forms like the uniform expanse of the sea.'[51]

In an unpublished and undated essay, 'Notes on the Relation of Art
and Morality', Symonds describes sex as the root of the aesthetic sense.
He argues that sex blinds most men to real beauty, for 'men regard the
female form as more essentially beautiful than the male. The contrary
to this belief can be abundantly demonstrated. The male form is infinitely richer in a variety of lovely qualities, and is incomparably nobler
in its capacities of energetic action.'[52] Elsewhere Symonds cites Benjamin Haydon, who recapitulated academic theory when he argued that
the ellipse is profoundly beautiful to the human eye.[53] Whereas Haydon
stated that the ellipse governs the female body, Symonds found it more
satisfying to cite examples of it in the male. In his *Studies* Symonds
describes 'the two wrestling boys at Florence, whose heads and faces
form in outline the ellipse which is the basis of all beauty, and whose
strained muscles exhibit the chord of masculine vigour vibrating with
tense vitality' (see Plate 3).[54]

In their intensely sensuous, even erotic, tenor such descriptions of
classical male sculptures echo Winckelmann's reflections on the apparent advantages of marble form over real bodies, whose physique is tra-
gically transitory. He prized the lasting beauty of a marble head that
came into his possession: 'You will recall the beautiful head of a
Faun . . . He is my Ganymede, whom I can kiss *nel cospetto di tutti i Santi**
without giving offence.'[55] (Symonds did not collect classical sculpture,
but he did exchange photographs of young male nudes with friends. All

---

*in the presence of all the saints

through Browning's funeral service in Westminster Abbey Edmund Gosse stole glances at a photograph Symonds had sent him.)[56]

No simple connection can be made between an author's homosexuality and his criticism; nevertheless, both Winckelmann and Symonds attempted to negotiate the complexities of sexual desire and aesthetic delectation. Symonds quotes Pater's sensitive translation of a letter Winckelmann wrote to a young man with whom he was in love:

> As it is confessedly the beauty of man which is to be conceived under one general idea, so I have noticed that those who are observant only of beauty in women, and are moved little or not at all by the beauty of men, seldom have an impartial, vital, inborn instinct for the beauty of art. To such a person the beauty of Greek art will seem ever wanting, because its supreme beauty is male rather than female. But the beauty of art demands a higher sensibility than the beauty of nature, because the beauty of art, like tears shed in a play, gives no pain, is without life and must be awakened and repaired by culture.[57]

Symonds responds: 'While it is true that "the supreme beauty of Greek art is rather male than female", this is due not so much to any passion of the Greeks for male beauty as to the fact that the male body exhibits a higher organisation of the human form than the female.'[58] He declares that 'the male body displays harmonies of proportion and melodies of outline more comprehensive, more indicative of strength expressed in terms of grace, than that of women'.[59]

Pater ventures to connect Winckelmann's worship of Greek sculpture with an admiration for the human flesh which it represents. He detects an affinity with the side of Plato represented by the 'brilliant youths in the *Lysis*, still uninfected by any spiritual sickness'.[60] He is, of course, referring to Platonic homosexuality, though he cannot say so. He moves on to discuss Winckelmann's own emotions:

> That his affinity with Hellenism was not merely intellectual, that the subtler threads of temperament were inwoven in it, is proved by his romantic, fervent friendships with young men . . . These friendships, bringing him in contact with the pride of human form, and staining his thoughts with its bloom, perfected his reconciliation with the spirit of Greek sculpture.[61]

The meaning of this seems clear enough today; to many of Pater's early readers, and perhaps to Pater himself, it was more opaque. His use of the word 'staining' exudes a faint scent of moral unease, yet Pater's description of the whiteness of sculpture – purged from the stains of passion – and the persuasive appeal of this metaphor allow him to rescue Winckelmann (and himself) from the taint of impropriety. 'Winckelmann fingers those pagan marbles,' writes Pater, 'with unsinged hands, with no sense of shame or loss.'[62]

In addition to reciting the metaphor of youth to personify a variety of sentiments, Victorian writers on Greece repeated such tropes as calm and light, which quickly degenerated into clichés. As with youth, the idea of Greek serenity may have derived from Winckelmann; to trace these images back to their German origins, however, is to give a false impression, for the secret of their power over the Victorian mind was that those origins were unappreciated. Calm, radiance, and childlikeness seemed to be qualities inherent in the Greek genius, plainly perceived across a distance of 2000 years; if the Victorians had distinctly told themselves that these ideas were merely the products of an outdated scholarship, they would not have accepted them so tamely.[63]

In his *Sketches in Italy and Greece*, Symonds wrote: 'Christianity decked her shrines with colour. Not so the Paganism of Hellas. With the Greeks, colour...was severely subordinated to sculpture; toned...to a calculated harmony with actual nature...Light falling upon carved forms...was enough for the Phoebean rites of Hellas.'[64] Symonds combined several contrasts in a single paragraph: between Christianity and paganism, North and South, painting and sculpture, the dark anguish of romantic art and the Greeks' Apollonian clarity. Light and colour bind these ideas together. Symonds also sought to moralize the mountains of Greece: 'Austerely beautiful, not wild with an Italian luxuriance..., they seem the proper home of a race which sought its ideal of beauty in distinction of shape and not in multiplicity of detail, in light and not in richness of colouring, in form and not in size.'[65] Symonds compares the austere, colourless landscape of the Greeks to their sculpture, and, like Pater, he uses the idea of austerity to redeem Greek sculpture from the taint of sin. He invites his readers to see the South as an unattainable land of lost content. By pursuing his hints about the clarity, sanctity, and nakedness of Southern scenery we can disentangle his paradox. While he is talking about landscape, his thoughts are with Greek art, which seemed to later Victorians to have the capacity simultaneously to soothe and to disturb. Classical sculptures are, undeniably, calm; but they force their nudity upon the spectator's notice. To a sexually tinged emotion the expressionlessness of the Greek statue, the absence of soul, and the lack of individual character are positive enticements. Blank and characterless expressions provided a vacant space upon which dreams and fantasies could be projected. Victorian passion could bring character enough. The Greek experience suggested to Symonds that fleshly passions had once been untroubling and free of guilt. This condition, however, would never be possible again: one could only gaze upon the innocence of the Greeks from afar, with *Sehnsucht*, like a northern sojourner in a southern land.[66]

Victorians believed that sculpture was the ruling art form of the ancient world. Symonds argued that the English nation had 'produced a drama that compete[d] with that of Athens' and that it also equalled Athens in painting, music, and architecture.[67] Yet 'a student who has tried, however imperfectly, to assimilate to himself the spirit displayed in the surviving monuments of Greek art, is brought back at every turn to sculpture as the norm and canon of them all.'[68] It is the very plasticity and solidity of sculpture that make it a suitable medium for Greek perfection; it allows the sensitive viewer to recapture the essence of Greece. Symonds's descriptions attempt to make visible the physical perfection of Greek bodies: 'Greek sculpture...brings us close to the...physical fulfilment of Greek life.'[69]

Almost all homosexual visitors to the Mediterranean who wrote about their experiences, from Winckelmann onwards, confessed to being overwhelmed by landscapes and personal contacts, and many ascribed the same feelings to their encounters with classical art and literature. The voyage south was a journey outside the library and into the 'real world', but it formed as well a symbolic regression from 'civilization' to the natural state of mankind, complete with the freedom to realize yearnings that might naturally (or, in the eyes of the bourgeois world, 'unnaturally') lurk in the breasts of visitors. As John Pemble remarks: 'In the South the intellectual rediscovered his instinctual humanity.'[70]

The classical world – at a time when homosexuality was despised, catalogued as an illness, sin, psychiatric disorder, and illegal act – suggested legitimate antecedents for the 'crime against nature'. The *Symposium*, the poems of Theocritus and Virgil, the friendships of Achilles and Patroclus and of Hadrian and Antinous, the myth of Ganymede, the statues of Apollo, all provided a canon of art, literature, and history that justified and authenticated homosexual love; the poets and painters of the Renaissance formed a link in this homosexual cultural genealogy.[71] For those in the cultured classes, homosexuality was literature and art; sex was transformed into an aesthetic act.[72] Hans Meyer argues that 'the existence of the homosexual outsider in the bourgeois society of the nineteenth century is conceivable only as an aesthetic existence... It was the homosexual writer and artist ... who was condemned to play a certain role, which is to say, condemned to an aesthetic existence. It is always the playing of a role, ... the aesthetic mimesis of reality.'[73] This approach idealized homosexuality, rendering it spiritual even to the point of preferring 'Platonic' friendships to actual sexual relations.

Furthermore, the general political circumstances sometimes made expatriation a way to escape harassment or persecution for both political and sexual renegades. The Criminal Law Amendment Act of 1885 was the outcome of investigations by the reforming editor of the *Pall Mall Gazette*, W. T. Stead, into the current traffic in adolescent girls. His zeal bore fruit in the passing of the law raising the age of consent from twelve to sixteen. However, with the memory of the Cleveland Street scandal and its revelations of male prostitution still in the minds of the shocked, reformers slipped in an extra clause, known as the Labouchere Amendment.[74] This legislation stated that any act of 'gross indecency' between males, in public or private, was a misdemeanour punishable with two years of hard labour; furthermore, connection *per anum* became a felony punishable with penal servitude for life. The Labouchere Amendment stood out conspicuously as the single most stringent law against a sexual offence in Europe. The advice of Maurice's psychologist and the real-life exile of Wilde provided the pragmatic legal and social reasons for English homosexuals to go south. Symonds's writings articulated an intellectual and cultural justification for doing so.[75]

In 1877 an irritable and tubercular Symonds settled permanently in Davos Platz for his health. Here and on visits to Italy, he enjoyed many forms of sexual activity with a wide variety of men. Because of the anguish he had suffered Symonds was almost obsessional about British hypocrisy, and he was particularly embittered by the Criminal Law Amendment Act. Symonds undoubtedly benefited from the clear air of Switzerland; nevertheless, in both his *Memoirs* and his *Sexual Inversion* he made a special point of stressing the fact that his health improved appreciably after he gratified his long-suppressed desires.[76]

It was during these years that Symonds confronted the issue of homosexuality directly. In the *Studies* he waxed lyrical in descriptions of Hellas, and carefully balanced evocations of young men and young women: 'Beneath the olive trees, among the flowers and ferns, move stately maidens and bare-chested youths.'[77] While working on the Greek poets for a broad public, Symonds also composed a 73 page essay aimed at a narrower, specialist audience. He privately printed an edition of ten copies of *A Problem in Greek Ethics* in 1883, which was later revised and appended to the first printing of Ellis's *Sexual Inversion* (1897). The 1908 edition, which appeared posthumously, was limited to 100 copies and bore the subtitle 'An Enquiry into the Phenomenon of Sexual Inversion Addressed Especially to Medical Psychologists and Jurists'. The booklet is the most eloquent and famous apologia for homosexuality, and the most scholarly study of homosexuality in Greece, written in English in the nineteenth century. Through the neutral idiom of 'science' it formulates a theory of homosexuality based on Antiquity. The first paragraph sets the tone:

> For the student of sexual inversion, ancient Greece offers a wide field for observation and reflection. Its importance has hitherto been under-rated by medical and legal writers on the subject, who do not seem to be aware that here alone in history have we the example of a great and highly developed race not only tolerating homosexual passions, but deeming them for the benefit of society. Here, also, through the copious stores of literature at our disposal, we can arrive at something definite regarding the various forms assumed by these passions, when allowed free scope for development in the midst of a refined and intellectual civilisation. What the Greeks called *paiderastia*, or boy-love, was a phenomenon of one of the most highly organized and nobly active nations. It is the feature by which Greek social life is most sharply distinguished from that of any other people approaching the Hellenes in moral or mental distinction.[78]

Whereas earlier works like the *Studies* depended on enthusiasm, in this essay Symonds manifests thoughtful analysis. He reviews, with extra-ordinary erudition and in lucid prose, the history of pederasty in Greek poetry and society. Symonds supersedes his previous aesthetic delibera-tions and uses sex to ignite the next level of argument: the political and social inequality of the Victorian establishment. The idealization of 'inversion' serves a distinct purpose in Symonds's theory, which aims at winning both social acceptance and the reform of the British criminal code. He championed 'Greek love' as honourable, devoted, and self-sacrificing; by appealing to the very virtues which Victorians prized, he subverts the dominant social order.

Symonds develops a representation of Greek homosexuality as a social construct, in which the overwhelming influence of Plato is always close to hand.[79] Symonds quotes Jowett's translation of the *Symposium* at length and summarizes it:

> The most salient characteristics of the whole speech are, first, the definition of a code of honour, distinguishing the nobler from the

baser forms of paiderastia; secondly, the decided preference of male over female love; thirdly, the belief in the possibility of permanent affection between paiderastic friends; and, fourthly, the passing allusion to rules of domestic surveillance under which Athenian boys were placed.[80]

His model of Greek love countered contemporary negative stereotypes, many of which still inform homophobia today. The masculinity of Greek pederasty was paramount: 'The fact remains that, till the last, Greek paiderastia among the better sort of men implied no effeminacy. Community of interest in sport, in exercise, and in open-air life rendered it attractive.'[81] Symonds harks back to his earlier calls for spiritual and intellectual freedom, and also evokes political liberty: 'Paiderastia...was closely connected with the love of political independence, with the contempt for Asiatic luxury, with the gymnastic sports, and with the intellectual interests which distinguished Hellenes from barbarians.'[82] Finally, Symonds places Greek pederasty into a context of closely allied aesthetics and ethics: 'The morality of the Greeks, as I have tried elsewhere to prove, was aesthetic. They regarded humanity as a part of a good and beautiful universe, nor did they shrink away from any of their normal instincts.'[83]

Symonds wrote at a time when the historical configuration of male homosexual desire was in rapid flux. Analysts were proposing models different from the construct of Greek love. Ulrichs and Hirschfeld, despite quotations from the classics, spoke of Urnings as a 'third sex'. Kertbeny's invention of the word 'homosexual' helped to separate such men and women into an entirely different category. Freud analysed homosexuality as an arrested stage in psychological development. More recently Alfred Kinsey's famous report on male sexuality has suggested that sexual behaviour and desire are located along a spectrum that ranges from exclusive homosexuality to exclusive heterosexuality. Current research in genetics suggests other possibilities. Not all of these theories are at variance with the ideas and practices of pederasty in Antiquity, but the new views have increasingly displaced antique notions of Greek love for both gays and the general public.

When the tendency to use the Greeks as a means of confirming private prejudgments became dominant, Hellenism soon ceased to be a vital cultural force.[84] It is not surprising, therefore, that Symonds's writings on ancient Greece held so little weight in the twentieth century. Just as Winckelmann's art history now seems culturally ethnocentric and ahistorical, so many of Symonds's theories appear naïve. We now understand that the choice of male or female partners in highly regimented Greece was more a function of social activity than of sexual identity.[85] The old view of homosexuality based on 'Greek love' was proudly élitist yet – curiously – rather apologetic, since it justified homosexuality by reference to great men and great ideas from the past, and such arguments exercised a strong appeal to Victorians of Symonds's class and background. Greek love, as understood by the Greeks, recast by the Romans, taken up by Renaissance writers and artists, and then revived and relived by homosexuals after Winckelmann – or as they tried, at least, to relive it – rests on certain presuppositions that are unfashionable, and no longer corresponds to sociopolitical realities. Ironically, while eighteenth- and nineteenth-century writers (including Symonds) thought that they had located in pederasty one of the major traits – indeed one of the major strengths – of classical civilization, they sometimes glossed over the social and political assumptions on which it rested. Responding to criticism of the first volume of his *Studies*, Symonds admits in the last chapter of the second volume that such abuses as slavery and the degradation of women existed in Greece, but he brushes them aside in a single paragraph.[86]

Nevertheless, in contrast to Winckelmann, it is unlikely that Symonds really desired to bring back the classical world. His ideals were generally more aligned with the liberal, socialist views of his own day (despite the élitism of his classical references). 'We must imitate the Greeks', he wrote,

> not by trying to reproduce their bygone modes of life and feeling, but by approximating to their free and fearless attitude of mind. While frankly recognizing that much of their liberty would for us be licence, and that the moral progress of the race depends on holding with a firm grasp what the Greek had hardly apprehended, we ought still to emulate their spirit by cheerfully accepting the world as we find it, acknowledging the value of each human impulse and aiming after virtues that depend on self-regulation rather than on total abstinence and mortification.[87]

By pointing to the sensuality of Greek culture, and its compatibility with spirituality, in writers such as Aeschylus, Sophocles, and Plato, Symonds hoped to demonstrate that a similar moral synthesis was possible for the nineteenth century. What had been true for the Greeks in regard to sex, love, and spirituality could also be true for contemporary British society.[88] Symonds's appeal to the model of ancient Greece was ultimately utopian, a quest for a new society in which homosexual desires would be accepted, philosophy and sexuality joined, and classical virtues recovered.

Notes

1   Centring on Foucault's historicizing of modern notions of sexuality, recent studies have highlighted the ways in which it can be misleading to use the word 'homosexuality' for contexts prior to the moment when it first came into use in the later nineteenth century, mainly because of its association with distinctively modern conceptions of identity as constituted through sexual desire. See M. Foucault, *The History of Sexuality, Volume Two: The Uses of Pleasure* (Harmondsworth, 1987); D. Halperin, *One Hundred Years of Homosexuality and Other Essays on Greek Love* (1990), 15–53.

2   Thomas Paine, *The Rights of Man*, pt. 2, ch. 3.

3   W. H. Auden (ed.), *The Portable Greek Reader* (New York, 1948), 1–38.

4   Percy Bysshe Shelley, *Hellas*, preface.

5   A. C. Swinburne, *The Swinburne Letters*, ed. C. Y. Lang (New Haven, CT, 1959–62), iii, 56.

6   J. A. Symonds, *Studies of the Greek Poets, Second Series* (1876), ii, 383.

7   J. A. Symonds, *The Memoirs of John Addington Symonds*, ed. Phyllis Grosskurth (Chicago, 1984), 17.

8   Ibid., 17.

9   Ibid., 77–8.

10   Ibid., 106.

11   L. Dowling, *Hellenism and Homosexuality in Victorian Oxford* (Ithaca, NY, 1994), xiii. See also G. Faber, *Jowett* (1957).

12   Dowling, *Hellenism*, 64, 77–8. See also the extensive analysis in Frank Turner, *The Greek Heritage in Victorian Britain* (New Haven, CT, 1981).

13   Symonds, *Memoirs*, 99, 286.

14   Ibid., 103.

15   R. Jenkyns, *The Victorians and Ancient Greece* (Oxford, 1980), 280–2. See also R. Aldrich, *The Seduction of the Mediterranean* (1993), 97–9.

16   Symonds, *Memoirs*, 286.

17   Phyllis Grosskurth, *John Addington Symonds* (1964), 43, 108–9.

18   Dowling, *Hellenism*, 89.

19   Grosskurth, *John Addington Symonds*, 266.

20   See, for example, Sir Joshua Reynolds, *Discourses Delivered to the Students of the Royal Academy*, ed. Roger Fry (1905).

21   Turner, *Greek Heritage*, 39–44; Aldrich, *Seduction*, 41–57; E. A. Adams, *Dandies and Desert Saints: Styles of Victorian Masculinity* (Ithaca, NY, 1995), 154–68.

22   J. J. Winckelmann, *Geschichte der Kunst des Altertums* (Dresden, 1764), Book 8. See also Alex Potts, *Flesh and the Ideal: Winckelmann and the Origins of Art History* (New Haven, 1994), 23–33, 50–4.

23   Müller's *Handbuch* was available in a popular translation by 1847. Other highly influential works were Brunn's *Geschichte der Griechischen Künstler* (1857) and Overbeck's *Geschichte des Griechischen Plastik* (1857–68) and *Die antiken Schriftquellen zur Geschichte der bildenden Künste bei den Griechen*

(1868). Each went through multiple revised editions. See E. Langlotz, *Über das Interpretieren Griechischen Plastik* (Bonn, 1947); Turner, *Greek Inheritance*, 42.

24 C. Justi, *Winckelmann und seine Zeitgenossen* (Leipzig, 1867–72); Potts, *Flesh and the Ideal*, 15.

25 For example, Pliny's *Natural History*, 34.54–65; Quintillian's *Institutio Oratoria*, 12.10; Cicero's *Brutus*, 70.9, and *Orator*, 9. These were also found in such compilations as Franciscus Junius's *The Painting of the Ancients*, available in numerous popular translations.

26 J. A. Symonds, *Studies of the Greek Poets, First Series* (1873), 208. Here Symonds compares the rise and fall of Greek tragedy with Greek sculpture in a manner that echoes Dionysos of Halikarnassos's study of rhetoric, *De Isocrate*, 3.

27 J. J. Winckelmann, *Reflections on the Painting and Sculpture of the Greeks*, trans. H. Fusseli (1765), 34. Winckelmann uses the distinction to compare Greek sculpture with classical literature, specifically the Socratic dialogues. Symonds used similar comparisons throughout his writings.

28 J. A. Symonds, 'The Ideal of Beauty in Greek Sculpture', *Journal of Pre-Raphaelite and Aesthetic Studies*, ii, 1 (1989), 99–105.

29 J. J. Winckelmann, *Geschichte*, 25ff; *Anmerkungen über die Geschichte der Kunst des Altertums* (Dresden, 1767), 1–2. Cf. Potts, *Flesh and the Ideal*, 57–8.

30 Jenkyns, *Victorians and Ancient Greece*, 165.

31 J. A. Symonds, *Sketches in Italy and Greece* (1874), 207. Byron also claimed to find in Attica and Ionia an excellence of climate strikingly different from the rest of the Mediterranean: *Childe Harold's Pilgrimage*, canto 2, stanza 73.

32 Symonds, *Greek Poets, First Series*, 400.

33 Ibid., 399.

34 Ibid., 310.

35 Winckelmann, *Geschichte*, 130, 132, 324. Cf. Potts, *Flesh and the Ideal*, 54–60.

36 Symonds, *Greek Poets, First Series*, 415.

37 Winckelmann, *Reflections*, 3, 5.

38 Symonds, 'The Ideal of Beauty', *loc. cit.*

39 W. Pater, *The Renaissance*, ed. K. Clark (1961), 203. Cf. Potts, *Flesh and the Ideal*, 250.

40 Symonds, 'The Ideal of Beauty', *loc. cit.*

41 For a recent evaluation of the problem see W. A. P. Childs, 'The Classic as Realism in Greek Art', *Art Journal*, xlvii, 1 (1988), 10–14.

42 Symonds, *Greek Poets, First Series*, 399.

43 Turner, *Greek Inheritance*, 41–2.

44 Symonds, *Greek Poets, Second Series*, 379.

45 In Wilde's *The Critic as Artist* Gilbert likens Plato's ideal education, conducted amid 'fair sights and sounds', to an education in Oxford.

46 Symonds, *Greek Poets, First Series*, 408.

47 Goethe, *Roman Elegies*, no. 5.

48 Jenkyns, *Victorians and Ancient Greece*, 142.

49 Potts, *Flesh and the Ideal*, 171.

50 Cf. W. Hogarth's *The Analysis of Beauty* (1753).

51 Winckelmann, *Geschichte*, 152–3.

52 Grosskurth, *John Addington Symonds*, 276 (citing 'Miscellanies', fol. 3, in the Houghton Library, Harvard).

53 Symonds, 'The Ideal of Beauty', *loc. cit.*, 99.

54   Symonds, *Greek Poets, First Series*, 407–8.
55   J. J. Winckelmann, *Briefe* (Berlin, 1952–7), iii, 127 (to Schlabbrendorf, 19 October 1765). See Potts, *Flesh and the Ideal*, 215.
56   Grosskurth, *John Addington Symonds*, 276.
57   J. A. Symonds, *A Problem in Greek Ethics* (1908), 68. For the original text, see J. J. Winckelmann, *Kleine Schriften, Vorreden, Entwürfe* (Berlin, 1968), 216.
58   Ibid., 68.
59   Ibid., 68.
60   Pater, *Renaissance*, 182.
61   Ibid., 182.
62   Ibid., 211–12. Cf. Adams, *Dandies*, 173–4.
63   Henry James, for example, also addressed these issues in his fiction. 'He left her . . . among the shining antique marbles. She sat down in the circle of these presences . . . , resting her eyes on their beautiful blank faces; listening to their eternal silence. It is impossible . . . to look long at a great company of Greek sculptures without feeling the effect of their noble quietude; which, as with a high door closed for the ceremony, slowly drops on the spirit the large white mantle of peace' (*The Portrait of a Lady*, ch. 28).
64   Symonds, *Sketches*, 168.
65   Ibid., 231.
66   German idealist writers, including Herder, Goethe, the Schlegel brothers, Schiller, and Hegel, imagined a historical divide separating the integrated wholeness of ancient Greek culture from its antithesis, the modern. Cf. Turner, *Greek Inheritance*, 43.
67   Symonds, *Greek Poets, Second Series*, 374.
68   Ibid., 375.
69   Symonds, *Greek Poets, First Series*, 405.
70   John Pemble, *The Mediterranean Passion: Victorians and Edwardians in the South* (Oxford, 1988), 155.
71   Aldrich, *Seduction*, 217.
72   Ibid., 222.
73   Hans Meyer, *The Outsiders: A Study in Life and Letters* (Cambridge, MA, 1982).
74   H. Montgomery Hyde, *The Cleveland Street Scandal* (1976); F. Whyte, *The Life of W. T. Stead* (1925).
75   Aldrich, *Seduction*, 99.
76   Symonds, *Memoirs*, 287. Cf. Winckelmann's letter of 10 November 1758: 'I am healthy and healthier than I ever was in Germany, free and contented, and I can say that I have begun to live for the very first time in Italy' (*Briefe*, i, 430).
77   Symonds, *Greek Poets, First Series*, 403.
78   Symonds, *Greek Ethics*, 1.
79   Ibid., 63. Nevertheless Symonds was convinced that his condition was innate. See Grosskurth, *John Addington Symonds*, 264, 293.
80   Symonds, *Greek Ethics*, 33. Symonds wrote to Jowett, who had criticized his opinions when translating the *Symposium*: 'Greek love was for Plato no "figure of speech" but a present poignant reality. Greek love is for modern students of Plato no "figure of speech" and no anachronism, but a present poignant reality. The facts of Greek history and the facts of contemporary life demonstrate these propositions only too conclusively' (Symonds, *Memoirs*, 102).

81 Symonds, *Greek Ethics*, 36. Cf. Adams, *Dandies*, 168–81.
82 Symonds, *Greek Ethics*, 51.
83 Ibid., 69.
84 Jenkyns, *Victorians and Ancient Greece*, 16.
85 K. J. Dover, *Greek Homosexuality* (1978); Halperin, *One Hundred Years*.
86 Symonds, *Greek Poets, Second Series*, 384. Cf. E. K. Sedgwick, *Between Men: English Literature and Male Homosexual Desire* (New York, 1985).
87 Symonds, *Greek Poets, First Series*, 422n.
88 Turner, *Greek Inheritance*, 115.

6

Pungent Prophecies of Art:
Symonds, Pater, and Michelangelo

Alex Potts

Juxtaposing Symonds's and Pater's intriguingly different studies of Michelangelo serves to illuminate crucial differences between the two men's highly influential writing on the Italian Renaissance. Their vividly contrasting images of Michelangelo represent two distinct ethical and aesthetic ideals – as if each condensed diverse facets of late Victorian self-understanding in his recreation of a figure who for some time had stood as a peculiarly dramatic type of the modern creative genius. Michelangelo deeply fascinated them both, though it would be only fair to say that Symonds's fascination was fuller and more wide-ranging – it gave rise to one of his most important late publications, the two-volume biography of Michelangelo he first published in 1892.[1] Pater's essay, on the other hand, betrays a haunting evasiveness, which like much apparent evasiveness in Pater proves on close inspection to have its own complex logic. In the 1870s, when Pater and Symonds were the two leading British writers on the Italian Renaissance, they quite literally crossed paths on Michelangelo.

The story begins with the publication of Pater's Michelangelo essay in the *Fortnightly Review* in 1871. It was called 'The Poetry of Michelangelo', and it is as much about the poetry as it is about the art, though in my view considerably more illuminating on the art. A reinterpretation of the poetry was a topical concern because a new scholarly edition of the poems had recently been published by Guasti,[2] based on a careful re-examination and collation of the manuscript sources. This exposed the previously available edition, issued by Michelangelo's great-nephew in 1623, as hopelessly bowdlerized and seriously misleading with regard both to the content and to the style of the poetry. Symonds too responded to this development. He was the first to make available new versions of Michelangelo's sonnets to the English-speaking public when he published his own translations of 23 sonnets (from Guasti's edition) in the *Contemporary Review* in 1872. In his introduction to these translations Symonds made very flattering reference to Pater's recent analysis of Michelangelo's poems, and went so far as to present his translations as a 'supplement' to Pater's work.[3]

Pater availed himself of Symonds's translations when he reissued his Michelangelo essay in a slightly revised form for the first edition of his *Studies in the History of the Renaissance*, which came out in 1873. He reproduced in an extended footnote the full text of Symonds's translations of three crucial sonnets, thereby making evident something which did not really emerge in the main body of his text – namely that some of the more passionate love poems were clearly addressed to men. While the first of the three sonnets was designated as being addressed to Vittoria Colonna,[4] and took as its theme an old man's incapacity to burn with love's flame, the loss of the 'blind desire' of his youth, the second was the famous sonnet to Tommaso de' Cavalieri, possibly the one in the whole sequence which gave most vivid expression to amorous feelings towards the addressee: 'Why should I seek to ease intense desire . . . No marvel if alone and bare I go/An armed Knight's captive and slave confessed' (in Italian 'knight' puns on the name Cavalieri). Pater did not acknowledge Symonds by name, though the article where the translations had appeared was signed.[5]

This omission did not seem to have offended Symonds at the time.[6] In his generally extremely favourable review of Pater's *Studies in the History of the Renaissance*, he characterized Pater's analysis of Michelangelo's poems as 'one of the triumphs of Mr Pater's criticism', and he singled out for special mention the most Paterian aspect of this analysis, namely the way Pater showed 'truest sympathy for what has generally been overlooked in this stern master – his sweetness'.[7] His only objection to Pater's interpretation had to do with the question as to whether the unfinished state of many of the statues was, as Pater claimed, central to Michelangelo's conception of sculpture. I shall return to this, because the point of difference illuminates the two men's very different interest in sculptural aesthetics.

From now on the story becomes clouded, and testifies to a growing split between the two men. In 1877, the year Pater, like Symonds, was obliged to stand down from his candidacy for the Oxford Professorship of Poetry, the *Renaissance* appeared in a new version under the title *The Renaissance: Studies in Art and Poetry*. Here Pater exercised considerable self-censorship, most notoriously in his omission of the controversial conclusion. He also excised the footnote with Symonds's translations of three Michelangelo sonnets. Generally speaking, his omissions and changes were designed to temper accusations of anti-Christian and amoral sentiment, and he left intact most of the passages evoking erotic bondings between men. Indeed, by adding the medieval story of undying love between Amys and Amile, a love which overrode familial bonds and asserted itself miraculously even in death, he intensified the possibly controversial overtones of this important dimension of his writing.[8] But by censoring the footnote which reproduced the three Michelangelo sonnets, he removed from his essay on the artist the one unambiguous reference to his involvement with male lovers, leaving the essay skewed by an almost conventionally anodyne focus on Vittoria Colonna as the principal addressee of the later poetry.

True, he criticized the Romantic heterosexualizing of Michelangelo's life as insinuating some kind of love-affair between him and the aged, and pious, aristocratic lady. He also kept the allusive comments about how 'beneath the Platonic calm of the sonnets there is latent a deep delight in carnal form and colour', and how, most evidently in his madrigals, Michelangelo 'often falls into the language of less tranquil affections . . . He who spoke so decisively of the supremacy in the imaginative world of the unveiled human form had not always been, we may think, a mere Platonic lover . . .'[9] 'Platonic lover' would have had powerful resonances for those prepared to hear them, as would Pater's insistence that, of two main poetic traditions available to Michelangelo for representing a 'pattern of imaginative love', he was more attuned to the newly revived Platonic tradition than to Dante's medieval Christian one. For most readers, however, Pater's censoring would successfully have sanitized his text, removing anything that might disturb a conventionally gendered understanding of the sexual dynamic of Michelangelo's poetry – or life. Not only was this bit of history effaced – so also was any acknowledgement of Pater's debt to and ties with Symonds.

At this moment, Symonds was publicly signalling his distance from Pater. His discussion of Michelangelo in the third volume of his *Renaissance in Italy* (on the fine arts), which appeared in the same year as the 1877 edition of Pater's *Renaissance*, makes no explicit mention of Pater, except to refer to him as a 'recent critic' who had wrongly suggested that 'Michael Angelo sought to realise a certain preconceived effect by want of finish' in his sculpture. Here, and more fully in his introduction to the volume of translations of Michelangelo's sonnets which he published in the following year, Symonds engaged in a critique of earlier commentators on Michelangelo, and even of Guasti, the editor of the new edition, for misleadingly representing Vittoria Colonna as the major addressee of the love poems, and ignoring or deliberately suppressing the clear evidence that many of these love poems were indeed addressed to men.[10] All this made Pater's treatment seem somewhat coy and evasive.

In the final round of this history, a somewhat perfunctory mutual recognition crept back in. Pater's 1888 edition of *The Renaissance*, which restored his controversial conclusion, included a brief footnote reference to Symonds, but without reinstating the translations of the sonnets included in the 1873 edition. Here Pater wrote: 'The sonnets have been translated into English, with much skill, and poetic taste, by Mr. J. A. Symonds.'[11] In turn, in the preface to his biography of Michelangelo, published four years later, Symonds made a passing reference to Pater, though its minimalism was possibly more subtly slighting than Pater's brief reference to his translations. 'Pater,' he commented in his survey of the Michelangelo literature, 'has touched upon the poems with his usual delicacy.'[12] Mostly a non-meeting of minds, then, which echoes the personal antipathy to the tenor of Pater's writing that Symonds began expressing in private when he first read the *Renaissance* in 1873, and which sharpened with time. Thus, in 1885, in a letter explaining his reluctance to read *Marius the Epicurean*, he wrote: 'I shrink from approaching Pater's style, which has a peculiarly disagreeable effect upon my nerves – like the presence of a civet cat.' (Civet cats emit a yellowish fatty fluid that has a powerful smell, a disagreeable substance that is, however, used for making perfume.) The man too came in for some stick – Pater's 'theory of life', according to Symonds, was that of one 'who has not lived and loved'.[13]

There are here two very different attitudes to life, as Symonds indicated – one activist, the other contemplative; one increasingly openly combating the homophobic prejudices of late-Victorian society, and moving towards an increasingly explicit, yet also necessarily carefully framed and moderated, defence of sexual relations between men; the other focusing on imaginative writing and a mode of critical interpretation where a latent sexual dynamic could dissolve the conceptual and ethical fixities of the time, where a homoerotic ideal would be evoked for those of like mind, but where there was an almost painful evasion of overt controversy. Symonds was an intelligent – and liberal – late nineteenth-century realist, confidently dealing with masses of historical fact and archival detail and trying to reconstruct the concrete fabric of the life of figures who intrigued him; Pater was a progenitor of modernist hermeneutic ambiguity, one of the more singular anti-positivists of his time, who threw into question the fixed categorizations that his contemporaries, including Symonds, brought to bear in their understanding of the past. For Symonds, the past was primarily of interest because it offered up vivid models for the conduct of life – ethics were his central concern, and were a necessary grounding for the artistic and the aesthetic; for Pater, not only were the aesthetic and the ethical inextricably intertwined, but an intensified openness to the aesthetic was integral to what it meant for him properly to be alive.

What makes it fruitful to see the one personality in the light of the other is not so much the contrast, but the fact that both were infused by that passionate late-Victorian quest for a value system that would function as a guide to the conduct of life. For both, this quest gained an exceptional intensity, because they found themselves in a situation where conventional understandings of love and desire were not only inadequate, but at some level intolerable.

Where Pater and Symonds did differ unequivocally was in the different definitions they gave of the Renaissance as a historical phenomenon – a phenomenon which fascinated as the crucible of both modern individualism and libertarianism. In the first volume of his study *Renaissance in Italy*, a political history of *The Age of the Despots* published in 1875, Symonds wrote:

> What the word Renaissance really means is new birth to liberty – the spirit of mankind recovering consciousness and the power of self-determination, recognising the beauty of the outer world, and of the body through art, liberating the reason in science and the conscience in religion, restoring culture to the intelligence, and establishing the principle of political freedom.[14]

Here we have a radical liberal, humanist view of the Renaissance as a moment in history which changed 'men's' minds, rather than as a state of mind in itself, as Pater conceived it. For Symonds the Renaissance was identifiable as a concrete historical moment when political changes and changes in the fabric of culture enabled humanity to discover a new freedom to act and to think, and made possible a new independence of, and ability to question, established hierarchies and conventions. With Pater, what was at issue was the formation of a new way of existing in and relating to the world, rather than a historical liberation of the human subject:

> For us the Renaissance is the name of a many-sided but united movement [note how the 'for us' undoes the idea of the Renaissance as a fixed historical object], [a movement] in which the love of the things

of the intellect and the imagination for their own sake, the desire for a more liberal and more comely way of conceiving life, make themselves felt, urging those who experience this desire to search out first one and then another means of intellectual or imaginative enjoyment, and directing them not only to the discovery of old and forgotten sources of enjoyment, but to the divination of fresh sources thereof – new experiences, new subjects of poetry, new forms of art.[15]

Symonds represented that scrupulous historicizing strain in late nineteenth-century culture, in which each age had a concretely definable mentality whose character could be reconstructed from a careful examination of historical documents, and from a full understanding of the larger historical forces – whether political or cultural – at play. Thus, for Symonds, the Renaissance had a clear historical location; and if he was quite aware that one could not fix precise limits to the emergence of a Renaissance spirit, one could at least start out from the idea that 'two dates, 1453 and 1527, marking respectively the fall of Constantinople and the sack of Rome, are convenient for fixing in the mind that narrow space of time during which the Renaissance culminated'.[16] Pater took almost the opposite view, stressing how no clear boundary could be drawn between the Christian middle ages and the Renaissance, not because there were always exceptions to such periodizings, but because fundamental distinctions of outlook, such as that between the traditionalism of the Christian middle ages and the antinomian libertarianism of the Renaissance, needed to be conceived dialectically. They existed for the historian as two distinct capacities of the human mind, two distinct modes of being, not as materially particularizable entities with a definite historical location. For Pater, the Renaissance, that 'general excitement and enlightening of the human mind', could 'be traced far back into the middle age itself'.[17] Symonds, on the other hand, insisted that any moments of liberation in the feudal middle ages were necessarily 'immature and abortive', making it inevitable that 'the first anticipations of the Renaissance were fragmentary and sterile.'[18] The solidly historicizing cast of Symonds's treatment of the Renaissance is perhaps most apparent in his very Victorian insistence on tracing the decline of the Renaissance and the material causes of this decline; while for Pater this just was not an issue. For him, the complex flow of history could not be firmed up in this way. That in part is what makes him seem more modern.

The difference of outlook extended to their different way of conceiving the interplay between the ancient pagan and the Christian currents within the Italian Renaissance. Symonds, particularly in his first volume on the Renaissance, took the anti-clerical liberal view as propounded by Michelet that the Christian and pagan spirit were fundamentally opposed. 'During the Middle Ages', he wrote, 'man had lived enveloped in a cowl. He had not seen the beauty of the world . . . The Renaissance shattered and destroyed [the fixed ideas of the ascetic medieval Church], rending the thick veil which they had drawn between the mind of man and the outer world, and flashing the light of reality upon the darkened places of his own nature.'[19] There are occasional passages like this in Pater, particularly in his essay on Winckelmann, but they are mediated by the general tenor of his analysis, which begins by locating some of the more vivid instances of 'that assertion of the liberty of heart . . . its antinomianism, its spirit of rebellion and revolt against the moral and religious ideas of the time', within the middle ages. Pater also argued against the idea that Renaissance rebirth was necessarily antithetical to the Christian culture from which it emerged. It was his view that fifteenth-century art, its 'great aim and achievement', 'as Christian art, is often falsely opposed to the Renaissance'.

Symonds's treatment of art in volume three of his *Renaissance in Italy* offers a more nuanced, and at times intriguingly complex, treatment of the duality between Christian and pagan on which he had insisted so categorically. By comparison with Pater, though, the intellectual categories which Symonds brings to bear in his aesthetic analysis of art and in his larger understanding of history are for the most part pretty mainstream – he was an intelligent, but not particularly original thinker at an abstract level. But the texture of his writing is a different matter: there it is not just the truth of things, but the fascination they have, that lies in the detail. What animates his narrative is the way that the details and the overall framework coexist in an unstable and sometimes energizingly antagonistic synthesis.

Symonds still insisted that the history of the visual arts in the Renaissance gave evidence of a fundamental incompatibility between the Christian-medieval and the pagan-Renaissance currents in early modern Italian culture, particularly in the case of sculpture,[20] the pagan art *par excellence* both in his view and in that of most of his Victorian contemporaries. But his discussion of certain individual artists, especially Niccola Pisano and Donatello, where he responded to a richly invested treatment of the male figure, effectively overrode the duality between Christian and pagan which framed his analysis. Thus on Donatello:

> The naked beauty of the boy David and the mailed manhood of
> St. George are raised to a spiritual region by the type of feature and

the pose of body selected to interpret their animating impulse ... [here there is a] power of expressing Christian sentiment in a form of perfect beauty, transcending the Greek type by profounder suggestion of feeling.[21]

For him the sculptures of Niccola Pisano were characterized by 'beauty and freedom', 'noble forms' and 'freedom of style'. As such they were 'a symbol of what happened in the age of the Revival. The old world and the new shook hands; Christianity and Hellenism kissed each other. And yet,' he added emphatically, 'they still remained antagonistic – fused externally by art, but severed in the consciousness that, during those strange years of dubious impulse, felt the might of both.'[22] He negotiated this and other 'Paterian' interminglings of the Hellenic and the Christian, as found in Raphael for example, by emphasizing that any apparent fusion between the two was necessarily momentary and fragile, and unable in the final analysis to overcome their deep-seated incompatibility.[23] This meant that, in his scheme of things, Italian Renaissance art, emerging as it did within an increasingly outworn and corrupted yet persistent Christian culture, was doomed never to realize itself fully. Nineteenth-century historians of art were very much in the sway of the Hegelian notion that Greek antiquity alone had been able to create a whole and stable, fully realized artistic and cultural ideal, a habit of thinking which in Symonds's case gained a further dimension from his identification with what he saw as the frank and healthy and at the same time ethically moderated sexuality of ancient Greece.

But I need to return to Michelangelo, with whose art Symonds did not have that easy identification he felt with Donatello's and Niccola Pisano's – or even Raphael's and that of certain other High Renaissance painters. What most fascinated Symonds about Michelangelo was not so much the power of his art, but rather the persona of the artist as hero, struggling against the odds to realize his higher aims. Michelangelo was for him of overwhelming importance as an ethical ideal, and the aesthetic dynamic of his art was something he admired but felt uneasy about. His biography presents the picture of a man who at some level magnificently realized himself against the odds and transcended the force of circumstance, but whose art was in a way incomplete and flawed, vitiated by tensions that were antithetical to the full realization of the artistic impulse.

This is nicely indicated in the following passage in the conclusion to his biography, where Symonds's deeply divided view of Michelangelo's art is projected outwards on to divisions of opinion among the artistic public at large:

> Michelangelo, then, as Carlyle might have put it, is the Hero as Artist. When we have admitted this, all dregs and sediments of the analytic alembic sink to the bottom, leaving a clear crystalline elixir of the spirit. About the quality of his genius, opinions may, will, and ought to differ. It is so pronounced, so peculiar, so repulsive to one man, so attractive to another, that ... 'it fascinates and is intolerable' ... The world of thoughts and forms in which he lived is habitually too arid, like an extinct planet, tenanted by mighty elemental beings with little human left to them but visionary Titan-shapes, too vast and void for common minds to dwell on pleasantly.[24]

The only sculptures of Michelangelo's to which Symonds responded in an unequivocally positive way were the early, most naturalistic and fully finished works, such as the Vatican Pietà and the large David in Florence, though he was also very drawn to the more finished of the two slaves in the Louvre (see Plate 5b), a sculpture whose 'charm', 'tranquillity', 'sinewy force' and 'languid pose', as he put it, affected one like a fine piece of music – it 'awakes no desire ... fills the soul with something beyond thought or passion ... '[25]

The overriding impression one has from reading Symonds's richly documented and carefully detailed exposition of Michelangelo's career is of the massive burden of circumstance that Michelangelo had to do battle with. One gets a vivid picture of the conflicting and difficult demands made on him by patrons, the tiresome and at times desperate negotiations he had to conduct in order to clear some sort of space for himself to think and work, the immensity and burden of the practical difficulties he continually faced, intensified by his own difficult personality. Positively, on the other hand, what also strikes one in this biographical portrait is the man's immense drive and force of personality, crotchety at times, generous at others, sustaining him in struggles which would simply have crushed most people; and also an immense dedication and single-minded sense of purpose. I sometimes wonder whether there is not a certain amount of self-projection here, coupled with an admiration for a personality who had something which kept eluding Symonds himself. Symonds, for all his immense output, often felt that he had been unable solidly to ground his life's work, to define a single coherent project that commanded his unequivocal dedication. The texture of life that had enabled Michelangelo to produce the art he did, rather than the texture of the art itself, the sense of project rather than the work as such, was Symonds's central concern.[26]

Pater's study of Michelangelo could not be more differently conceived. Pater performs a kind of phenomenological reduction, focusing on what he sees to be the essence of Michelangelo, the distinctive qualities that strike one most deeply when one confronts the art, and momentarily bracketing out the mass of biographical detail and material circumstance. With Pater, we have no re-creation of the artist's self struggling to invent and then realize his art – for a moment, one is left alone in front of the works. Pater focuses on a few chosen pieces, the painting of the Creation of Adam from the Sistine Chapel, above all the four famous sculpted allegories of Night, Day, Dawn, and Dusk from the Medici chapel in San Lorenzo in Florence, as well as the Vatican Pietà and some later drawings of the dead Christ to which he alludes only briefly. It is in communion with these that the unique sense of things embodied in Michelangelo's art was to be appreciated: 'The pure type of the Michelangelesque,' as Pater put it, 'sweetness and strength, pleasure with surprise, an energy of conception which seems at every moment about to break through all the conditions of comely form, recovering, touch by touch, a loveliness found usually only in the simplest natural things – *ex forti dulcedo.*'[27]

Of course, this bracketing is to an extent illusory. Pater moulds a very careful portrait of Michelangelo and the driving preoccupations of his art from biographical detail, and from a particular reading of the poetry. The poetry after all is flagged in the title of the essay. But his interpretation of the poetry, his intriguing discussion of the Dantesque and Platonic registers of imaginative love on which the poetry plays, the sparely selected and allusively narrated biography, form a kind of frame from within which the essence of the Michelangelesque, made intensely present to us in the art, emerges.

Pater is particularly concerned with the material embodiment of this essence in sculpted stone; and the effective incompletion of many of the more compelling sculptures is seen by him as integral to their impact and to their value, regardless of whether this incompletion was or was not a consciously articulated artistic strategy on Michelangelo's part. For Pater, Michelangelo's sculpture is about living form emerging from hard stone, something which he feels plays a role even in the more powerful paintings.[28] This tension between the breath of life and dead stone, the vivid sense of recalcitrant stuff being animated, or reanimated as Pater would have it, is – for Pater – Michelangelo's distinctive achievement: an achievement not inferior to or better than, but radically different from the self-contained plastic ideal of ancient Greek art.[29] So much is clear from Pater's definition of the poetics of Michelangelo's approach to sculpture:

> ...as his persons have something of the unwrought stone about them, so, as if to realise the expression by which the old Florentine records describe the sculptor – *master of live stone* – with him the very rocks seem to have life. They have but to cast away the dust and scurf that they may rise and stand on their feet.[30] (See Plate 6a)

At issue here, too, were more general formal determinants of sculpture as an art-form. If sculpture simply imitated and realized in solid three-dimensional shape the plastic forms of painting, it would in Pater's view make these forms hard and recalcitrant. An evoked form would become a literal object – and mere objecthood, as a modern critic famously put it, would take over from art. The task of sculpture, then, was to find a means of avoiding 'a too heavy realism, that tendency to harden into caricature which the representation of feeling in sculpture is apt to display'. Michelangelo's incompleteness was one way of achieving this, 'of etherealising pure form, of relieving its stiff realism, and communicating to it breath, pulsation, the effect of life'.[31]

In his 1877 study of the fine arts in the Renaissance, Symonds directly took issue with Pater for 'assuming...that Michelangelo sought to realise a certain preconceived effect by want of finish'. His critique reads as very much in line with current art-historical opinion. The 'distracted circumstances of his life', Michelangelo's wayward temperament, the fraught history of his larger commissions, and the immense manual labour involved in seeing though such ambitious commissions as he took on – these facts alone, Symonds believed, would explain the large number of unfinished works. That Michelangelo did not deliberately cultivate unfinish but, on the contrary, 'always aimed at...high finish' was for him demonstrated conclusively by the fact that several of his most famous works were 'executed with the highest polish it is possible for stone to take'.[32]

In his biography of Michelangelo, doubtless written when he was no longer so motivated by the need to set his interpretation apart from Pater's, Symonds suggested that the matter might not be so clear-cut. Though he was still convinced that Michelangelo, had he had the time, would have brought all his work to that same level of finish as was found on sculptures such as the Pietà, the David, and the Moses,[33] there was still a question as to 'whether he preferred to leave off when his idea was sufficiently indicated, or whether his numerous engagements prevented him from excavating the lowest surfaces, and lastly polishing the whole'. This 'is a question which must for ever remain undecided'. And he even went on to speculate, in rather conventional terms, on the possible aesthetic logic of this incompletion: 'There is no doubt that he must have been pleased, as all true lovers of art are, with the picturesque effect – an effect as of things half seen in dreams or emergent from primeval substances – which the imperfection of the craftsman's labours leaves upon the memory.'[34] However, the point as Pater conceived it was not the incompletion as such, but rather a larger formal logic of stone carving – a logic which did not interest Symonds. In Pater's view, what was so compelling about Michelangelo as a sculptor was that he had developed a way of realizing sculpted figures so that one's sense of their stone-likeness, instead of submerging suggestions of living form in inert materiality, became integral to the aesthetic drama of vital animation that they evoked.

Pater was not putting forward the conventional Romantic cliché that the sculpture came alive for the viewer because he or she could imagine reliving the drama of the artist's creative act; watching form, as it were, take shape from raw stuff under the master's magic touch as the stone was being cut away. Rather it was a drama to be had from a direct communion with the sculpture as a fully realized work of art, and it was driven by a tension between the sense of tangible inanimate stone and the elusive sense of an insubstantial 'breath of life' – the latter perhaps no more than a passing effect of light and shadow vivifying the sculpture's surfaces. Such a tension echoed a double sense to be had of the human body as, on the one hand, a solid substantive thing and, on the other, elusive, immaterial, living impulse, brought into focus by thinking of the body in transition from life to death. This complex of ideas underpins the *tour de force* of his essay, the magnificently eloquent and suggestive account he gives of the four allegories of the times of day in the Medici chapel (see Plates 6a and 6b):

They concentrate and express, less by definite conceptions than by the touchings, the promptings of a piece of music, all those vague fancies, misgivings, presentiments, which shift and mix and are defined and fade again, whenever the thoughts try to fix themselves with sincerity on the conditions and surroundings of the disembodied spirit . . . Of all that range of sentiment he is the poet . . . – dumb inquiry over the relapse after death into the formlessness which preceded life, the change, the revolt from that change, then the correcting, hallowing, consoling rush of pity; at last far off, thin and vague, yet not more vague than the most definite thoughts men have had through three centuries on a matter that has been so near their hearts, the new body – a passing light, a mere intangible, external effect, over those too rigid, or too formless faces; a dream that lingers for a moment, retreating in the dawn, incomplete, aimless, helpless; a thing with faint hearing, faint memory, faint power of touch; a breath, a flame in the doorway, a feather in the wind.[35]

What convinces in Pater's analysis is not only the way he has tried to imagine a life-and-death drama being played out in the substantive material presence and the evanescent optical texturing of these sculptures, but also the fact of his singling them out. For there is no denying, when you see them in the Medici chapel, that they are amongst the most intense and telling pieces of sculpture in Western art, and that this is highlighted by the way they literally stand out from their setting. The whole elaborate architectural structure becomes an arena where these amazing things are suspended. Pater's phenomenological reduction has a very real logic – these works do linger in one's consciousness as something almost apart from the whole panoply of Michelangelo's art, and from the fraught and fragmented history of the Medici-tomb project which gave rise to them.

Symonds had some sense of this too, but his take on these sculptures is intriguingly different from Pater's. He projects on to them an almost violent conflict between, on the one hand, the limits imposed by the plastic forms of sculpture and, on the other, the animating drive of the artist's creative impulse and the deep inner feelings to which he was giving expression. They work in his view because they go beyond the limits of sculpture as an art, somehow conveying to the viewer a sense of artistic form being blown apart by tortured human intensity. The disturbing eloquence of the sculptures is generated by the clash between a plastic shape and a tragic torment that the former could never contain:

> ...sculpture has passed beyond her old domain of placid concrete form. The anguish of intolerable emotion, the quickening of the consciousness to a sense of suffering, the acceptance of the inevitable, the strife of the soul with destiny, the burden and passion of mankind: – that is what they contain in their cold chisel-tortured marble.[36]

Michelangelo's art, Symonds writes, renders love as

> spasms of voluptuous pain; and the sleep of Night (see Plate 6b) is troubled with fantastic dreams, and the Dawn starts into consciousness

with a shudder of prophetic anguish. There is not a hand, a torso, a simple nude, sketched by this extraordinary master which does not vibrate with nervous tension, as though the finger that grasped the pen (and we might add the hand that grasped the chisel) were clenched and the eyes that viewed the model glowed beneath knit brows.[37]

Symonds was fascinated by what he saw as a peculiar, almost painful, intensity – a version of the *terribilità* traditionally ascribed to Michelangelo, but in this case something much more interesting and subtly differentiated (and human) than the usual guff about sublimity and agonized genius. But equally he was disturbed by it. 'Surely also we may regret, not without reason,' he wrote at the conclusion of his dramatic evocation of the raw Beethovenian power of the allegorical figures in the Medici chapel with their 'strained postures and writhing limbs', 'that in the evil days upon which he had fallen, the fair antique *Heiterkeit* and *Allgemeinheit* were beyond his reach.' The problem as Symonds saw it was partly political – Italy by this time had been carved up by foreign powers, its political liberty extinguished, and the papal and Medici courts fallen into corruption.[38]

But there was also a sexual dimension to Symonds's unease. Michelangelo lived in a culture which blocked the return to a 'frank and in the true sense pagan' sensuality, to 'Greek sincerity'. The sensuality which flourished in the Renaissance, he explained in his volume on the fine arts, was one of base lust and animality. The conditions which had given rise to that Platonic cultivation of the sexual and the sensual, that Greek fusion of ethical restraint and sensibility for beauty, had disappeared; liberated from the prohibitions of a Christian denial of the flesh, people simply indulged in unconstrained and bestial gratification.[39] Thus, while Symonds celebrated the way in which the Italian Renaissance 'achieved for the modern world...the liberation of the reason, the power of starting on a new career of progress', he deplored 'the corresponding sensual debasement of the race who won for us the possibility of freedom'.[40]

Symonds's attitude is very complex. Certainly there is more than a residue of Victorian moralizing, almost Ruskinian at times. But he is also arguing in a very un-Ruskinian way that the Christian culture of Michelangelo's time lacked the free and open, and at the same time ethically grounded, practice of sexual relations – at least of sexual relations between men – which had been found in ancient Greece and which had generated a true appreciation of bodily beauty. He was thus signalling the distance between sensuality as it was conceived, and lived, in the modern Christian world, and that fusion of physical impulse with the mental and the ethical that had been realized in Greek antiquity. Though on one level he was clearly echoing an idealizing of Greek antiquity which was almost a cliché in the late eighteenth- and early nineteenth-century German idealist thought that he admired, he was also making a more particular and potentially highly controversial point about 'Greek ethics', and what he saw as a civilizing frankness of sexual self-understanding and mutual bonding between men in ancient Greece which was blocked in the modern world.[41] Something of the latter is at issue when he represents Michelangelo's often tortured intensity, his 'seclusion' and his 'renunciations', and his desperate appeal to Platonic speculations to help him in 'his warfare with the flesh and roving inclination', in the following terms:

> The total result of this singular attitude towards human life, which cannot be rightly described as either ascetic or mystical, but seems rather to have been based on some self-preservative instinct, bidding him to sacrifice lower and keener impulses to what he regarded as the higher and finer purpose of his being, is a certain sense of failure to attain the end proposed, which excuses, though I do not think it justifies, the psychologists, when they classify him among morbid subjects.[42]

Symonds here is arguing against late nineteenth-century studies such as those by Lombroso, which attributed Michelangelo's genius to a 'radical psychical unsoundness', inferred, among other things, from, as Symonds put it, his 'indifference to women and his partiality for male friends';[43] he was suggesting that a certain 'frigidity' in Michelangelo, and his tortured struggle with his sexual inclinations (which Symonds made clear were evidently awakened by men rather than by women), stood in the way of the fullest artistic self-realization, even as it held him back from the common and brutish sensuality that took over the sensibility of many of his heterosexual contemporaries – artists and patrons alike.[44] For Symonds, this 'repression' and the tensions it generated meant that Michelangelo never was able to achieve a classical perfection such as that attained by Jacopo Sansovino in a statue of Bacchus, where 'realism' was 'irradiated and idealised by the sculptor's vivid sense of natural gladness'.[45] By contrast, Michelangelo's attempt in this vein, an early Bacchus, was lacking in 'Greek inspiration', and was no more than the imitation of 'a physically desirable young man in a state of drunkenness'.[46]

The closest Michelangelo came to Greek sensuality, in Symonds's view, was in the famous *ignudi* of the Sistine Chapel, with their endless 'variations on one theme of youthful loveliness and grace' (see Plate 7). For Symonds, though, these figures were to a certain extent abstract and schematic – they were 'adolescent, but the adolescence is neither that of the Greek athlete nor that of the nude model. Indeed it is hardly natural; nor yet is it ideal in the Greek sense of that term. The physical gracefulness of a slim ephebus was never seized by Michelangelo.'[47] There was something missing, a serene ease and frankness combined with an ideality of bodily beauty found in the finest figures of ancient Greek art. He rounded out his discussion with the comment: 'It is an arid region, the region of this mighty master's spirit.' And yet Symonds's description of the 'feminine delicacy and poignant fascination' of Michelangelo's *ignudi* was more intense than anything he wrote about antique statuary. Here again he differs from Pater, for he seems not to have had a language for moving beyond the straightjacketing of nineteenth-century aesthetic and moral categories – in this case the abstract privileging of antique beauty – so as to do justice to the complexities of his fascinating and deeply invested responses to art such as Michelangelo's, where canonical notions of beauty and of a classical fusion of sensuality and ideality did not apply. Pater, on the other hand, was fascinated precisely by an aesthetic sensuality which no longer had the frank and shameless quality of the antique – one where a fevering of the conscience, a certain pain and torment in desiring, a splitting and division of the self characteristic of modern consciousness, generated an intense intoxication unknown to ancient Greek sensibility.[48]

The difference goes deeper than Pater's personal allusiveness about his homosexuality – it is not just a matter of Pater accommodating himself to public condemnation of homosexuality by cultivating a sensibility that was simultaneously fascinated by sexual impulse and by its prohibition. At issue is a very different conception of desiring, Pater's more fluid and errant, envisaged, one might say, more psychoanalytically, as impelled by lack; Symonds's more substantive and objectifying and also more concretely libertarian – not in a 1960s sense, but in one appropriate to a freethinking, liberal, Victorian ethic. The tensions occasioned by sexual impulse were conceived by Symonds as conflicts, often of a violent nature, between instinctual forces and forces opposing them; while, for Pater, tension was internal to the dynamic of desiring.[49] There is a passage in Pater's *Studies in the History of the Renaissance* where he is describing the differences between an antique understanding of liberty and a modern one embodied by a figure such as Goethe, but where he might easily be seen as characterizing differences between Symonds and himself in their treatments of Michelangelo:

> That naïve, rough sense of freedom, which supposes man's will to be limited, if at all, only by a will stronger than his, he can never have again . . . The chief factor in the thoughts of the modern mind concerning itself is the intricacy, the universality of natural law, even in the moral order. For us, necessity is not, as of old, a sort of mythological personage without us, with whom we can do warfare. It is rather a magic web woven through and through us, like that magnetic system of which modern science speaks, penetrating us with a network, subtler than our subtlest nerves, yet bearing in it the central forces of the world.[50]

Pater was wrong only to historicize this distinction in the way he did, rather than to recognize that he was tapping a fundamental distinction within late Victorian culture – two different and equally modern ways of imagining the individual self's freedom. What he described as 'that naïve rough sense of freedom' was a powerful paradigm in late Victorian Britain, and nowhere more intriguingly and complexly so than in Symonds's case. And this difference underpins the very different, but equally resonant images the two men offered of Michelangelo. Arguing against those who sought to classify the artist as a morbid personality, and who pathologized his struggles and his intense and volatile temperament, as well as his failure to conform to heterosexual norms, Symonds wrote:

> The essential point about Michelangelo is that he never burned out, and never lost his manly independence, in spite of numerous nervous disadvantages. That makes him the unparalleled personality he is, as now revealed to us by the impartial study of the documents at our disposal.[51]

It is appropriate to conclude with one of the most intensely moving passages in Symonds's writing, where he envisages the very difficulty of coming to terms with Michelangelo as the source, for us, of his most formidable strengths. Symonds could be every bit as subtle and evocative as Pater about the complexities of an artistic personality that truly compels us and touches the very fibre of our being:

> The sweetness that emerges from his strength, the beauty which blooms rarely, strangely, in unhomely wise, upon the awful crowd of

his conceptions, are only to be apprehended by some innate sympathy or long incubation of the brooding intellect. It is probable, therefore, that the deathless artist through long centuries of glory will abide as solitary as the simple old man did in his poor house at Rome. But no-one, not the dullest, not the weakest, not the laziest and lustfullest, not the most indifferent to ideas or the most tolerant of platitudes and paradoxes, can pass him by without being arrested, quickened, stung, purged, stirred to uneasy self-examination by so strange a personality expressed in prophesies of art so pungent.[52]

Notes

1 For an account of the genesis of the work see Phyllis Grosskurth, *John Addington Symonds: A Biography* (1964), 257–61.
2 This had appeared in 1863. See Walter Pater, *The Renaissance: Studies in Art and Poetry*, ed. D. L. Hill (Berkeley, CA, 1980).
3 Ibid., 360. When he published a complete translation of Michelangelo's sonnets in book form in 1878, he tempered this, referring simply to 'the refined study of Mr W. H. Pater'. See J. A. Symonds, *The Sonnets of Michael Angelo Buonarroti*, new edn (1904), p. xix.
4 In the original edition of Symonds's translation of Michelangelo's sonnets (1878), Vittoria Colonna is not named as a possible addressee of this particular sonnet (No. LI). In the introduction he notes that, while 'Vittoria Colonna and Tommaso de' Cavalieri, the two most intimate friends of his old age in Rome, received from him some of the most pathetically beautiful of his love poems . . . to suppose that either . . . was the object of more than a few well-authenticated sonnets would be hazardous.'
5 Pater made mention only of Guasti, the editor of the new Italian edition that Symonds had used.
6 Pater, *Renaissance*, 360.
7 Ibid., 343.
8 See A. Potts, 'Walter Pater's Unsettling of the Apollonian Ideal', M. Wyke and M. Biddis (eds), *The Uses and Abuses of Antiquity* (forthcoming).
9 Pater, *Renaissance*, 63–4.
10 Symonds, *Sonnets*, pp. xiv–xix.
11 Pater, *Renaissance*, 65.
12 J. A. Symonds, *The Life of Michelangelo Buonarroti* (1893), i, p. xix.
13 D. Donoghue, *Walter Pater, Lover of Strange Souls* (New York, 1995), 40, 43–4.
14 J. A. Symonds, *Renaissance in Italy, I: The Age of the Despots*, new edn (1902), 22.
15 Pater, *Renaissance*, 1–2.
16 Symonds, *Despots*, p. viii.
17 Pater, *Renaissance*, pp. xxii–xxiii.
18 Symonds, *Despots*, 8.
19 Ibid., 11.
20 Ibid., 7, 88–9.
21 J. A. Symonds, *Renaissance in Italy, III: The Fine Arts*, new edn (1899), 100–1. Symonds is referring to Donatello's famous bronze statue of David and his

marble statue of St George in armour from Or San Michele, both now in the Museo Nazionale in Florence.

22   Ibid., 76–8. A work by Niccola Pisano that had a particular significance for him was the nude male figure of Fortitude on the pulpit in Pisa cathedral.

23   Ibid., 25–6. Symonds took the neo-Hegelian view that a more permanent synthesis, moving on to a 'further point outside both Christianity and Paganism, at which the classical ideal of a temperate and joyous natural life shall be restored to a conscience educated by the Gospel' would not be attained by the 'figurative arts', but only perhaps by philosophy or, as he put it, 'the scientific method'.

24   Symonds, *Michelangelo*, ii, 373.

25   Ibid., ii, 87. On the Pietà in St Peter's Rome, see *Fine Arts*, 285. On the large marble David, now in the Accademia in Florence, see *Michelangelo*, i, 98–104.

26   In the introduction to his *Michelangelo* he made it clear that he was going to 'concentrate attention on his personality' and the documenting of the detailed circumstances of his life. A prioritizing of context over aesthetic analysis is also evident in his study of the fine arts of the Italian Renaissance.

27   Pater, *Renaissance*, 57.

28   See, for example, his remarks on the Sistine Adam: ibid., 59.

29   'And it is in this penetrative suggestion of life that the secret of that sweetness of his is to be found' (ibid., 60).

30   Ibid., 60.

31   Ibid., 52–3.

32   Symonds, *Fine Arts*, 308.

33   He cited the finish of the early Bacchus (Museo Nazionale, Florence) as 'alone . . . sufficient to explode a theory favoured by some critics, that, left to work unhindered, he would still have preferred a certain vagueness, a certain want of polish in his marbles' (*Michelangelo*, i, 61).

34   Ibid., i, 113–14.

35   Pater, *Renaissance*, 75–6.

36   Symonds, *Michelangelo*, ii, 34.

37   Ibid., i. 253.

38   Symonds imagined that what Michelangelo had in mind when he was creating Night, 'the nightmare-burdened, heavy-sleeping woman', was evoked in the following lines of a sonnet by the sculptor: 'Dear is my sleep, but more to be mere stone,/ So long as ruin and dishonour reign:/ To hear naught, to feel naught, is my great gain;/ Then wake me not; speak in an undertone.'

39   Symonds, *Fine Arts*, 126–9, 332–3.

40   Ibid., 30.

41   Symonds's fascination with the Greek cult of the beautiful male nude, and his insistence on the 'healthy human tone' and 'ethical rightness' of Greek sculpture already featured prominently in early published writings such as *Studies of the Greek Poets* (1873).

42   Symonds, *Michelangelo*, ii, 370.

43   Ibid., ii, 382.

44   See, for example, *Fine Arts*, 332–3.

45   Ibid., 122–3. He is referring to the marble statue now in the Museo Nazionale in Florence.

46 Symonds, *Michelangelo*, i, 61. The statue represents a youthful Bacchus holding up a cup from which he appears to be about to drink.
47 Ibid., i, 278–9. See also i, 244–6.
48 Pater, *Renaissance*, 177.
49 For further discussion see Potts, 'Walter Pater's Unsettling', *loc. cit.*
50 Pater, *Renaissance*, 184–5.
51 Symonds, *Michelangelo*, ii, 370.
52 Ibid., ii, 374. On the larger role played by the figure of Michelangelo in Victorian culture, see L. Østermark-Johansen, *Sweetness and Strength: The Reception of Michelangelo in Late Victorian Britain* (Aldershot, 1998). This appeared after the present chapter had been submitted for publication.

7
Into Forbidden Territory: Symonds and Tiepolo

Rosella Mamoli Zorzi

How can words paint this warmth of blues,
Blended with black, white, brown, all hues?
Longhi we want, Tiepolo,
To make us moderns feel blue so:
They knew the deep Venetian night,
The values of Venetian light... [1]

One of Symonds's claims to distinction is that he was the first English critic to write with appreciation and at length on the Venetian painter Giambattista Tiepolo.

It is well known that the eighteenth century was looked upon with disdain during the greater part of the nineteenth century. It was considered a century of 'decadence':[2] a verdict that had originated while Tiepolo was still alive, in the change of taste to Neoclassicism. The Venetian artist was in fact partially eclipsed even at the court of Spain, in Madrid, where he had been regarded as one of the great artists of the century, and where he died, aged 74, in 1770. The new ascending star, Raphael Mengs (1728–79), a representative of the Neoclassical idiom, obfuscated his glory. The fact that leading Neoclassical figures such as Antonio Canova and Dominique Vivant-Denon owned some Tiepolos, and that famous eighteenth-century travellers such as Charles Nicolas Cochin (1758) and Goethe (1786) admired the artist, and that even at the beginning of the nineteenth century, and through the century, collectors bought Tiepolo drawings and paintings,[3] does not change the fact that Tiepolo was relatively neglected for decades.

In the English-speaking world, in addition to the general nineteenth-century distaste for the art of the previous century, there were further reasons for relegating Tiepolo to the background: a basic suspicion against the sensuous art of the Venetians. This had been forcefully expressed in one of Sir Joshua Reynolds's famous discourses, and it was repeated a century later in Ruskin's veto against anything that belonged to what he called the 'Grotesque Renaissance' – which included the art and architecture of the eighteenth century. These views prevented artists and writers from actually *looking* at Tiepolo until late in the nineteenth century.

This English-culture silence was broken forcefully by Symonds, in his long essay 'On an Altar Piece by Tiepolo', collected in *In the Key of Blue and Other Prose Essays*, and published in 1893,[4] the year of his death. The essay, however, was completed earlier, as it was first published in October 1891 in the *Century Guild Hobby Horse*.[5] Symonds's interest in Tiepolo, furthermore, dated back to at least ten years before that, because on 3 November 1883 he had written to Horatio Forbes Brown, from Davos, enquiring whether his Anglo-Venetian friend and future biographer[6] knew the fresco of 'Henry III's entrance into Venice at the Pisani Villa':

> Do you know it? I should very much like a photo of it, if there is one. What a fool one is about Italy – always finding some treasure that has escaped notice in a score of visits to a place! This fresco would have interested me deeply and have made a pleasant object for an excursion.[7]

Symonds had found mention of these particular frescoes in the *Souvenirs littéraires* of Maxime du Camp. Du Camp, a friend of Flaubert, had written, referring to his Venetian visit of the 1850s:

> Je m'intéressais aux Tiepolo; j'avais contemplé tous ceux que garde la ville, depuis le 'Portement de la Croix', qui est à S. Alvise, jusqu'à l' 'Antoine' et à la 'Cléopatre' du palais Labia; j'allai sur la Brenta afin de voir la grande fresque représentant l'entrée de Henry III à Venise, qu'il a peinte à la villa Pisani et que l'on a trop retouchée.* [8]

It is quite obvious that the other paintings mentioned by Maxime du Camp were also well known to Symonds. These included *The Ascent to the Calvary*, *The Flagellation*, and *The Crowning with Thorns*, in the church of S. Alvise – incidentally the only paintings by Tiepolo which

---

*I was interested in the Tiepolos; I had studied all those kept in the city, from 'The Carrying of the Cross', which is in S. Alvise, to the 'Antony' and the 'Cleopatra' of the Palazzo Labia; I went to the Brenta in order to see the great fresco depicting the entry of Henry III into Venice, which he painted in the Villa Pisani, and which has been over-restored.

Ruskin ever mentioned (in *St. Mark's Rest*, 1884) – and the *Antony and Cleopatra* cycle in the Palazzo Labia, at that time a 'much dilapidated' palace, which guidebooks had started to mention only in the late 1870s. Murray's *Handbook for Travellers in Northern Italy* for 1860, for instance, did not have one word for the Palazzo Labia frescoes, nor did it have one word on the huge ceiling of the Scalzi church, though it did mention the Tiepolos in the Villa Valmarana ai Nani in Vicenza. The *Baedeker* guidebook for 1879, *A Handbook for Travellers: Northern Italy*, mentioned the Labia frescoes, and so did the 1885 Mueller guidebook, *Venice, Her Art Treasures and Historical Associations*. There was however no mention of the Scalzi ceiling, which was noticed for the first time only in the 1899 *Baedeker*.

The *Henry III* frescoes were destined to a strange fate in the course of very few years. In 1893 Mme Nélie André, a well-known portrait painter, by then the wife of Monsieur Henri André, a very wealthy banker, was offered, and bought, the Tiepolos Symonds had been enquiring about.[9] The subject, linked to French history, seemed ideal for such buyers: the Villa Contarini cycle of frescoes represented the arrival of Henry III, King of France, at the villa, on his way back from Poland, in 1574. The king is represented on the steps of the villa, with the Brenta and the boats in the background, and with Procuratore Contarini (the owner of the mansion) welcoming him before the entrance. In the original disposition of the frescoes, the ceiling had been painted with a balustrade all around it, so that the painted guests seemed to be looking down to admire the royal visit.[10] Because of the 'French' subject, Henry de Chennevières, writing in the *Gazette des Beaux Arts* in 1896, praised the Andrés as benefactors of France; but he also fully realized the artistic importance of the purchase, since he was one of the first critics to launch again the cult of Tiepolo:

> Jamais peut-être dans son oeuvre pourtant surabondante de gaietés d'âme et de brosse, Tiepolo ne donne davantage la sensation de la peinture heureuse de peindre et devenue le besoin d'un esprit et d'un oeil obsédés de la ligne et du ton, comme le musicien l'est de sa libre chanson. La qualité du coloris participe de la joie, plus spéciale encore, de cette composition.*[11]

*Perhaps nowhere else in his work, overflowing though it is with lightness of heart and of brushstroke, does Tiepolo convey such an impression of painting delighting in painting, of painting become the need of a soul and an eye obsessed with line and colour, as a musician is obsessed with his free-flowing song. The quality of colouring partakes of the even more special joy of this composition.

Although in 1883 Symonds seems to know and appreciate Tiepolo, in 'The Gondolier's Wedding' (1882)[12] the narrator (a persona of Symonds) does not enjoy the early-morning ceremony of the wedding and wonders if this has to do with the 'ugliness of a very ill-designed barocco building'.[13] Ruskin's[14] anathema seems still to be at work here, since the building is the Church of the Gesuati on the Zattere and the narrator does not have a word for the Tiepolo ceiling and painting inside.

Ignoring the huge Tiepolo ceilings of the Gesuati and the Scalzi, and even those of Ca' Rezzonico, not to mention the Udine frescoes, was, then, the rule. A number of English-language artists described at length the interiors of those churches, and the 'surfeit of marbles' in the Scalzi, but they never seemed to raise their eyes to the *Transportation of the Holy House of Loreto*, with its swirling house carried by the Angels. This was the case, for example, with two American painters, Samuel B. Morse (1831) and James De Veaux (1843).

After Ruskin's veto on the 'Grotesque Renaissance' no-one, not even Henry James, seemed really to *look* at Tiepolo. In 1872 James wrote about Tiepolo for the first time, reviewing an exhibition in New York. He noticed a lack of sincerity in 'this florid master of breezy drapery and fastidious pose'. More than 30 years later he remembered having written *A London Life* in the Palazzo Barbaro, in a 'room with a pompous Tiepolo ceiling': a *pompous* ceiling – hardly an appreciative adjective. (It does not matter that the ceiling was not, in fact, a Tiepolo. The Tiepolo ceiling, *The Glory of the Barbaro Family*, had been sold before the Curtises rented and bought the palace where James was several times a guest; but James was unaware of this.) In spite of his change of taste regarding the eighteenth century, James never really liked Tiepolo: there is a 'Tiepolo ceiling' in one short story, 'Collaboration' (1892), but it is not really relevant.[15] The reference to the 'pompous' ceiling was made as late as 1908, that is years after the celebrations of the bicentenary of 1896 – when Tiepolo's fame was rising again – and many years after James's own reaction against some of Ruskin's diktats.

Without doubt in the English-speaking world there lingered a strong influence of Sir Joshua Reynolds's general strictures on Venetian art. Reynolds in fact loved this art, but he felt obliged to criticize it in his public lectures. Referring mainly to Veronese, he had written in Discourse IV:

Young minds are indeed too apt to be captivated by this splendour of style; and that of the Venetians is particularly pleasing; for by them, all those parts of the Art that gave pleasure to the eye or sense, have been cultivated with care, and carried to the degree nearest to perfection...

The Venetians, however, according to Sir Joshua, had 'uninteresting subjects', 'capricious composition', 'violent and affected contrasts', and 'total inattention to expression'; and

> even in colouring, if we compare the quietness and chastity of the Bolognese pencil to the bustle and tumult that fills every part of a Venetian picture, without the least attempt to interest the passions, their boasted art will appear a mere struggle without effect; *a tale told by an ideot [sic], full of sound and fury, signifying nothing.*[16]

Reynolds, it is true, was criticizing Venetian mannerism of the Cinquecento – not his contemporary Tiepolo; but the undercurrent of suspicion for the 'bustle and tumult', and the allusion to Bolognese 'chastity', betray persistent misgiving about an art that 'gave pleasure to the eye [and] the senses', an art that somehow seemed too sensual and morally loose for the English climate. It is precisely the sensuous beauty of his work which seems to have been an obstacle to the appreciation of the Venetian painter even in the later part of the nineteenth century, and especially for such writers as Henry James, who adored Tintoretto, loved Veronese and Titian, but could not bring himself to appreciate the hovering and half-naked goddesses of Tiepolo.

If one reads Symonds on the Renaissance, one can see quite clearly why he could appreciate Tiepolo, and write on him. In the Renaissance, 'art...became the exponent of the majesty and splendour of the human body',[17] the flesh was no longer 'entombed in "hair shirts and cerements"', as John Pemble has observed.[18] What seems in fact rather surprising is that no other celebrator of Renaissance 'paganism' should be led to admire Tiepolo.

Symonds described the great art of Renaissance Venice as an art linked to power and to the exhibition of the greatness of the Republic in mythopoetic terms. He also wrote: 'To trace the history of Venetian painting is to follow through its several stages the growth of that mastery over colour and *sensuous beauty* which was perfected in the works of Titian and his contemporaries'[19] (my italics). Discussing the art produced after the Renaissance, and even modern art, in the first chapter of the third volume of *Renaissance in Italy*, Symonds argued:

> ...painting has lost its hold upon the centre of our intellectual activity. It can no longer give form to the ideas that rule the modern world. These ideas are too abstract, too much a matter of the understanding, to be successfully handled by the figurative arts; and it

cannot be too often or too emphatically stated that these arts produce nothing really great and universal in relation to the spirit of their century, except by a process analogous to the mythopoetic. With conceptions incapable of being *sensuously apprehended*, with ideas that lose their value when they are incarnated, they have no power to deal. As meteors become luminous by traversing the grosser element of our terrestrial atmosphere, so the thoughts that art employs must needs immerse themselves in *sensuousness* . . . [my italics].

Our deepest thoughts about the world and God are incapable of personification by any aesthetic process; they never enter that atmosphere wherein alone they could become through fine art luminous. For the painter, who is the form-giver, they have ceased to be shining stars, and are seen as opaque stones; and though divinity be in them, it is a deity that refuses the investiture of form.

As Phyllis Grosskurth has noted, Symonds found in Venetian painting 'vivid, pulsating life'.[20] The Venetians were not 'angelic as the fancy-fostered Florentines, not merely human like the sober Flemish, not abstractedly intellectual like Duerer'.[21]

It is no wonder that Symonds, pursuing these lines of thought, could appreciate Tiepolo, with his 'glowing colours . . . the imitation of fruits, rich stuffs, architectural canopies, jewels, and landscape backgrounds' – words, these, that do not refer to Tiepolo, but to the great Renaissance Venetian painting,[22] yet which could be applied, without changing a comma, to the Settecento artist. One could say that this view of what painting was, or should be, was what led Symonds to interrupt the long English silence on Tiepolo, allowing him to *look* at Tiepolo's paintings and to write about them, in spite of his somewhat limited appreciation of the baroque. In Venice, of course, admiration for Tiepolo had never really died out, as is shown by Antonio Berti's *Elogio di Gio: Batta Tiepolo* of 1856 and Urbani de Gheltoff's work of 1879. So local information might have helped.

In his essay on Tiepolo Symonds dealt first with the Settecento, represented for him by four painters, Tiepolo, Canaletto, Guardi, and Longhi. Symonds's re-evaluation of these painters, and partially, but only partially, of the eighteenth century, was part of a general tendency, marked by Gosse's studies of the Settecento (Symonds wrote to Gosse in 1889: 'Your book has been my companion'),[23] and by Cornelius Gurlitt's *Geschichte des Barock Stiles in Italien* (1887), which actually rhapsodized on the Scalzi Tiepolo ceiling. Symonds also admired Vernon Lee's *Studies of the Eighteenth Century in Italy* (1880) in spite of his dislike for the author.[24] These were just a few of the important works which indicated that the century generally considered a century of decadence was returning to favour. This recuperation of the eighteenth century seems to have been easier for French and for German culture than for English: Burckhardt, the first edition of whose *Cicerone* is dated 1855 (but the book was written in 1853–4), admitted of some eighteenth-century talented painters 'that they fortified themselves by following the example of Paolo [Veronese], creating a few works of notable importance. This is true of Lazzarini, Angeli, Fiumani, and also of Tiepolo'.[25] Symonds had read Burckhardt, and his own translation of Gozzi's *Useless Memoirs* (1890) may also be a sign of this interest, although Symonds was not enthusiastic about the book. The French writers and painters who praised Tiepolo, from Delacroix to Taine, the de Goncourts, and then de Chennevières, could also have stimulated his appreciation.

Among the 'four eminent painters' mentioned by Burckhardt, Symonds focused on Tiepolo: 'Of these Tiepolo was by far the greatest, in natural endowment, in splendour of performance, in fecundity of production.'[26] Then, as one might expect, he went on to discuss Tiepolo as an incarnation of Veronese:

> Believers in metempsychosis might have sworn, seeing his [Tiepolo's] grand style bud and bloom in that degenerate age, that Paolo Veronese lived again in Tiepolo's body. He has the same sincerity of conception, the same firmness of execution, the same largeness, breadth, serenity and sanity, that we admire in the early master.

Symonds comments on the 'sincerity of conception' in Tiepolo – a comment that is exactly the opposite to the lack of sincerity observed by James, who had, however, also compared Tiepolo to Veronese, in less enthusiastic terms. (James had written: Tiepolo 'offers a desperately faint but not unmusical echo from the azure-hearted ceilings of Paul Veronese').[27] Symonds's admiration for the Antony and Cleopatra cycle is without bounds: 'largeness, breadth, serenity and sanity' are seen in the

> frescoes of Palazzo Labia, where the loves of Antony and Cleopatra fill immense spaces with mundane pomp and insolent animalism. How grandly the great scenes are planned; how large and luminous the sky-regions, where masts bristle and pennants flutter to the breeze of Cydnus; how noble the orders of architecture, enclosing groups of men and women, horses, dwarfs, dogs, all in stately movement or superb repose!

There is a sort of wonder that the greatness and power of these frescoes should belong to the century of 'castrati and cicisbei, of wanton Casanova and neurotic Rousseaus and effeminate abbés'. With the Palazzo Labia frescoes we have a 'master of the heroic age', painting in a century still perceived as a century of decadence. Symonds then proceeds to evaluate Tiepolo *per se* rather than for his 'affinity to Veronese'. There is still some reserve in his description of the 'vast decorative schemes for ceilings . . . with flying Angels, allegorical figures upon clouds and cornices, in all possible attitudes of violent movement and perilous foreshortening', which he described as 'works in the barocco taste of the Italian decadence, upon which the noble artist spent too much of his energy and time'. These great frescoes, 'soulless compositions', are in fact contrasted with the Labia cycle. But Symonds then goes on to evaluate the real quality of Tiepolo's painting:

> The specific strength of Tiepolo as an artist lay, I take it, in a peculiar and just perception of certain atmospheric and colour qualities in his Venetian birthplace; the employment of which for the realisation of very original and bold conceptions placed him in advance not only of Veronese, but also of all his contemporaries. Tiepolo, in spite of his *barocco* decorative schemes, his frigid allegories and conventional 'machines', was a *plein air* master in a sense of this term which is wholly inapplicable to men like Guardi, Canaletto, Longhi . . .
>
> His originality consisted in the fact that he seems to have been aware of the imminence of a radical change in art principles, and in the effort to bring *plein air* into the studio, where hitherto a conventional scheme of light and colour held undisputed sway. His key of colour, wonderfully clear and luminous, is settled by the harmonies between weather-mellowed marble, light blue sky, russet or ochre-tinted sails, vivid vegetable greens, sunburnt faces, and patches of bright blue in the costume of sailors and the common people, all subdued and softened by the pearly haze 'of moisture bred' which bathes the Venetian landscape in the warmth of a Venetian summer.[28]

Tiepolo's visual art seems to be based on the same principles as Symonds's own verbal description: one thinks of Symonds's description of Venice in 'A Venetian Medley', where the first impression of the city is described as follows:

> Venice inspires at first an almost Corybantic rapture. From our earliest visits, if these have been measured by days rather than by weeks,

we carry away with us the memory of sunsets emblazoned in gold and crimson upon cloud and water; of violet domes and bell-towers etched against the orange of a western sky; of moonlight silvering breeze-rippled breadths of liquid blue; of distant islands shimmering in sunlitten haze; of music and black gliding boats . . . [29]

Symonds loves Tiepolo because the painter feels and reproduces 'the living rapport which exists in nature between colour, light and atmosphere', because he 'has detached and fixed for us a fragment of the whole wide scene around him and ourselves'.[30] (This last sentence echoes strangely James's much more tragic comment on a much more tragic painter, Tintoretto: 'He habitually conceived his subject as an actual scene . . . not as a mere subject and fiction – but as a great fragment wrenched out of life and history, with all its natural details clinging to it and testifying to its reality.')[31] This focusing on this rapport has interested art-critics, especially Francis Haskell and J. R. Hale,[32] for its modernity. Symonds declares he could use *Christ's Ascent to Calvary* to show how Tiepolo 'breaks the tradition . . . of a conventional chiaroscuro and a conventional system of decorative tinting';[33] but he does not, and it is no coincidence that he should discard the one painting described by Ruskin in terms of its chiaroscuro. According to Ruskin, this was one of 'two notable pieces of plausible modern sentiment . . . Tiepolo is virtually the beginner of Modernism: these two pictures of his are exactly like what a first-rate Parisian Academy student would do . . . Look thoroughly at them and at their dramatic chiaroscuro for a little time, observing that no face is without some expression of crime or pain, and that everything is always put dark against light, or light against dark.'[34]

The painting Symonds chose to illustrate his viewpoint is a fairly small canvas, which was temporarily exhibited at the Accademia (see Plate 8):

It is a tall and narrow canvas, divided, after old Venetian custom, into two almost equal sections; the upper portion being occupied with sky and architecture, the lower with a group of figures in which the subject-interest of the composition concentrates. On the marble pavement of the palace, in the open air, kneels a female saint supported by praying women, and backed by mundane figures – a hard-featured old man, a dainty page, and so forth. The saint, whose head and flowing fair hair is surrounded with an opalescent aureole, like greenish water of the lagoon flashed through with silvery sunbeams, kneels in an attitude of physical prostration. She is clearly dying . . . [35]

Observation on masses and colour culminates in the description of the *plein air* effect

> gained by the most subtle and adroit interworking of tint with tint; not any one of the dominant hues (except in the very highest lights) being allowed to assert its own unmodified quality. The hair of the bending priest, for instance, looks black at a certain distance. Yet it is almost entirely painted in strokes of blue upon a dark ground.[36]

The 'richly-glowing but subdued ochre, like gold dulled and smouldering', the white of the saint's robe, 'all the shades and semitones of which have been worked with greens and yellows and faint suggestions of greyish blues', tend to form 'a chromatic scheme' akin to the *plein air* effect.

The rest of the description of the painting underlines the extreme suffering of the saint, and aims at formulating a theory of art where the subject (a 'distressing motive') 'counts for little'. When a subject is treated as Tiepolo treats it,

> we can quit the subject and ascend into regions of pure art... The final meaning of Tiepolo's work lies in its interpretation of a world delightful to our senses by lines and hues, naturally derived from the great source of universal beauty: form, and stuff, and substance, flooded by the light of day; things closest to our senses, yet capable of subtlest transformation at the poet-artist's bidding.[37]

The artist achieves poetry through 'the revel of his light and colour sense'. This *pala* is a masterpiece of art, somehow cancelling the (distressing) subject, and as such it becomes the exemplum of art for art's sake, of pure beauty and sensuous enjoyment. Symonds describes in detail his surmisings in seeing it, before theorizing on the result.

Tiepolo has 'skirted the very border of the abyss of physical torment' in depicting St Lucy. Before appreciating exactly the quality of art that renders its subject irrelevant, Symonds has long passages on the actual suffering, indulging in the very descriptions that the painting cancels:

> ...the saint is a woman of exquisite and natural beauty, a lily of whiteness, a princess of dignity and grace. The ashen pallor of her face shows that she has suffered some sudden and terrible shock to her vital system; and on her exquisite throat there is just one little stain of crimson, indicating blood. The heavy bluish lids droop

downward to her ivory cheeks; and as we gaze intently, we seem to feel that they cover no eyes but only empty orbits. This impression is so vaguely, yet so tenderly communicated, that at first I rebuked my fancy for having trespassed on some region of unimaginable horror, which existed not in the manly painter's eye, but in my own too curious imagination. Then I perceived upon a step below the marble platform where the saint is kneeling, a silver plate with two eyes placed upon it, by the side of a bloody stiletto. It seemed that the pity and terror I had taken from those drooping eyelids were not fanciful . . .[38]

It is at this point, after observing the eyes and the bloody stiletto, that Symonds indulges in listing what Tiepolo manages to avoid: the horror of

jocund women carrying their eyes or bleeding breasts on plates; [the reference is to St Agatha, whose breasts were cut off] . . . the butcherly abominations of Italian or Flemish or French naturalists – Caravaggio's flayings, Rubens's flakes of spear-divided flesh with blood and water gushing from a gaping wound, Poussin's bowels wound like ropes on capstans by brawny varlets.

Art cancels the 'abyss of physical torment'; but the horror of physical torment is carefully evoked, in the details of the 'flakes of spear-divided flesh', the gaping wound, the 'bowels wound like ropes'. Symonds indulges in algolagnia, and the discourse is strung between the trappings of the Decadents and a purely formalist aesthetics. Of course one is also tempted to view this tension as that of the ideal of art against the abyss of life, rendered in the Victorian discourse – though with as much literary gloss as possible – of Symonds's 'unpublished' autobiography.[39]

Symonds lists the horrors that other non-Catholic viewers observed with revulsion: Mrs Jameson, in the mid-nineteenth century better known than Ruskin as an art critic, discussed at length the 'atrocious subject' of martyrdoms, where 'in spite of all possible discretion on the part of the painter, and every attempt to soften the circumstances' martyrdoms 'remain in the highest degree horrible and revolting. [St Agatha] is usually bound to a pillar . . . undraped to the waist, and on each side a slave or executioner with a pair of shears'.[40] With Symonds, the reaction to gory martyrdom is distinctly different. Before theorizing the purifying effect of art in Tiepolo's rendering of St Lucy's martyred body, he dwells on examples of tortured bodies, presenting verbally, insistently, what art finally hides: revelling, one could say, in this listing, not simply registering the horror, as Mrs Jameson did. A propos of Tiepolo, one writer only, a Frenchman, was to move a further step forward in the interpretation of this joyful Settecento artist as a Decadent. Maurice Barrès read his own melancholy and feverish attitude in Tiepolo's paintings: 'Ciel, drapeaux, marbres, livres, adolescents, tout ce que peint Tiepolo est eraillé, fripé, devoré par sa fièvre et par un torrent de lumière, ainsi que sont mes images intérieures que je m'énerve à éclairer dans mes longues solitudes.'*[41]

Tiepolo has been wonderfully 'read' by Symonds, a critic who finally looked at his paintings and wrote on them. In 1890 no English writer was looking at his art so carefully and so closely; the return of fame did not come until the bicentenary celebrations of 1896, with the work of Chennevières, Molmenti, Centelli, Zanetti, Meyer, Blanc, and de Gheltoff. Yet even today Tiepolo is often seen as fickle and sensuous. Remnants of the Victorian attitude to the glorious and joyous Settecento can be detected in such unsuspecting writers as Mary McCarthy, who comments with irony on 'the charming unruffled fashion of the northern Italian saints; St Lucy carrying her eyes, like a *plat du jour*, and St Agatha, her breasts, in a clean white saucer',[42] but refers to the 'theatrical warehouse patronized by Tiepolo for his floats in the sky'.

The case of Symonds and Tiepolo seems to suggest that the sensibility and sensuousness of a life lived outside the conventional norms of Victorian behaviour, especially sexual, are essential in 'allowing' the eye to roam on paintings of sensuous beauty without being blindfolded by handed-down prohibition norms. Unconventional sensibility and behaviour in life seem to go together with an ability to read 'forbidden' pictorial texts. One wonders what the historiography of art, from Winckelmann to Symonds, might have been without the special homoerotic sensibility of these men, whose idealization of Greek culture opened up new vistas on new ages. As for Tiepolo, it was a woman, liberated intellectually and sexually, and able to enjoy the taste for life and freedom of the Settecento, who was to bring the phantasmagoria and visual riches of his frescoes into the novel. Edith Wharton proceeded triumphantly on the way that John Addington Symonds had opened.

*Sky, banners, marbles, books, youths: everything that Tiepolo paints is frayed, crumpled, devoured by his fever and by a torrent of light – just like my own inner imaginings, which, wearing myself out, I strive to elucidate in my long solitudes.

Notes

1   J. A. Symonds, *In the Key of Blue and Other Prose Essays* (1893), 16. One wonders about the possible relation between Symonds's 'symphonies' and those
of Whistler. In a letter of 1882 Symonds called the 'sad sumptuous days' of
the Venetian autumn 'a divine Whistlerian Symphony'. See *The Letters of
John Addington Symonds*, ed. Herbert Schueller and Robert Peters (Detroit,
1967–9), iii, 768–9.

2   Book VI of the second volume of *The Handbook of Painting*, based on Kugler
and rewritten by Waagen and then by J. A. Crowe (1874), is called, significantly, 'The Decline of Art, 1700–1810'.

3   The Cheney Collection was made between 1842 and 1852. See George
Knox, 'Description and Provenance of the Cheney Album', in *Catalogue of
the Tiepolo Drawings in the Victoria and Albert Museum* (1975), 3–9.

4   On Symonds's essay, see Francis Haskell, 'Tiepolo e gli artisti del secolo XIX',
in Vittore Branca (ed.), *Sensibilità e razionalità nel Settecento* (Florence, 1967),
ii, 495–7; and John Hale, *England and the Italian Renaissance* (1954), ch. 8.

5   Percy L. Babington, *Bibliography of the Writings of John Addington Symonds*
(1925), 191. See also J. A. Symonds, *The Letters and Papers of John Addington
Symonds*, ed. Horatio Forbes Brown (1923), 250.

6   On the friendship between Brown and Symonds, and the burning of Symonds's
papers after Brown's death, see John Pemble, *Venice Rediscovered* (Oxford,
1995), 54–6, 67. See also Phyllis Grosskurth, *John Addington Symonds: A Biography* (1964), and J. A. Symonds, *The Memoirs of John Addington Symonds*, ed.
Phyllis Grosskurth (1984), Preface.

7   Symonds, *Letters and Papers*, 161; *Letters*, ii, 858.

8   Maxime du Camp, *Souvenirs littéraires* (Paris, 1892), ii, 160.

9   On the Jacquemart-André purchase, see Henri de Chennevières, 'Les Tiepolo
de l'Hotel Edouard André', *Gazette des Beaux Arts*, xv (January 1896), 126.

10 The frescoes were installed in the new boulevard Hausmann residence of the
Andrés, where they are still. Bernard Berenson discussed Tiepolo in his *Italian Painters of the Renaissance* (1896). The section on Tiepolo was written in
1894 – see new edn (1952), i, 35. See also *The Letters of Bernard Berenson and
Isabella Stewart Gardner*, ed. Rollin Van H. Hadley (Boston, 1987), 142.

11 De Chennevières, 'Les Tiepolo', *loc. cit.*

12 *Cornhill Magazine*, xlv, 265, (January 1882), 80–93. Reprinted in *Italian
Byways* (1883).

13 Ibid.

14 Symonds read Ruskin, and visited Italy as a young man following Ruskin's
indications. But, like most young men of his generation, he gradually with-
drew from his initial devotion. See *Letters*, iii, 39–40, 310.

15 Rosella Mamoli Zorzi, 'Tiepolo, Henry James, and Edith Wharton', *The Metro-
politan Museum Journal*, xxxiii (1998), 211–29.

16 Sir Joshua Reynolds, *Discourses on Art*, ed. R. R. Wark (New Haven and
London, 1959), 64.

17 J. A. Symonds, *Renaissance in Italy, I: The Age of the Despots* (New York, 1888), 19.

18 John Pemble, *The Mediterranean Passion* (Oxford, 1988), 199.

19 J. A. Symonds, *Renaissance in Italy, III: The Fine Arts* (1877), 38–9, 361.

20 Grosskurth, *John Addington Symonds*, 60.

21 Ibid.
22 Symonds, *Fine Arts*, 361.
23 Grosskurth, *John Addington Symonds*, 313.
24 Ibid., 224.
25 Jakob Burckhardt, *Il Cicerone*, new edn (Florence, 1952), 1079.
26 Symonds, *Key of Blue*, 43.
27 Henry James, 'The 1871 Purchase', in John Sweeney (ed.), *The Painter's Eye: Notes and Essays on the Pictorial Arts* (1956), 58.
28 Symonds, *Key of Blue*, 45–6.
29 J. A. Symonds, *New Italian Sketches* (Leipzig, 1884), 169.
30 Symonds, *Key of Blue*, 47.
31 Henry James, *The Letters of Henry James*, ed. Leon Edel (Cambridge, MA, 1974–84), i, 140.
32 Haskell, 'Tiepolo e gli artisti', *loc. cit.*; Hale, *England and the Italian Renaissance*, ch. 8.
33 Symonds, *Key of Blue*, 47.
34 John Ruskin, *St Mark's Rest: The History of Venice* (Sunnyside, Kent, 1887), 30.
35 Ibid., 48.
36 Ibid., 49.
37 Ibid., 52.
38 Symonds, *Key of Blue*, 50.
39 Symonds, *Memoirs*.
40 Anna Jameson, *Sacred and Legendary Art* (1848), 612.
41 Maurice Barrès, *Un homme libre* (Paris, 1912), 199.
42 Mary McCarthy, *Venice Observed* (New York, 1956), 73, 112.

8
Versions of Antinous: Symonds between Shelley and Yourcenar

Stephen Bann

Symonds belongs with a pair of imaginary siblings, both of whom were born shortly before him and survived him by a brief time: Walter Pater, born one year before and dying just one year later, and (perhaps a less obvious choice) Samuel Butler, the oldest of the trio and also the most long-lived, having been born in 1835 and surviving till 1902. I would not wish to imply any degree of special personal contact between these uneasy Victorian men of letters whose especially diverse interests and writing practices resulted in their being resolutely excluded from the 'Great Tradition' when it was put together in the second quarter of the twentieth century, and who have had to wait until our own times for a more catholic appreciation. Butler, no doubt, is the extreme case: he has the most tyrannical father, but makes the most successful bid for freedom when he emigrates for a few years to New Zealand and returns with a fortune; he is also the most blatantly unorthodox of the three in his cultural preferences, singling out for intensive study the Lombard painter Gaudenzio Ferrari, whom Symonds conventionally dismissed as a mere eclectic, and making a significant contribution to the new visual art of photography.[1] Pater has neither father nor fortune to blight or facilitate his adult life. His taste for the unorthodox stops short, perhaps, at something as nuanced as the defence of Botticelli as a 'secondary painter', and he would never have attempted so substantial a piece of revisionism as Symonds's *Life of Michelangelo*. But his success at channelling his literary gifts into the forms most suited to them – the 'imaginary portrait', the essay in aesthetic criticism, and the discursive, essayistic novel – results in a consistency of achievement which neither Butler nor Symonds can match.[2]

Symonds has both father and fortune, the latter by the good grace of the former. His writing never approaches the wonderful idiosyncrasy of

Butler, who was willing to argue at length and with uncanny persuas-
iveness that Nausicaa was in fact the true author of the *Odyssey*; nor
does it have the ostentatious marks of style that characterize the essays
of Pater. Symonds, indeed, appears to have held Pater's writing in an
aversion almost physical in its intensity, comparing its effect on him
with that of the odour of a civet cat.[3] What Symonds does share, however,
with both Butler and Pater is a pervasive homoerotic disposition that
colours his work as a writer, just as it complicated his everyday life. Yet,
from a superficial point of view, we might say that the differences
within the similarity are again striking. Butler is the most cheerfully
self-mocking of the three. Already in correspondence sent home to his
aunt while making his fortune in New Zealand, he confesses (if that is
the word): 'If I had three or four thousand a year I should much like to
buy a young conscientious artist with a dash of pre-Raphaelitism in him,
and keep him for my edification and instruction.'[4] Though Butler's
biography does present one instance of his being fleeced by an unscru-
pulous person answering to this description, it may be suggested that
he was, at any rate, able to settle for capturing the desired image in his
chosen medium of photography. (I am thinking of the fine portrait,
dated 1870, of 'Johnston Forbes-Robertson in armour'.)[5] By contrast,
Pater steers a skilful, and prudent, path in the contemporary artistic
milieu, not hesitating to lend tacit support when necessary to such
egregious figures as the artist Simeon Solomon, but tempering his attitudes so that they remain compatible with his position as fellow of an
Oxford college. His passionate friendships, such as that with Charles
Shadwell, the dedicatee of *The Renaissance* and subsequently his literary
executor,[6] mature in the homosocial atmosphere of academic life. Only
one illustration occurs in the whole of his published work: the drawing,
attributed to Leonardo, of 'a face of doubtful sex' which is placed as a
frontispiece to *The Renaissance*.

I would not wish to pursue much further this generalized comparison
between Symonds, Butler, and Pater, but simply to single out the
elements in play that will be of significance in the further discussion. It
would be possible to use the data that have already been assembled, and
to develop them further, in reaching an entirely predictable conclusion
about the degree to which Symonds contrived to distance himself from
the other two members of the cohort, in respect of his declared sexuality.
Butler successfully took charge of his own life and, in writing *The Way
of All Flesh*, effectively imposed his authorized commentary. Pater gave as
part of his legacy to Shadwell the duty of warding off any intrusive investigations into his private life, and the connivance of his redoubtable

sisters ensured that the only extensive biography published within a generation was the almost comically unbalanced effusion of Thomas Wright.[7] Symonds had his own Shadwell, of course, in the person of Horatio Brown, who contrived in his authorized biography to deflect the issues concerning Symonds's troubled sexuality on to the more acceptable ground of the Victorian crisis in religious belief. But Brown's biography can be seen now as merely a holding operation. As Phyllis Grosskurth has testified, it certainly provided an incentive to Symonds's more recent biographer to return to the original autobiography and fill in the gaps which had come to seem all too glaring in the disciple's complicit account. Now that such a wealth of autobiographical material has been assembled, including the extensive personal testimony of the letters and indeed the very detailing of sexual fantasies that was supplied under seal of anonymity to Havelock Ellis, it is hard not to see him as infinitely closer to our period than either Butler or Pater. The writer who was so circumspect as to circulate privately his essay, *A Problem in Greek Ethics*, when it first appeared in 1883, and subtitle it 'an Enquiry into the phenomenon of sexual inversion addressed especially to medical psychologists and jurists', has gained a wider audience amongst all those who are attentive to the construction of what Michel Foucault called a 'scientia sexualis'.

Yet there is a danger that the proleptic Symonds – the Symonds who so courageously anticipates the currency of what we can afford to take as a matter of course – may crowd out the historical Symonds: the Symonds whose life proceeded parallel to those of Butler and Pater. While there can be no doubt that he deserves substantial credit for the demythologizing tendency of his work, at least in his last years, it must also be said that this was sustained, on occasions, at the expense of the subtle and fastidious spirit that had informed his earlier writings. For example, nothing could be more proleptic of Symonds's later reputation than his article 'The New Spirit', first published in March 1893, a month before his death, in which he proclaims: 'St Sebastian might have been a Christian martyr, and Antinous the deified mignon of a pagan emperor; but art only saw their common qualities of beauty, convenient opportunities for depicting naked young men in the prime of life.'[8] It comes as a surprise, surely, that Symonds should be content with so banal and functional a definition of what 'art' sees, particularly when he has devoted the opening passage of an essay published only 14 years before to a careful and learned discrimination between the representations of St Sebastian and Antinous in Western visual culture. The aim of this article will be to open up the issues implicit in the 'Antinous' essay of 1879, and indeed those to be found in Symonds's other allusions to the 'deified mignon', rather than to mimic the radical shorthand of 'The New Spirit', whose tone is only too close to some regrettable examples of contemporary art-historical discourse. In line with this objective, the context provided by Butler and Pater is important. It will be impossible to avoid the conclusion that Symonds's exploratory range of literary forms – from the poetic through the essayistic to the designedly scientific – offers far less precise a focus than the perfumed prose of Pater. Equally, it will be interesting to note, in the consideration of the particular image which Symonds chooses to relate to the 'Antinous' essay, the different relation to visual culture implied by Pater's reproduction of the red-chalk drawing attributed to Leonardo – and indeed by the photographic image of Butler's 'Johnston Forbes-Robertson in armour'. Such a reference to the different technologies of visual art in the nineteenth century is no mere connoisseur's detail, but an indication of the wider cultural context within which all three writers, and their respective differences and connections, may be adequately assessed. In the end, as will be seen, my aim will be to reinforce my first trio – Butler, Pater, Symonds – with a second trio spanning a range from Romanticism to the present day. If the link in the first instance is provided by the contemporaneity of the three writers, in the second it comes from the transformations over a century and a half of the image and meaning of Antinous.

Why should a leading French woman novelist, writing in the aftermath of the Second World War and herself in a stable, same-sex relationship, take particular note of Symonds's writing? Why should she single out for special attention a phrase which Symonds himself quotes from Shelley (the English poet to whom he devotes a critical study, not to mention the opening essay of one of his travel books)? The answer is, in the first place, that what is transmitted from one author to the other – from Shelley, through Symonds, to Marguerite Yourcenar – is a certain image of Antinous, the oriental favourite of the Emperor Hadrian whose fictional *Memoirs* Yourcenar published to considerable acclaim in 1951. To this tripartite sequence, which spans a century and a half and the passage from Romanticism into modernism, there must, however, be added for the purposes of this analysis a further tripartite sequence within the work of Symonds himself. In brief, he offers in his historical reflections on the enigma of Antinous first of all a poem, published in 1878 in *Many Moods* though it was probably written more than ten years earlier;[9] secondly, an essay, which appeared in *Italian Sketches* in 1879; and finally, a footnote, this being all that can be found of Antinous (though

for good reason, as I shall argue) in *A Problem in Greek Ethics* (1883).
Symonds, as will be seen, makes Antinous the focus of these very different
styles of enquiry, just as Shelley and Yourcenar display very different
types of investment in his elusive image.

I emphasize the point that it is above all with an image that all of these
writers are preoccupied, in order to make the necessary reservation that
Antinous is virtually absent from the Western literary tradition. There
is not a single reference to him in the poetic works of Milton, Blake,
Coleridge, Wordsworth, Keats, or Shelley (the single appearance for which
he is indebted to the latter being in a fragmentary piece of prose). Browning
is one poet contemporary with Symonds in whose poetry the name
Antinous makes an appearance, but this is in the rather puzzling guise
of one of Penelope's suitors.[10]

By contrast, the visual tradition emerging from the Renaissance, and
refreshed by the Neoclassicism of the eighteenth and early nineteenth
centuries, had enshrined the figure of Antinous as one of the pre-eminent
types of male beauty. As early as the mid-fifteenth century the Floren-
tine artist Benozzo Gozzoli draws in his sketchbook the sculpture of
Antinous now in the Museo Nazionale at Naples, which also serves as
a model shortly afterwards for the bronze statue of Jonah in the Chigi
chapel of S. Maria del Popolo at Rome, placed there under Raphael's
direction.[11] It is, however, the discovery at Rome in 1543 of what was
taken to be a full-size portrayal of Antinous (now usually regarded as a
Mercury or Hermes) that launched a period of more than two centuries
during which this statue, the so-called Belvedere Antinous, was taken as
the privileged representation of the second-century suicide to whom his
lover, the Emperor Hadrian, had devoted a posthumous cult. One index
of its popularity is the figure of the dying Hyacinthus in Domenichino's
fresco of *Apollo and Hyacinthus*: according to the testimony of Richard
Jackson, at any rate, it was an engraving after this early seventeenth-
century work that suggested to Pater the theme of his late essay, 'Apollo
in Picardy'.[12]

By the mid-eighteenth century, however, the Belvedere Antinous
had begun to lose its place alongside the Apollo, also in the papal collection, as a paragon of classical art. As Alex Potts has explained, its
historical identity was challenged by Winckelmann, who could not
accept that so pure a specimen had been produced in or after the
period of Hadrian, and proclaimed it to be an earlier representation of
the Greek huntsman, Meleager.[13] Simultaneously, both critics and artists began to subject the tradition which it embodied to much closer
scrutiny. In the section on 'Expression', from his 'Notes on Painting'

appended to the survey of the Paris Salon of 1765, Diderot has fun with the idea of an actor or dancing master enjoining the statue of Antinous: 'Come along, you ninny, brace those knees, show off that figure; hold your nose up a bit.'[14] If Diderot intends to show the difference between the grace of art and the artificial pose which turns the statue 'into the most insipid of fops', we cannot be certain whether the same purpose is served by Hogarth when he incorporates the well-known serpentine form, together with those of Hercules and Venus, in the sculptor's yard depicted in the didactic section of his *Analysis of Beauty*. Peter Wagner has pointed out the element of mockery involved in juxtaposing the powerless male nude with an over-attentive and effeminate dancing master.[15]

With the coming of the nineteenth century, and the gradual displacement on historical grounds of the Belvedere Antinous from its pre-eminence, the image of Hadrian's favourite continues to assert its presence in the studio and the academy. Ingres, that great defender of the classical tradition, seems almost to have viewed Antinous as one of the family: a note preserved in the archive of the Getty Research Center records his despatching to Montauban 'my portrait and that of my wife Madelaine and the Greek head of Antinous. 3 marbles.'[16] Yet his contemporary as a pioneer in the new art form of photography, Auguste Bayard, invokes Antinous in a very different fashion when he exploits for thematic purposes the very different mode of reproduction implicit in the new technique. Among the most original of all early photographic sequences is the set which he began around 1840, involving his own head and naked torso in the posture of a 'drowned man'. The intended reference to the legendary demise of Antinous in the river Nile is made plain by 1845, when Bayard deliberately rings the changes between his own figure and a cast of Antinous in a series which brings into play the ontological link between the sculptural cast and the medium of photography: *Bayard surrounded by Statues.*[17]

This mention of the arrival of photography, and its capacity to put in question the tradition of reproduction through prints and casts that had empowered the Western academic tradition, is a timely reminder of the anti-idealist backlash against classicism which made headway throughout the nineteenth century, and to which Symonds becomes a late recruit. It is worth noting that Samuel Butler, who qualified as a passable painter before he became a remarkably original photographer, was drawing from a plaster cast of 'Antinous as Hermes' as early as 1868, with the object of securing a place in the Royal Academy's quota for the Paris Schools.[18] Twenty years later he was producing as a photographer an image of a male nude torso that would hardly have disgraced Robert Mapplethorpe. But he felt constrained to point out that the model of his choice had acquired his finely chiselled musculature not by athletics, but by the unremitting daily labour of working the handle of a sausage machine. This materialist explanation of a feature of masculine beauty can be identified not only with Butler's ebullient iconoclasm, but also, of course, with the special kind of 'reality effect' that photography engendered. A body thus traced from the life could not but have its referent in a practice unknown to the classical tradition.

Where then does Symonds stand in relation to these various revisionist strategies – historical, satiric, and materialist? It is interesting to note that he was enthusiastically commending to his friends as late as 1864 his own father's elaborately argued attempt to define the *Principles of Beauty*. John Addington Symonds senior, the noted physician and disciple of the Scottish aesthetician David Ramsay Hay, endeavours to provide for the pleasurable effects of the fine arts upon our senses a mathematical explanation that goes much further than Hogarth's serpentine line of beauty. Antinous makes no appearance in his gallery of line-drawings carved up into significant divisions and proportions. But there is an omnipresent tension between the writer's unalloyed allusions to manifestations of beauty in the arts implicitly characterized as feminine – 'the finely-proportioned and exquisitely-chiselled contour . . . the hue of the delicately-tinted cheeks, the ruby colour of the lips, the brilliancy of the eyes, and the flow of the raven or golden tresses' – and the intended reduction of these effects to their measurable components. 'Very wonderful it is,' exclaims Dr Symonds, 'that the proportionate vibrations of the air, and the harmonic ratios of sculptured marble, should give so keen a sense of delight to the ear and eye.'[19]

Very wonderful it undoubtedly is. But Dr Symonds, improving on Hay, is determined to reduce it to 'the mysterious molecular actions of the ultimate vesicles of the nervous tissue'.[20] His son had a longer trajectory to take, in his search for a suitably materialist explanation of the troublesome effect of bodily attraction: one that would lead him not to the 'ultimate vesicles' but to the historical origins of 'the phenomenon of sexual inversion', in a pamphlet which was none the less addressed to 'medical psychologists and jurists' of the professional class to which his father belonged. But it is with the whole course of that trajectory, rather than its point of arrival, that we are concerned here. In placing this abbreviated account of the shifting image of Antinous, especially in Symonds's own period, in advance of the further questioning of the relation to Shelley and Yourcenar, I am drawing attention to the multiple purposes which it could serve, both as a historical reference point and as a sign situated within an evolving regime of representation. Butler, as I suggested, punctured the skin of male beauty by his sly allusion to the craft of sausage making. Pater, in the frontispiece which adorned *The Renaissance* on its first appearance in 1873, sedulously reproduced the 'little drawing in red chalk' attributed to Leonardo which he had examined at the Louvre: 'A face of doubtful sex, set in the shadow of its own hair, the cheek-line in high light against it, with something voluptuous and full in the eye-lids and the lips.'[21] This could stand for the two forces, sometimes conflicting and sometimes in union, of Leonardo's genius: 'Curiosity and the desire of beauty'.[22] But Symonds, in choosing his own frontispiece a few years later than Pater, would endorse neither the sardonic spirit of disavowal implied in the story of Butler's photography, nor Pater's shy complicity in Leonardo's 'type of subtle and serious grace'. His reproduction of the 'Ildefonso Group', in a delicate stipple engraving (see Plate 5a), manifests a sculptural work which he had never himself seen, except in the form of a cast, but whose problematic rendering of Antinous could pose both an erotic enigma and a test of his historical and philological acuity.

In the historical sequence within which this enquiry is cast, there is a curious and illuminating symmetry between Yourcenar's interest in Symonds – as regards the fluctuating image of Antinous – and Symonds's interest in Shelley. Yourcenar's great novel of 1951, *Les Mémoires d'Hadrien*, is supplied with a long bibliographical note in which Symonds is singled out for special attention among the mass of Winckelmann's epigones, nearly all of whom are taxed with 'confused idealism' and have become mere 'curiosities'. Symonds's essay of 1879 in *Sketches and Studies in Italy*, however, remains 'of great interest' despite some dated aspects.[23] The same is true, states Yourcenar, of 'his remarkable and very rare essay on antique inversion, *A Problem in Greek Ethics*'. This bibliographical passage tells us quite a lot about her research, so far as Symonds is concerned. She has managed to track down the privately printed, and certainly 'very rare' pamphlet-essay of 1883. She has also read the 'Antinous' essay from 1879 and, evidently, picked up the Shelley quotation as it appears in Symonds's opening pages. That she does not have either of them to hand when actually compiling the *Mémoires* is made more than likely by the inaccessibility of the essay, and by the fact that she misquotes the brief passage from Shelley. Shelley wrote – and Symonds correctly quoted – 'effeminate sullenness'. Yourcenar has inverted the phrase but, with its meaning essentially unchanged it still functions for her as a kind of hieroglyph, revealing the divided character of Antinous *in the same way* as it comes across through the images of him:

> Everything that can be said about Antinous' temperament is inscribed in the least of his images. *Eager and impassionated* [sic] *tenderness, sullen effeminacy*: Shelley, with the admirable candor of the poet, says in six words what is essential, where most art critics and nineteenth-century art historians only knew how to expatiate in virtuous declamations, or to engage in false and vague idealisation.[24]

Symonds is therefore for Yourcenar the authority on Antinous who, with poetic insight, can recognize the truth about his subject as it has already been conveyed in a vivid, imagistic formula (and we shall see that his note to the 1883 pamphlet also, for her, performs the same role). Shelley, for Symonds, is also the precursor whose precious texts are celebrated for their very rarity, and in part for the transgressive character which accounts for that rarity. In the little book on Shelley's life and works which Symonds wrote in the summer of 1878, few passages stand out so vividly in the rather sub-standard prose as the one in which he recalls finding 'two uncut copies in boards at a Bristol bookshop' of the original publication of the *Revolt of Islam*.[25] If we take into account the fact that Symonds was writing to Gosse in January 1878 about the sources for a possible essay on Antinous, the parallel between the two subjects of research comes to appear significantly close – as if Shelley's six lapidary words were indeed a trigger for his more intensive study or, alternatively, the fascination with Antinous, already anticipated in the earlier poem, fuelled a new interest in Shelley.[26]

I should point out at this stage, however, that there is nothing simple in the way in which Shelley pays tribute to the instantly recognizable type of Antinous, and hijacks it for his own purposes in 'The Coliseum: A Fragment':

> It was a face, once seen, never to be forgotten. The mouth and the moulding of the chin resembled the eager and impassioned tenderness of the statues of Antinous; but, instead of the effeminate sullenness of the eye, and the narrow smoothness of the forehead, shone an impression of profound and piercing thought; the brow was clear and open, and his eyes deep, like two wells of crystalline water which reflect the all-beholding heavens. Over all was spread a timid expression of womanish tenderness and hesitation, which contrasted, yet intermingled strangely, with the abstracted and fearless character that predominated in his form and gestures.[27]

Shelley therefore explicitly modernizes Antinous, fitting the character visually identified for his futuristic dialogue with the neo-pagan exemplar of beauty amid the ruins of the Coliseum. He refashions him, giving him a post-Cartesian power of thought, yet still insists on the androgynous impression of his facial features. Symonds is thus faithful to Shelley in his 1879 essay precisely in the degree to which he, too, refines his interpretation of the well-known image and supplants it with a new reading that penetrates the inner state of mind:

> But, after longer familiarity with the whole range of Antinous's portraits, and after study of his life, we are brought to read the peculiar expression of his face and form somewhat differently. A prevailing melancholy, sweetness of temperament overshadowed by resignation, brooding reverie, the innocence of youth touched and saddened by a calm resolve or an accepted doom – such are the sentences we form to give distinctness to a still vague and uncertain impression.[28]

Both Shelley and Symonds, therefore, invest the Antinous type with a measure of inferiority. In Symonds's case, this is seen as the result of long study of the images and the records pertaining to him, as a result of which 'what seemed sullen, becomes mournful'.[29] This seems the point at which to ask how far Symonds's image of Antinous, as traced in his early poem, in his essay, and in the subsequent note to *A Problem in Greek Ethics*, does indeed reflect the process of learning that he implies in the quoted passage. To what extent can we measure Symonds's own development – the process that he himself was self-consciously engaged in marking throughout his life – in terms of the floating signifier of Antinous?

Symonds's poem, 'The Lotos-Garland of Antinous', published in *Many Moods* in 1878 but (as mentioned previously) written perhaps a decade before, participates fully in what its author proclaimed to be the 'unity of tone' in that collection, which was defined by 'the themes of Love, Friendship, Death, and Sleep'.[30] It can be viewed, however, as a prefigurement of Symonds's later and perhaps most celebrated poem, 'In the Key of Blue', in that the image of the crimson lotos-blossom is employed to intensify the erotic charge of the imagined youthful body, with accumulating metonymies leading up to a vivid synecdoche as the statue-like form of Antinous takes flesh, so to speak, before our eyes. Two passages can be used to demonstrate this strategy:

> He rose, and from his shoulder's ivory
> The veil fell fluttering to his rounded thigh:

> Naked he stood; then on his forehead set
> A crimson wreath of lotos, cool and wet...[31]

If this is the moment when the 'ivory' starts into life, the death scene is foreshadowed by an even more lubricious exchange of material properties:

> ...and in the glow
> The ruddy lotos-flowers upon his brow
> Blazed ruby-like, and all his form divine
> Blushed into crimson, and the crystalline
> Bowl of the gleaming beryl flashed, and dim
> With dusky gold the fur that mantled him,
> Spread tawny splendour.[32]

One senses here the poetic logic of the process whereby the ideal body, whose pleasure cannot be conveyed in explicitly sexual terms, finds a kind of equivalent erotic intensity through the consummation of a self-appointed death. Indeed, Symonds in a sense re-enacts the same process, over a wider narrative sequence, in the opening essay of his travel book, *Italian Byways* (1883) – with Shelley taking the place of Antinous. He presents himself as leaving the frigid Alps, taking the long descent into northern Italy, and hardly pausing for breath before he has reached the Ligurian coast, where Shelley's memory vividly excites him. Whilst he is being entertained at the same villa near Lerici in which Shelley had stayed, Symonds laughs to himself to think of 'that luncheon party, when Shelley lost his clothes, and came naked, dripping with sea-water, into the room, protected by the skirts of the sympathising waiting-maid'.[33] This has to be, of course, the prelude to the inevitable visit 'to the spot where Shelley's body was burned'.[34]

By the time of this visit, however, Symonds has written and published, with the bibliographical assistance of Horatio Brown, the long essay on Antinous that earned Yourcenar's particular admiration. Shelley had struck a neo-pagan note in his 'Coliseum' fragment, providing a spokesman for unorthodox, anti-Christian sentiments, and Symonds likewise sees his first task as the discrimination of the two types of martyrdom so crudely conflated in the 1893 essay on 'The New Spirit': Antinous and St Sebastian. In this comparison, the superior interest of Antinous resides first of all in the fact that his story is no mere legend, telling us 'nothing to be relied upon' but, in principle, ascertainable fact. 'In spite of the perplexity and mystery that involve the death of Antinous in impenetrable gloom, he is a true historic personage, no phantom of myth, but a man as real as Hadrian, his master.'[35] Here the metonymic process is evidently working in a rather different way from the poetic logic of 'The Lotos-Garland'. Hadrian was a real man; therefore Antinous too was a real man, and not merely a sculptural representation. But, paradoxically, the best documentary evidence from which we can deduce the reality of Antinous remains the spate of artistic representations that were produced after his deification by the grieving emperor.

Symonds's essay thus becomes a close reading of the image tradition, which is at the same time a powerful attempt to clarify the motivation of the historical Antinous. To this end, he points out from the start the intrinsic contradictions which constitute and identify the sculptural type: Antinous's body combines, as he puts it, 'Greek beauty of structure with something of Oriental voluptuousness'.[36] Its distinctive status as a concatenation of forms, rather than a unitary and ideal form, can be traced specifically in the 'fusion of diverse elements' distinguishing the different features of the head.[37] This is precisely where it becomes apposite to cite Shelley's six words on the subject – 'eager and impassioned tenderness . . . effeminate sullenness' – but to substitute for the 'sullenness' a note reminiscent of Winckelmann: 'The unmistakable voluptuousness is transfigured in tranquillity.'[38]

Symonds's essay cannot avoid being led, at this stage, in a hermeneutic circle bounded by the twin spectres of Winckelmann and Lessing. We are taken through many examples of the sculptural type for clues as to the real Antinous, but these sculptures return to us, in the last resort, only the kinds of effect which sculpture as a medium is specially qualified to convey. This is why the investigation suddenly changes gear when it arrives at the 'Ildefonso group', known only as a cast to Winckelmann and his fellow Roman-antiquarians and taking its name from the collection to which the original marble sculpture had gravitated in Madrid.[39] Having already positioned an engraving of the group as his frontispiece, Symonds is ready to use it as a prop for his historical investigations. He has already, in discussing the inadequacy of the conventional historical sources, introduced the crucial issue of the motivation of Antinous: 'Whether he was drowned by accident, whether he drowned himself in order to save Hadrian by vicarious suffering, or whether Hadrian sacrificed him in order to extort the secrets of fate from blood-propitiated deities, remains a question buried in the deepest gloom.'[40]

It is from this impenetrable gloom induced by the historical record, however, that the Ildefonso group will rescue us, since it provides sufficient narrative potential to allow these different possibilities to be played off one against another. It was the sculptor Tieck who first suggested

that the three figures in the group represented Antinous (on the left),
the Genius of Hadrian, and a miniature Persephone; his gloss on this
identification is that Antinous's decision to drown himself is conveyed
by 'the loving, leaning attitude of the younger man, and by his melancholy look of resolution'.[41] The weakness of this case is, as Symonds
admits, the improbable equation of the figure carrying the inverted
torch with the Emperor Hadrian, which led a further commentator to
modify the theory by classing this figure as a sacrificial daemon. But
Symonds is more interested in exploring the ingenious variant of the
German scholar Bötticher, who proclaims the group as representing 'not
a sacrifice of death, but a sacrifice of fidelity on the part of the two
friends, Hadrian and Antinous, who have met before Persephone to
ratify a vow of love till death'.[42] Support for Bötticher's interpretation,
Symonds concludes, can be found in the likely significance of the action
of the 'Hadrian' figure, who is kindling a torch at the sacred fire and
will shortly transfer it to Antinous's waiting right hand, before lighting
the second torch in its turn. Yet he cannot completely accept the explanation, as he confesses, because it is unclear how such a scene could possibly engender the mood of 'melancholy and solemnity' investing the
faces of both young men: 'Antinous is not even looking at the altar, and
the meditative curves of his beautiful reclining form indicate anything
rather than the spirited alacrity with which a friend would respond to
his comrade's call at such a moment.'[43]

One may well ask at this point what is really at stake for Symonds in
this debate, and the answer comes back very clearly in Whitney Davis's
discussion of the significance of Antinous for Winckelmann. As Davis
explains, Winckelmann's view of Greek art 'reflects his experience of
line-engraving in books and of the silhouettes of lost masterworks
offered on gems and coins'. In direct alignment with this point of view,
modern love itself can be only 'an imitation of a teleology that was fulfilled elsewhere, always partly unavailable in the present moment in
which the desiring observer is actually placed'.[44] Symonds's frontispiece
of the Ildefonso group also offers the experience of an engraving, setting at a distance the original sculpture which he had most probably
never seen, and thus marking the positionality of the 'desiring observer'. One might say indeed that Pater's engraved vignette reproducing
the supposed Leonardo drawing, which takes the colour of the original
'red chalk', attempts, by the biographical sleight of hand so cleverly
practised in his 'imaginary portraits', to espouse the desire of Leonardo;
the stipple engraving commissioned by Symonds designedly exposes
his own.[45]

Moreover the fact that the choice should fall upon a group hypothetically involving Antinous makes opportune a further comparison with Winckelmann. As Davis explains, Winckelmann antedates Symonds in seeing Antinous's distinctiveness precisely in the fact that he postdates the classical period:

> The image of Antinous is on the more modern side of the 'high style' of classical art, of the Phidian age, and so works towards a vision of the possibility of homoerotic teleology in a present moment. In this position it can display a fullness or suffusion of homoerotic teleology that the 'empty' earlier image must logically reserve . . . [46]

Symonds's preoccupation over many years with the image of Antinous can indeed be associated with Antinous's availability as a shifter between the classical and the modern. Symonds himself indeed shifts perceptibly in the act of narrativising the figures of the Ildefonso group when he invokes in a Whitmanesque idiom the 'spirited alacrity with which a friend would respond to his comrade's call'.

Yet Antinous's position on the cusp of modernity ultimately devalues him in Symonds's eyes, and deprives him in *A Problem in Greek Ethics* of his 'suffusion of homoerotic teleology'. Here it is no longer a question of the Ildefonso group, but of the authentic relief depicting Antinous in the Villa Albani, which shows the youth in a coiffure and posture specifically ancient Greek in their connotations. According to Winckelmann, 'the boy himself . . . presumably adopted his pose to attract his lover's regard'.[47] For Symonds, however, when he comes to write the 1883 pamphlet, the issue of Antinous's motivation is less clear, and none the less crucial: did he act freely, or was he simply obeying Hadrian's behest? Symonds set up the issue by explaining Alexander the Great's 'love of males' as a borrowed trait: 'A kind of spiritual atavism moved the Macedonian conqueror to assume on the vast Bactrian plain the outward trappings of Achilles Agonistes.'[48] A note then directs us to two brief sentences on Hadrian and Antinous that appear to fly in the face of all that he has written on the subject so far: 'Hadrian in Rome, at a later period, revived the Greek tradition, with even more of caricature. His military ardour, patronage of art, and love for Antinous seem to hang together.'[49]

It has to be remembered, of course, that Symonds is here addressing 'medical psychologists and jurists' in a work of very small circulation. It is not, as with the foregoing essay, a piece of exploratory critical writing in which he can make play with the presence and absence of the desired body through the medium of engraving. Indeed Symonds is so anxious, in 1883, to defend the Greek ethic of comradely love against the contagion of 'effeminacy' and 'pederastic lust' that he must presumably exorcise an image that looms so inconveniently on the threshold between antiquity and modernity.[50] Antinous is now a mere 'caricature', to be revived oxymoronically in the essay of 1893 as a 'deified mignon' or just a 'naked young m[a]n in the prime of life'.

Yet Symonds's comment about the aspects of Hadrian's life 'hanging together' must have struck a chord in Yourcenar, and justified her listing in her bibliography a work containing just two sentences. Yourcenar is no longer burdened by the confusing iconography of classical sculpture, confining her interest in the image of Antinous to the few engraved gems that might have belonged to Hadrian himself.[51] Nor does she have doubts about Antinous's motivation. Possessed by the conviction that he must sacrifice himself to avert the predictions of the Egyptian oracles foreshadowing Hadrian's death, Antinous has to lie and deceive his lover in order to carry out his plan. Hadrian arrives too late at the sacrifice when Antinous has already offered the clippings of his hair to the flames, and he can only retrieve the cold body from the river's mud. But Hadrian's grief is tempered by the fact that he has an empire to run: it is his supreme lucidity in this, as in other matters, that gives Yourcenar the tone for these fictitious but historically founded memoirs. So far from being a caricature of the Greeks whose culture he so admired, Hadrian becomes for Yourcenar the single person who stands, by virtue of his unique historical role, above the religious practices and mythologies of both ancient and modern worlds. As early as 1927, she had signalled this perception by underlining, in her volume of Flaubert's letters, a sentence by the novelist which pinpointed the idea: 'The gods being no longer and Christ being not yet, there was, from Cicero to Marcus Aurelius, a unique moment in which there was man alone.'[52] Her strategy is to cite this moment between the demise of paganism and the rise of Christianity in the ecumenical vision of Hadrian, 'cet homme seul et d'ailleurs relié à tout': the man who stands alone and in whom all things hang together.[53]

Hadrian's conspicuous achievement, for Yourcenar, is to transcend the dichotomy of Ancient and Modern: not in an equivocal way, as the late antique image of Antinous presented itself to Symonds, but with a clarity of vision which enables him to stand above the fatal recurrence of forms. One might indeed say that in his telling relegation of Hadrian as mere caricaturist, just as in his earlier effort to make the mutual relationship of Hadrian and Antinous leap out of history into the present,

Symonds testifies to his own profound sense of belatedness. He can no longer, like Shelley, blithely alter the features of Antinous to suit his own, forward-looking purposes. 'Je suis venu trop tard dans un monde trop vieux,'* Brown quotes him as saying.[54] The avowal is all the more poignant for being itself a quotation from the French Romantic poet Alfred de Musset.

This essay has been concerned with two sets of three: Butler, Pater, and Symonds, at the outset; and Antinous as envisaged by Shelley, Symonds, and Yourcenar. It is indeed revealing to note that, when Symonds himself takes into account such triple sequences, it is in order to depreciate his own position as a latecomer. His relationship to his father and grandfather, he explains, is analogous to that of Euripides to Sophocles and Aeschylus, or of the late Flamboyant style to the Decorated and the original Gothic. In each case, according to Symonds, the second term is superior to the first, and immeasurably superior to the third. Such a series of triads has nothing in it of the Hegelian dialectic. But it does suggest, at least so far as the literary and artistic parallels are concerned, the cycles of discourse which Lévi-Strauss, following Jakobson, uses to analyse the development of musical language in his 'Overture' to *Le Cru et le cuit*, where Bach is taken as a musician of the 'code', Beethoven as a musician of the 'message', and Wagner a musician of the 'myth'.[55]

It would take another essay to work out in any detail the implications of this model for the discursive styles of the nineteenth-century writers mentioned here. Let me end speculatively, however, by suggesting that Butler, the failed painter and successful photographer, sustained through the techniques of ironic dispersal and reversal the mythic role of a post-Romantic writer. Pater (the civet cat) so ingeniously reworked the mythic material of the age that his elaborate prose became a shifter to the new codes of modernism. Symonds, a member of the Decadent generation who passionately rejected Parnassian language games, desperately wished to break out of the latecoming phase and be a writer of the 'message'. This condemned him to be a stifled voice for his own generation and the next. But it may well be that, the cycle of modernism now having run its course, his message can sound more clearly than at any time in the past century. It may also be the case that, for some readers at any rate, the interferences complicating this message will provide an arresting subject of study.

*I have come too late into a world too old

Notes

1   See Elinor Shaffer, *Erewhons of the Eye: Samuel Butler as Painter, Photographer, and Art Critic* (1988).

2   For a conspectus of recent views on Pater's significance, see Elinor Shaffer (ed.), *Comparative Criticism Yearbook*, xvii (Cambridge, 1995). Also Stephen Bann, 'Walter Pater', in Michael Kelly (ed.), *Encyclopedia of Aesthetics* (Oxford, 1998), ii, 445–7.

3   Quoted in Horatio F. Brown, *John Addington Symonds: A Biography*, 2nd edn (1903), 401. It is perhaps worth recalling that the civet is a component in some exquisite perfumes.

4   Quoted in Shaffer, *Butler*, 23.

5   Ibid., 204.

6   The dedication to Shadwell ('C.L.S.') is dated 1873, and appears in the first edition. The engraved vignette was the subject of much discussion between Pater and his editor, and appears for the first time in the second edition of 1877. See W. Pater, *The Letters of Walter Pater*, ed. Lawrence Evans (Oxford, 1970), 18–20.

7   See Thomas Wright, *The Life of Walter Pater* (1907).

8   J. A. Symonds, *Last and First* (New York, 1919), 37.

9   J. A. Symonds, *The Letters of John Addington Symonds*, ed. Herbert Schueller and Robert Peters (Detroit, 1967–9), i, 832. Commenting on a letter to Dakyns dated 29 July 1868, the editors identify Symonds's mention of a poem on 'The Sacred Theban Band' as 'probably "The Last Garland of Antinous"'. Although the basis for this conclusion remains opaque, the poem does indeed relate to the poetic themes developed by Symonds in this period.

10   The reference comes in 'Pippa Passes', and is in fact a quote from *Odyssey*, 22: Robert Browning, *The Poems*, ed. John Pettigrew (New Haven, CT and London, 1981), 317.

11   See Phyllis Pray Bober and Ruth Rubinstein (eds), *Renaissance Artists and Antique Sculpture: A Handbook of Sources* (1986), 58, 163.

12   See Shaffer, *Comparative Criticism Yearbook*, xvii, 124–6. Originally reproduced in Wright, *Pater*, ii, 191.

13   See Alex Potts, *Flesh and the Ideal: Winckelmann and the Origins of Art History* (New Haven, CT and London, 1994), 146–50.

14   See John Goodman (ed.), *Diderot on Art* (New Haven, CT and London, 1995), i, 214.

15   See Hans Peter Wagner, 'Eroticism in Graphic Art: The Case of William Hogarth', in Patricia Craddock (ed.), *Studies in Eighteenth-Century Culture* (1991), 67. The reference comes in Plate 1 of *The Analysis of Beauty*.

16   MS note (undated) with correspondence between Ingres and the Pastoret family (Getty Research Center, Los Angeles, 860026).

17   See Geoffrey Batchen, *Burning with Desire: The Conception of Photography* (Cambridge, MA, 1997), 157–62.

18   Shaffer, *Butler*, 21.

19   John Addington Symonds Sr, *The Principles of Beauty* (1857), 50, 55.

20   Ibid., 55.

21   Walter Pater, *The Renaissance*, 6th edn (repr. 1906), 115. The vignette is not explicitly related to the drawing mentioned in the essay, but it has been universally assumed that the one refers to the other.

22 Ibid., 109.
23 Marguerite Yourcenar, *Les Mémoires d'Hadrien*, new edn (Paris, 1974), 358.
24 Ibid., 336.
25 J. A. Symonds, *Shelley*, new edn (1887), 97.
26 The letter to Gosse, dated 19 January 1879, is already quoted in Brown, *Symonds*, 334.
27 Percy Bysshe Shelley, *Complete Works*, ed. Roger Ingpen and Walter E. Peck (1926–30).
28 J. A. Symonds, *Sketches and Studies in Italy and Greece, Third Series*, new edn (1927), 186.
29 Ibid., 186.
30 J. A. Symonds, *Many Moods* (1878), p. v.
31 Ibid., 125.
32 Ibid., 127.
33 J. A. Symonds, *Italian Byways* (1883), 18.
34 Ibid., 19.
35 Symonds, *Sketches and Studies*, 185.
36 Ibid., 185.
37 Ibid., 185.
38 Ibid., 186.
39 See Francis Haskell and Nicholas Penney, *Taste and the Antique* (New Haven, CT and London, 1981), 173–4.
40 Symonds, *Sketches and Studies*, 191.
41 Ibid., 224.
42 Ibid., 225.
43 Ibid., 225.
44 Whitney Davis, 'Winckelmann's "Homosexual" Teleologies', in Natalie B. Kampen (ed.), *Sexuality in Ancient Art* (Cambridge, 1996).
45 Stipple engraving, which uses dots rather than intersecting lines to build up texture, was widely used in the eighteenth century. Arguably it stresses the presence and absence of the referent more poignantly than the *burin*, because of its dependence on a simple code that anticipates digital printing.
46 Davis, 'Winckelmann', *loc. cit.*
47 Ibid.
48 J. A. Symonds, *A Problem in Greek Ethics* (1901), 4.
49 Ibid., 4.
50 Ibid., 66.
51 See her listing of portraits of Antinous in *Mémoires*, 336–7.
52 Ibid., 321.
53 Ibid., 321.
54 Brown, *Symonds*, 185.
55 See Claude Lévi-Strauss, *Le Cru et le cuit* (Paris, 1964), 37–8.

9

'A Certain Disarray of Faculties': Surpassing the Modernist Reception of Symonds

Howard J. Booth

In February 1912, nearly 20 years after Symonds's death, A. C. Benson gave a paper in Cambridge. The biographer of Walter Pater had an audience of 20 that included Bertrand Russell and, Benson recorded in his diary, 'a strange bearded man who turned out to be Lytton Strachey. It was rather a fiasco; I was tired and stupid. There was no discussion. The paper was on J. A. Symonds. Not worth the trouble – never mind, one must just go on.'[1] Benson did not record in his diary Strachey's after-the-paper question, which probably contributed to his depression. Strachey asked: 'But tell me, had Symonds *any* brain?'[2] The sustained attention given by Benson was greeted with a flippant phrase, placing Symonds as an eminent figure of the past that a 'modern' outlook could see through.

This account of a Cambridge evening suggests that Symonds's reputation was failing to carry into the new century, and indeed a number of the new generation of writers viewed Symonds as an aesthete who wrote unfocused and over-ripe prose. Aldous Huxley, at Oxford and attending Walter Raleigh's lectures on sixteenth-century plays, changed from initial approval of Symonds's *Shakespere's Predecessors in the English Drama* (though he thought from the outset that the style was 'a shade too lush') to disapproval of Swinburne and Symonds on Elizabethan playwrights.[3] The young T. S. Eliot had a similar view, arguing in a letter that the critical legacy on the English Renaissance (he mentions Lamb, Swinburne, and Symonds) had been flabby and amateurish.[4] Eliot used imagery of soap and water when, in the version of *The Waste Land* that received Pound's scalpel, he described the writers from the end of the nineteenth century: 'Fresca was baptised in a soapy sea/Of Symonds – Walter Pater – Vernon Lee'.[5] When D. H. Lawrence wanted a name for a narcissistically self-conscious aesthetic protagonist in an early short story, 'The Shades of Spring', he called him John Adderley Syson – a clear echo of Symonds's name.[6] Young writers of the rising generation, on this evidence, seem briefly to have negotiated a relation to Symonds in their early careers. Behind the identification of a diffuse style there hovers the suggestion of a figure who was insufficiently balanced and focused in life.

My project here is to look at the persistence through the twentieth century of a response to Symonds that condemned his style as deviating from what is right and proper, with, behind it, more or less hidden, the view that the 'pathology' of Symonds's style could be linked to his sexual 'pathology'. Of course, it has been argued in wider terms that aestheticist and Decadent writing were linked to homosexuality in the public imagination by the Wilde trials, and that such artwork was held to be 'suspect'.[7] Conrad's sea-tales were one early manifestation of a modernist concern with a hard, purposeful, and heterosexual 'masculine' writing. Such a view of modernism leaves out much – including, as many critics have pointed out over the last 30 years, the impact of writing by women and homosexual men in the first half of the twentieth century; but it does identify an important aspect of the movement. More recently, changing social attitudes have aided a rise of interest in Symonds the man, seeing him as an early proponent of the validity of homosexual experience. But the critical views of Symonds's texts, literary judgements that were linked to modernism and gained the centre ground in the academy after the Second World War, have remained unquestioned. The wider body of his writing has been largely ignored in accounts of Symonds from within lesbian and gay studies. Assessments of the quality of the work have continued to come from within a line of responses that, at its inception, was closely connected to a phobic response to Symonds's sexuality.

Arthur Symons's review of Horatio Brown's biography can stand as a founding text in this response. But Arthur Symons's central claim there – of a 'certain disarray of faculties' as *both* a man *and* a writer – had been aired in Symonds's own lifetime. It was held, when he was in a self-loathing and self-pitying mood, by Symonds himself – as Arthur Symons notes in his quotations from the Symonds's *Memoirs* excerpted in Brown's volume. While today we might well alight with interest on how Symonds stretched the sexual conventions of his day, in his own time this was beginning to be seen as a sign of the absence of the 'quality of reserve'. This was the phrase used towards the end of Walter Pater's 1875 review of the first volume of Symonds's *Renaissance in Italy* (*The*

Age of the Despots). To quote in full the closing sentences of Pater's piece:

> Notwithstanding Mr Symonds's many good gifts, there is one quality which I think in this book is singularly absent, the quality of reserve, a quality by no means merely negative, and so indispensable to the fullest effect of all artistic means, whether in art itself, or poetry, or the finer sorts of literature, that in one who possesses gifts for those things its cultivation or acquisition is neither more nor less than loyalty to his subject and his work. I note the absence of this reserve in many turns of expression, in the choice sometimes of detail and metaphor, in the very bulk of the present volume, which yet needs only this one quality, in addition to the writer's other admirable qualities of conception and execution, to make this first part of his work wholly worthy of his design.[8]

Pater was of course to influence modernism with his views on how strong feeling needed the counterweight of Hellenic balance and form. As recent Pater critics have brilliantly demonstrated, he also tried to subvert heterosexual mores and conventions in his writing.[9] Symonds was much more overt in his writing strategies, and more of an 'outsider' than Pater, but he also internalized the emerging tenets on the artist's life and the successful work of art, and consequently often viewed his own work in terms of 'failure'.

In his review, Arthur Symons, an important figure in establishing the critical ground for modernism (and a great admirer of Pater), cleverly seeks to nail Symonds as man and author using the literary tenets of this nascent modernism. Arthur Symons had known and corresponded with Symonds, and certainly knew of his sexuality, having helped bring about the collaboration between Symonds and Ellis on *Sexual Inversion*.[10] He begins his review with a series of coded references to Brown's failure to mention Symonds's sexuality, noting that the book had 'so careful and successful a reticence'. These remarks on the opening page made clear to those readers who already knew about John Addington Symonds's sexuality, that Symons would, in an understated way, bring this knowledge to his evaluation. Arthur Symons claims that the view taken of Symonds by Brown is 'absolutely the creation of the biographer', but paradoxically it also maintains a 'remarkable subtlety and insight'. Homosexuality cannot, in the same year as the Wilde trials, be mentioned directly if a serious argument is to be sustained by the critic,[11] so Arthur Symons prefers instead to intimate a general sense of the outcome of such a sexuality for a personality and a literary career.[12] After quoting Symonds on his own feeling that there was a gap between what he wanted to be and what he achieved – 'I wish and cannot will' – Arthur Symons rushes in to agree with him:

> Here, indeed, we seem to be at the root of the great spiritual tragedy of his life, a tragedy of noble ambition thwarted on every side, physically, morally, mentally. It was quite true that Symonds could create nothing, neither a well-balanced personality nor an achieved work of art. No one ever had a higher ideal of perfection, or strove more earnestly to reach it. But, as he well knew, there was something lacking, a certain disarray of faculties, and the full achievement never came.[13]

All the faults that held Symonds back are located within himself, none is said to stem from society's attitudes, and the reference to the moral aspect of his 'tragedy' alludes to homosexuality. Arthur Symons goes on to note Symonds's commitment to life – 'Life therefore first' – wishing that he had made more of his 'personality' in his writing, as this might have brought him the fully successful work of art. What Symons wants, though, is a writing from the self that disciplines out anything that stems from the homosexuality.

In 1914 the American critic Van Wyck Brooks again saw a lack of integrated personality and approach to art in John Addington Symonds. There are few direct references to homosexuality in the Brooks biography of Symonds, but for reasons different from those of Arthur Symons. Brooks worked from published sources on Symonds, and while drawn to homosexuality he refused to admit it in the authors that he admired, such as Symonds and Whitman. He refers to 'crass misunderstandings' of Symonds's statements on male beauty, but seems particularly responsive himself to Symonds's writing on the male body.[14] Van Wyck Brooks was writing a kind of non-Freudian psychobiography, locating the failings of Symonds in the father-induced split between a fluent surface and impenetrable depths. But he does reach further than Arthur Symons:

> The lack of that final, absolute touch in any of his writings is due, I think, to the confusion and intertwining of the subjective and the objective – the impenetrable reserve and the rhetorical candor. True literature strikes a middle term, where self and theme coalesce. In poems, essays, subjective work, theme is harmoniously submerged in personality, just as in really great histories and biographies personality is harmoniously submerged in theme. Symonds, not in his biographies, not in his *magnum opus* [the seven-volume *Renaissance in*

Italy], reaches this point; certainly not in his poems or essays. He is not quite the true historian, the true biographer, who finds satisfaction in a just view of objects. In all his pseudo-objective books the history of the man or the epoch is, one feels, continually being utilized, restlessly, half-consciously, in place of strictly creative work, to test the point of view of its author.[15]

Symonds fails the modernist test of impersonality, and the work therefore fails as art. But Brooks glimpses here what is so fascinating about Symonds – the homosexual outsider attempting to make sense of his own place in the world by reconfiguring the understanding of cultural history to give a sense of belonging to himself and those like him. The view of Symonds as generally disordered in self, and therefore in art, has had a long life. Though Phyllis Grosskurth's biography of Symonds was a groundbreaking text in objective lives of homosexuals, she also evoked the figure of the aesthete (with homosexuality hovering just out of sight) before condemning the writing style for wanting reserve: 'Today Symonds's writings can be analysed as the expression of the unreconciled elements of his nature. Sensuous and artistic, he loved the colour and texture of words, but he lacked the restraint of the true artist in handling his medium.'[16] This was not, I have been arguing, a new view for the 'today' of 1964, the year Grosskurth's biography was published, but one that already had a long history. The link between the 'pathology' of personality and that of style in Symonds survived for so long because the role in it of a phobic response to homosexuality was not foregrounded, but recessed (if nevertheless important and structural). It also continued because it drew easily on modernist views on the relation between how the creative author should live and approach his art and what made for 'good' or 'bad' writing – views that in 1964 were part of the mainstream of university English studies.

In the rest of this chapter I want to look at a number of writers who were at a distance from the heterosexual centre in society, and explore how they came to take other views of Symonds. After looking at Henry James's very different focus in his tale stemming from the relation between Symonds's life and art, 'The Author of "Beltraffio"' (1884), I shall examine the against-the-grain responses to Symonds in the twentieth century of Virginia Woolf, E. M. Forster, and Norman Douglas. At the end an approach to Symonds's vast output that might begin to surpass the modernist reception will be sketched.

James had met Symonds in 1877, and he described him in a letter to his brother William as 'a mild, cultured man, with the Oxford perfume'.[17] It was later, in 1884, that he heard from Edmund Gosse that Symonds's wife Catherine did not approve of his work. This provided James with the '*donnée*' of a story, one in fact at a considerable distance from the facts of Symonds's own life.[18] The narrator of the story is a young American admirer of Mark Ambient, a novelist whose views on art seem to be closer to those of Pater than of Symonds, but James gives Ambient an interest in the Renaissance and in Italy. The narrator of 'The Author of "Beltraffio"', on his first visit, tries to press his enthusiasm for Ambient's writings on to the wife, who refuses even to read her husband's work. Her aim in life is to protect her beautiful son, Dolcino, from his father's influence, indeed from his very touch. She appears to yield to the narrator's wish to read Ambient's latest work, but her actual aim is to evaluate the likely impact it will have on her son when he comes to read it. She looks over the sheets while nursing her son, who has become ill. Fearing for the child's inevitable corruption by his father's work she locks the door, keeps the doctor away, and the child dies. Summarized in this way – always dangerous with a Henry James text – the story appears to be a condemnation of bourgeois British philistinism that takes an unpleasantly misogynistic form. But there are also many ambiguities. James's support for the narrator can be called into question, and the boy can be seen either as a symbol of the achieved beauty of the father's art or as a demonstration of the frailty of that beauty. James heard confirmation from Gosse of Symonds's sexuality only after the tale was written, but a number of commentators have written about the homosexual aspects of the tale.[19] They note descriptions of Ambient's lifestyle and writings, the speedily established relationship between the narrator and Ambient, and the wish of the narrator to touch the beautiful young boy (the narrative of Mann's *Death in Venice* hovers in embryonic form here, perhaps). Maurizio Ascari has pointed out in his recent consideration of aesthete figures in Henry James that Ambient is depicted as the aesthete of 'elsewhere', of Italy.[20] James was generally sceptical about aestheticism, and his stories about artists from the decade after 'The Author of "Beltraffio"' suggest that, though writers should be dedicated to their art, this should not permeate every aspect of their being, that they still need a 'private life'. Perhaps the main Jamesian preoccupation with Symonds springs from his belief that marriage can get in the way of writing (a point he developed with the figure of the greedy Mrs St George in 'The Lesson of the Master').[21] 'The Author of "Beltraffio"' is a characteristically Jamesian distillation of what is of interest in Symonds's life, and it is at a distance from the already developing modernist response to Symonds. It shows that various reactions to Symonds were possible, and that the position that linked homosexuality to a generally disordered personality and a flawed writing style was not simply 'the truth'.

In the first part of the twentieth century there were a number of responses to Symonds from homosexual and bisexual authors who drew on his example of a life and a body of writing produced in a society and culture antagonistic to homosexual desire. The major modernist writer who had known Symonds as a child was Virginia Woolf.[22] Symonds features in her moving and impressive memoir of her childhood, 'A Sketch of the Past', written between 1939 and 1940, specifically in the section that deals with her memories of summers spent by the Stephen family at their holiday home in St Ives. Woolf writes about the distinguished male Victorians she remembers as visitors (they were not all there at the same time). Distant from her then, they are still more distant and 'other' in memory:

> The great figures were of course on the horizon: Meredith, Henry James, Henry Sidgwick, Symonds, Haldane, Watts, Burne-Jones: they were figures in the background. But the kind of memory I have of them is of figures only, looming very large, but very far away.
>
> I remember looking down at J. A. Symonds from the landing at Talland House; and noting his nerve-drawn white face; and the tie that was a cord with two yellow blobs of plush. I remember Watts, in his frilled shirt and grey dressing gown: and Meredith, invoking a damsel in a purple petticoat – a flower. I remember Meredith's voice; and the irony with which he said 'a book of mine'. I remember not what they said, but the atmosphere surrounding them. I remember the ceremony of being taken to see them and the way in which both father and mother conveyed that a visit to Meredith was something altogether out of the way. Both shared a reverence for genius. The reverence impressed me. And the eccentricity, the individuality: how Meredith dropped a round of lemon into his tea. How Watts had bowls of whipped cream and minced meat; how Lowell had a long knitted purse, with rings round it, and sixpences always came from the slit. What I received was some general impress of strength, of oddity. What they said I have forgotten. But I remember the roll of Meredith's voice. I remember the hesitation and qualification, the humming and hawing of Henry James' voice. So that no doubt I was supplied very early with a vision of greatness and great men. Greatness still seems to me booming, eccentric, set apart; something that we are led up to by our parents and is now entirely extinct.[23]

Symonds is portrayed here as more sensitive and less assertive than the other great men (and one notes that 'greatness' was wholly an attribute of men). Both here, and in another description of Symonds, worn by illness, 'peering' *up* a staircase at her, the suggestion is of a non-threatening exchange of glances between Symonds and the young Virginia Stephen.[24]

The consideration of her childhood in 'A Sketch of the Past' brought Woolf back over the ground she had previously reworked in her novel *To the Lighthouse* (1927). She drew in the novel on her memories of her mother for the depiction of Mrs Ramsay, seeing such women as helping others, supporting men, and finally exhausting themselves. The needy figure of her father Leslie Stephen, demanding consolation and support from his female relatives, contributed to her creation of Mr Ramsay. Virginia Stephen's family context was also used for the novel's concern with death, loss, and return. In 'A Sketch of the Past', the description of the bay and St Ives is linked to an account of a trip, initially frustrated by death but eventually undertaken, to the fishing boats. There is in the first part of this description another presence by Woolf's side, a non-threatening older male, John Addington Symonds. To give just the opening:

> From the Lookout place one had then a perfectly open view of the bay. Mr Symonds said it reminded him of the Bay of Naples. The bay was a large lap, many-curved, sand-edged, silver green with sandhills, flowing to the Lighthouse rocks at one end, which made two black stops, one of them with the black and white Lighthouse tower on it.[25]

Symonds looks at the Cornish view through the eyes of a lover of Italy (the Bay of Naples was of course often appropriated as a 'homosexual' space; one thinks of Wilde, Lord Rosebery, Norman Douglas, and the homosexual 'colony' on Capri) but he is not seen as interfering with the view of the young Virginia Stephen. Symonds in 'A Sketch of the Past' can be seen as taking a role similar to that of Mr Carmichael at the end of *To The Lighthouse*. Carmichael does not intervene – though Lily finds herself unable to share her feelings with him – when Lily struggles to complete the painting. His presence if anything aids her work, unlike that of the invasive, patriarchal, and heterosexual figure of Mr Ramsay.[26] Early in the novel, Mrs Ramsay finds Mr Carmichael disturbingly self-sufficient and unreceptive to her charms – she puts it down to his unpleasant wife. Given that he is a poet and may also be an opium addict, Woolf is perhaps suggesting homosexuality – that Carmichael is a decayed relic of the *fin de siècle*.[27] Woolf responds to Symonds as someone who does not invade and colonize women's space, and not in terms of failure in life and art.

E. M. Forster's interest in symonds came late in his life, when he became the writer active in the modernist period who engaged with the full, unexpurgated text of Symonds's embargoed *Memoirs*. Sitting on the committee of the London Library in October 1939 he had to consider the request of Dame Katherine Furse, one of Symonds's daughters, to see her father's text. (She was writing a memoir of her father, and Furse had been encouraged to be true and frank about Symonds's sexuality by Woolf, who said in a letter to her: 'I'm glad to think that now we needn't hush up so much.' This comes as something of a surprise given Woolf's own reticence about homosexuality in her autobiographical writings and in her biography of her friend Roger Fry.)[28] Himself homosexual, Forster was not shocked by the likely contents of Symonds's *Memoirs*, though he noted that one fellow member of the committee, the director of the National Portrait Gallery, had homophobic views from the 'Dark Ages'.[29] It was not until 1961 that Forster actually got to read the *Memoirs* in full, and he made a long and penetrating entry on them in his *Commonplace Book*.[30] As one would expect from an account of an unpublished embargoed text, there is a lot of summary, but one sees the twentieth-century homosexual responding to the ways in which this nineteenth-century man made sense of his dissident desires. Forster has an eye for the key events and trends, focusing on the denunciation of the Harrow headmaster Vaughan for his affair with Symonds's friend Alfred Pretor, the early dreams and the idealization of physical desire, how the Symonds's marriage worked, and the increasing expression Symonds gave to his homosexuality. He is alert to Symonds's use of cultural material in his effort to make sense of his desires, singling out the 'unerring choice of myths appropriate to his own development'.[31] Also, Forster is interested in the accommodation that Symonds and his wife came to, and this brings out that characteristic Forsterian tone of admiration for tolerance when dealing with life's imperfections: 'But they seem to get through their lives in a way that happens in life and not in poetry and fiction.'[32] (One could turn this insight into a response to Henry James's Symonds-based narrative: in life people with differences often muddle through.) Forster copied out a number of quotations from Symonds's text, and the last, prefaced with the words 'A literary resolution', quotes Symonds as saying, 'I struggled long to conquer fluency.' One can imagine Foster, as he copied this, smiling both to himself and to any future reader who might pick up the fact that fluency was never

Forster's problem. He was a novelist who wrote no novels for the last 45 years of his life, in part because he felt he could not address homosexual love directly.[33] Forster's homosexual novel *Maurice* was to be published only posthumously in 1971, and to him Symonds's strategy of making a voyage of discovery through cultural history in his writing, in an age even more proscriptive than his own, must have seemed admirable.

The novelist and travel writer Norman Douglas, who had a high-profile career in the first half of the twentieth century, but whose reputation faded rapidly after his death in 1952, neither knew Symonds personally nor read the *Memoirs* in full. He shows how readers away from such knowledge responded to Symonds's efforts to foreground male–male desire, and how Douglas, as a writer himself, sought to recycle these sources of positive identification for the homosexuals of a new generation. That said, Symonds had taken more risks than did Norman Douglas before the First World War; but perhaps the context of publishing that prevailed before the Wilde trials gave Symonds greater liberty of action. In the mid-1910s Douglas was assistant editor of the *English Review*, and he seems to have had free reign over what he reviewed himself. The books he chose often sought to validate homosexuality in some way. Among these reviews – unsigned, of course – were pieces on such early pro-homosexual texts as George Ives's *A History of Penal Methods* and Edward Carpenter's *Intermediate Types Among Primitive Folk*. Douglas also reviewed the Van Wyck Brooks book on Symonds in March 1915, dryly suggesting that Brooks may have idealized Symonds's project in his writings.[34]

In these reviews Douglas was at once keeping the general *English Review* readership content and also writing for an audience that was looking for references and further material on same-sex desire and its cultural history. The problem with this strategy was that it was likely to reach only those already able to catch the references. The best example of Douglas's extreme reticence in print at this time (he was outspoken in life, and would venture stronger statements in print in later years) comes from the end of chapter 15 of his travel book *Old Calabria*, published in 1915. Douglas moves from talking about Sappho (you have to know about the association with lesbianism), to eminent Victorian Hellenists like Swinburne and Symonds, to Plato, and then on to third-sex theories. (Associated with the Ulrichs–Hirschfeld line in German homosexual sexology – disseminated in Britain through Carpenter's rather woolly writings on the 'intermediate sex' – these argued that to be (say) a woman who loved another woman you had, in your biological make-up, really to be a man, and so to be part of a third sex of mixed male and female attributes.)[35] The passage is at once allusive and elusive; many of its readers must simply have been baffled. He talks about a writer who believed the lost poems of Sappho to be the greatest treasure still missing under Italian soil:

> The lost poems of Sappho – a singular choice! In corroboration whereof he quoted the extravagant praise of J. A. Symonds upon that amiable and ambiguous young person. And he might have added Algernon Swinburne, who calls her the greatest poet who ever was at all.
>
> Sappho and these two Victorians, I said to myself. . . . Why just these two? How keen is the cry of elective affinity athwart the ages! *The soul, says Plato, divines that which it seeks, and traces obscurely the footsteps of its obscure desire.*
>
> The footsteps of its obscure desire –
>
> So one stumbles, inadvertently, upon the problems of the day concerning which our sages profess to know nothing. And yet I do profess to see a certain Writing on the Wall setting forth, in clearest language, that 1 + 1 = 3; a legend which it behoves them not to expunge but to expound. For it refuses to be expunged and we do not need a German lady to tell us how much the synthetic sex, the hornless but not brainless sex, has done for the life of the spirit while those other two were reclaiming the waste places of earth, and procreating, and fighting – as befits their horned anatomy.[36]

Douglas here defends those who make culture and contribute to the 'life of the spirit', which he sees as the third sex, as opposed to those who make war and have children. But if Douglas sees the 'Writing on the Wall' as being in 'the clearest language' then this excerpt from *Old Calabria* is clear only to those able to follow the references – references which Symonds was amongst the first to disseminate, and where he has become for Douglas a link in a chain of homosexual cultural material.[37]

The writers on whom I have been concentrating from the modernist period – Woolf, Forster, and Douglas – suggest in their different ways, following on from the different contexts in which they lived and wrote, a way of moving past the account of Symonds's life and writing in terms of 'failure'. Symonds's efforts to understand his world, to consider his wider place as a man who loved other men using large areas of cultural history as his laboratory, and to find a way of writing in a hostile society, have to come to the fore.

Two articles, by Ed Cohen and Peter Allen Dale, point to an approach to Symonds beyond the emphasis on literary quality compromised by personal flaws. Cohen examines how the homosexual subject in late Victorian England was formed in and by powerful forces, at a time of changes in the experience and analysis of subjectivity. For Cohen, the first wave of lesbian and gay theory had emphasized broad trends and had often failed to find ways of writing about the individual subject's relation to emergent identities in an environment everywhere seeking to naturalize heterosexuality and negative about homosexuality. Cohen puts forward his project in his own inimitable prose:

> Unfortunately, following Foucault, most of us working on 'queer' topics in the Victorian period have focused our analyses at the level of what we might call 'governmental' discourses (in the broadest possible sense) such as law, medicine, education, religion, literature, and the arts, as well as those nineteenth-century discourses designated as the 'human sciences' (biology, sociology, anthropology, criminology, sexology, psychology, etc.). As a consequence, while we have begun to develop a relatively comprehensive sense of the ways in which a privileged range of sexualized meanings and practices systematically coalesced within these discourses, offering subject-positions that legitimated the asymmetrical distribution of power and resources, we have a much more rudimentary notion of how what I would call sexually 'ec-centric' subjects lived out their dis-positions, let alone how they made sense of them.[38]

Cohen's argument is that Symonds's autobiography shows, in the decades before Freud, how a split subject – and more than that a subject with a sense that they were a split subject – came into being. Internalized heterosexual and class norms led to a certain surface, while Symonds was keenly aware of a hidden, what he saw as 'real', homosexual self. One can see a split in Symonds parallel to that noted by Cohen in terms of his attitudes to writing and to style. Writing cultural history in order to re-use and repoint the material in a way relevant to his own positioning in society, Symonds nevertheless internalized, and felt the need to judge himself against, the emerging modernist canons of taste. But, even after the self-condemnatory statements in the *Memoirs*, Symonds continued to pursue his well-established strategy, publishing, amongst other texts, his biography of Michelangelo and his book on Whitman.

Peter Allen Dale's piece suggests how a wider examination of Symonds's work could be pursued through a reading strategy that finds in

Symonds's interest in the past more than a search for other men he could say were 'homosexual'. Dale looks at Symonds as a cultural historian in relation to other cultural historians, a line of approach that had lain largely dormant since the 1890s, when Frederic Harrison had compared Symonds and Ruskin on the Renaissance.[39] Looking at Symonds's 'emplotment' of the Renaissance, Dale sees him as moving beyond other writers on the period in that he no longer sees the period as the battle of religion versus humanism, but casts it in terms of a debate between hermeneutics and science. Symonds does not rest in the view that the Renaissance shows a period that offers a synthesis, of however brief duration, between pagan and Christian and which provides an example to the nineteenth century. In beginning with this question Dale sees Symonds as following Hegel, not Ruskin. However, for his answer Symonds turned not to Hegel but to Michelet, with his emphasis on nature and the praise of the natural in the Renaissance period. Symonds goes along with Michelet in his view that the lesson of the Renaissance is 'follow nature', rejecting the opinion held by many other writers – Renan, Arnold, George Eliot, and Burckhardt are all cited by Dale – that the period offers an example of the possibilities of a reasoned culture. Symonds, even more than Michelet, equated nature with political and sexual freedom, and judged the Counter-Reformation as tragic. However, the overall course of history, in Symonds's view, was one of gradual improvement. Symonds, as Wallace Furgusson explained back in the 1940s, was the first British writer of *Kulturgeschichte*, of a many-stranded approach to cultural history that seeks to reach an insight into a period's characteristic mental structure. Such an approach has to find a way of seeing order somewhere, of deciding what material is to be selected. Dale sees Symonds eventually finding his guiding principle in 'cosmic enthusiasm' and in his views of evolution. Not for Symonds Michelet's Goethean historical 'metamorphosis', but rather a theory of evolution towards a better state (and so it is not evolution as Darwin understood it). Symonds saw the Renaissance as a time when man had ridden with nature rather than against it, and his view was that repression could make ill a whole period and the people who lived in it.[40]

Dale's history-of-ideas approach tends to see writers as constructing arguments like chess openings, playing a number of moves, and then introducing clever variations from precedent. Symonds's own complex positioning in relation to these arguments, and why various positions would have appealed to him, is insufficiently addressed. Examined with Symonds's own experience as a homosexual man in the nineteenth century in mind, his course through this material makes much sense. It leads him to a suspicion of 'reason' (because it often sought to naturalize a rejection of homosexuality), to an interest in repression (following from his own understanding of his sexual development), and to the necessity he felt for a positive view of life if he was to carry on functioning as a person and a writer.

Combining Cohen's work on how Symonds tried to make sense of his life as an 'ec-centric' subject with Dale's approach to Symonds as a historian of ideas, opens up the possibility of examining Symonds's sexuality and writing in a way that reaches beyond the modernist reception, and takes investigations of Symonds and of homosexuality beyond the privileged ring of the texts on Greek and modern male–male desire which, along with the *Memoirs*, are usually considered in accounts of Symonds from within lesbian and gay studies. I would argue that it is wrong to ask whether or not Symonds lives up to those notions of what writing should be that finally achieved dominance in the following generation, ideas that at best colluded in the exclusion of the representation of homosexual desire and which attempted to pass themselves off as self-evidently true and universal. Rather, Symonds's writing needs to be seen as a remarkable body of texts that sweeps out from a complex, pressured present to pursue his concerns in examinations of large tracts of Western culture.

Notes

1 A. C. Benson, *The Diary of Arthur Christopher Benson*, ed. Percy Lubbock (n.d.), 234.

2 Michael Holroyd, *Lytton Strachey: A Critical Biography, Volume 1, The Unknown Years (1880–1910)* (1967), 203.

3 Huxley's criticism was mainly directed, though, at what he regarded as the overvaluation of Elizabethan dramatists. See *The Letters of Aldous Huxley*, ed. Grover Smith (1969), 48, 67.

4 See *The Letters of T. S. Eliot, Volume 1 1898–1922*, ed. Valerie Eliot (San Diego, 1988), 277.

5 T. S. Eliot, *The Waste Land: A Facsimile and Transcript of the Original Draft including the Annotations of Ezra Pound*, ed. Valerie Eliot (1971), 27.

6 D. H. Lawrence 'The Shades of Spring', *The Prussian Officer and Other Stories*, ed. John Worthen (Cambridge, 1983), 98–112, 260.

7 On the impact of the Wilde trials see Ed Cohen, *Talk on the Wilde Side: Toward a Genealogy of a Discourse on Male Sexualities* (1993); and Alan Sinfield, *The Wilde Century: Effeminacy, Oscar Wilde and the Queer Moment* (1994). Jonathan Dollimore has noted that: 'One of the many reasons why people were terrified by Wilde was because of a perceived connection between his aesthetic transgression and his sexual transgression. "Inversion" was being used increasingly to define a specific kind of deviant sexuality inseparable from a deviant personality.' Jonathan Dollimore, *Sexual Dissidence: Augustine to Wilde, Freud to Foucault* (Oxford, 1991), 67.

8   Walter H. Pater, review of John Addington Symonds, *The Age of Despots, The Academy*, clxix (31 July 1875), 105–6.

9   See Richard Dellamora, *Masculine Desire: The Sexual Politics of Victorian Aestheticism* (Chapel Hill, NC, 1990); Linda Dowling, *Hellenism and Homosexuality in Victorian Oxford* (Ithaca, 1994); and Laurel Brake, *Walter Pater* (Plymouth, 1994).

10   Phyllis Grosskurth, *Havelock Ellis: A Biography* (1980), 174–5.

11   Witness the unstable writing of William Barry's review article on Brown's biography of Symonds and key works by Symonds and Pater in *The Quarterly Review*, clxxxii (July 1895), 31–58, which gets sucked into the table-thumping of the time around Hellenism, aestheticism, and homosexuality. Barry reprinted this review in his *Heralds of Revolt* (1904).

12   Arthur Symons, 'John Addington Symonds', *Studies in Two Literatures* (1897), 248.

13   Ibid., 252.

14   See James Hoopes, *Van Wyck Brooks. In Search of American Culture* (Amherst, MA, 1977), 22; and Van Wyck Brooks, *John Addington Symonds: A Biographical Study* (1914), 18–20, 160–3.

15   Brooks, *John Addington Symonds*, 136–7.

16   Phyllis Grosskurth, *John Addington Symonds: A Biography* (1964), 324–5.

17   Henry James, *The Letters of Henry James*, ed. Leon Edel (Cambridge, MA, 1974–84), ii, 101.

18   See Henry James, *The Complete Notebooks*, ed. Leon Edel and Lyall H. Powers (New York, 1987), 25–6.

19   For an account of the origins of the tale and the correspondence with Gosse see Leon Edel, *Henry James, Volume 4: The Treacherous Years, 1895–1901* (1969), 114–21. See also Leland S. Person, 'James's Homo-Aesthetics: Deploying Desire in the Tales of Writers and Artists', *Henry James Review*, xiv, 2 (Spring 1993), 188–203; and Leland Monk, 'A Terrible Beauty is Born: Henry James, Aestheticism and Homosexual Panic' in Thomas Foster, Ellen E. Barry and Carol Siegel (eds), *Bodies of Writing, Bodies in Performance* (New York, 1996), 247–65.

20   Maurizio Ascari, *In the Palatial Chamber of the Mind: Comparative Essays on Henry James* (Pescara, 1997), 134–8.

21   Henry James, *The Figure in the Carpet and Other Stories*, ed. Frank Kermode (1986).

22   One of Virginia Stephen's earliest passions was for Madge Symonds, who provided the basis for Sally Seton in *Mrs Dalloway*, and for Mrs Dalloway's memories of her feelings for Sally. Leslie Stephen and Symonds were friends and, as well as Symonds's visit to St Ives, members of the Stephen family visited him at Davos. Woolf and Symonds were also related by marriage when Madge Symonds married Virginia's cousin William Wyamar Vaughan.

23   This quotation comes from the manuscript version of 'A Sketch of the Past', in the first edition of Virginia Woolf, *Moments of Being: Unpublished Autobiographical Writings*, ed. Jeanne Schulkind (Brighton, 1976), 136. The 1985 second edition of *Moments of Being* substitutes the text of Woolf's typescript in this section.

24   Virginia Woolf, *Moments of Being* (1st edn), 83.

25   Ibid., 112.

26 Virginia Woolf, *To the Lighthouse*, new edn (1977), 141–6, 158–67, 191–2.
27 Ibid., 41–3.
28 Indeed Woolf, quoting Fry, provoked Furse's ire when she called Symonds's work 'pornographic', Hermione Lee, *Virginia Woolf* (1996), 12, 288, 709.
29 E. M. Forster, *Commonplace Book*, ed. Philip Gardner (Aldershot, 1988), 353.
30 Ibid., 224–7, 228–9.
31 Ibid., 225.
32 Ibid., 227.
33 For a discussion of why Forster stopped writing novels see P. N. Furbank, *E. M. Forster: A Life, Volume 2: Polycrates' Ring, 1914–1970* (1988), 131–3.
34 The review of the Ives book was in the *English Review* for June 1914, 422–3; the piece on Carpenter is in the September 1914 issue, 271–2; and the review of the Van Wyck Brooks volume can be found in the March 1915 issue, 509. For the attributions to Douglas see Cecil Woolf, *A Bibliography of Norman Douglas* (1954).
35 See Jeffrey Weeks, *Sexuality and its Discontents: Meanings, Myths and Modern Sexualities* (1985); Hubert Kennedy, *Ulrichs: The Life and Work of Karl Heinrich Ulrichs, Pioneer of the Modern Gay Movement* (Boston, MA, 1988); Charlotte Wolff, *Magnus Hirschfeld: A Portrait of a Pioneer in Sexology* (1986); and Edward Carpenter, *The Intermediate Sex: A Study of Some Transitional Types of Men and Women* (1908).
36 Norman Douglas, *Old Calabria* (1915), 116.
37 Other, negative uses of the link between Symonds and homosexuality were possible. In the first of Compton Mackenzie's two 'Capri novels', *Vestal Fire* (1927), Mackenzie has the young admirer of Count Marsac claim that Marsac's feelings for a young boy are part of 'an ideal love in the key of blue'. His mother does not understand the reference, and it does not help her when Dawson refers her to 'John Addington Symonds, of course'. Mackenzie shows no knowledge of Symonds's writings on 'the key of blue' in either prose or verse. His project in the novel is to make homosexuality appear to have a laughable semi-private language rooted in the excesses of aestheticism.
38 Ed Cohen, 'The Double Lives of Man: Narration and Identification in the Late Nineteenth-Century Representation of Eccentric Masculinities', *Victorian Studies*, xxxvi, 3 (Spring 1993), 353–76, 354.
39 Frederic Harrison, *Tennyson, Ruskin, Mill and Other Literary Estimates* (1900), 126–48.
40 Peter Allan Dale, 'Beyond Humanism, J. A. Symonds and the Replotting of the Renaissance', *Clio*, xvii, 2 (1988), 109–37.

10

Bringing Symonds out of the Closet: Some Recollections and Reflections

Phyllis Grosskurth

It is an extraordinary experience to re-read one's first book – especially one written more than thirty years ago. I must have consulted it when I was editing Symonds's *Memoirs*, but so far as I know I have not opened and read it carefully for all those years because I had gone on to become engrossed in the lives of other people.

And so I picked it up earlier this year, and began to read. But before I discuss my reactions to this unfamiliar work, I should describe something of the myriad of memories that came flooding back as I recalled that exciting period. In 1960 I came to England to work on my doctoral dissertation under Professor Geoffrey Tillotson. At that time I was very enthusiastic about Matthew Arnold and wished to explore his influence on nineteenth-century literary criticism. Professor Tillotson was not in the best of moods on the day we met, and more or less superciliously remarked that so much had been written on Arnold that he did not think I could add anything of significance. He suggested a number of names of lesser-known Victorian figures whom he felt might justify investigation. John Addington Symonds was one of those names.

A few days later I was browsing in a bookstall in Broadstairs where I came upon a biography of Symonds by Horatio Brown. I returned to my hotel and sat up most of the night engrossed in it. What particularly intrigued me was the fact that it had been published in 1895, only two years after Symonds's death. Most of it consisted of extracts from Symonds's autobiography interspersed by linking commentary from Brown, Symonds's literary executor. Why, I asked myself, had the original autobiography not been published? I was more mystified than enlightened by Brown's explanation that the decision not to publish the full autobiography had not been made for 'ordinary or obvious reasons which render the immediate publication of autobiography undesirable'. My potential biographer's curiosity had been whetted. There was some mystery here, and I was determined to get to the bottom of it.

On returning to London I encountered a mellower Professor Tillotson. 'I have changed my mind,' he said. 'If you have your heart set on Arnold I have no objection to your proceeding with your project.' 'As a matter of fact,' I replied, 'I too have changed my mind. I think I should like to work on Symonds.' I proceeded to tell him about the Brown biography and expressed my determination to find the original manuscript. Not unexpectedly – or unreasonably – he pooh-poohed the idea. He suggested that almost certainly it had disappeared, that Brown had extracted the sections he used, discarding the others in the wastebasket.

I was not be to deterred. At the same time as I began to read through Symonds's work chronologically I started to haunt antiquarian dealers like Maggs and Quaritch in search of the elusive manuscript or any letters relating to John Addington Symonds. My next step was to insert a query in *The Times Literary Supplement* requesting information about Symonds. Since I did not then keep a daily journal, as I have done now for several years, I can only rely upon my memory to reconstruct events. What is certain is that I had an unexpected response to that small item in the *TLS*. First, there was a note from Professor Herbert Schueller of Wayne State University informing me that he and Professor Robert Peters had already started working on a collected edition of Symonds's letters. I sent him those few letters that I had already collected, assuring him that I was simply embarking on a Ph.D. thesis.

At some point that same year I was contacted by the descendants of Symonds's friend, Graham Dakyns, who had masses of letters in a trunk in Hatfield. Then the librarian of Bristol University, Dr Shum Cox, wrote that there was a collection of unsorted letters in their archives. I can well remember the first day I arrived in Bristol and Dr Cox took me into a room where he had to unlock a sort of cage. As he fumbled with a large ring of keys, I was literally hopping up and down with excitement. He gently suggested that I try to calm myself. These letters were even more personal than those in Hatfield. In those far-off days photocopying was in its infancy, and I had to copy out all the relevant passages by hand. The Dakyns family kindly lent me their letters for a time. At one point I had a trail of letters arranged chronologically winding around my whole bedroom floor.

Ah, but the best was yet to come! In the post one morning was a letter from the Librarian of the London Library, Mr Stanley Gillam, suggesting that I come and see him. He told me that he possessed the precious manuscript of the autobiography in a safe right there in his office; but, alas, that there was an embargo on it until 1976. Since I was a bona fide scholar I would be given permission to read and quote from it in my thesis. However, if I were to write a book some day, he continued, I could use only the facts I had discovered in it. (I remember thinking at the time that such an idea was inconceivable.) In subsequent years I have worked in many archives, but in none have I encountered the liberal attitude and kind assistance that I received both from the London Library and from the University of Bristol.

The perusal of the manuscript was an extraordinary experience. From my reading of Symonds's work, particularly his poetry, I had already surmised that he was a homosexual and was conveying an oblique message to his readers. Brown had been extremely hypocritical, in my view, to suggest that Symonds's problem had been religious doubt. Why bother to publish such a misleading account? The whole burden of the memoir is the account of Symonds's tormented attempt to hide his proclivities from a Victorian society which only two years after his death exerted its moral wrath on Oscar Wilde.

Of course this was not the sort of material which one would put into a doctoral thesis in those days. I was using Symonds as a focal point for the distillation of a number of trends I believed characteristic of nineteenth-century literary criticism, although I did refer to the oblique references to homosexuality. It never occurred to me to write a biography, which as a genre had never been of particular interest to me. However, the literary world of London is small; and a number of publishers, hearing about this Canadian scholar in the British Museum, got in touch with me. John Guest of Longmans told me that he would commission me on the spot, but he did not know whether I could write. His suggestion was this: that I submit to him a synopsis of a biography in addition to a sample chapter.

This was one of the greatest challenges of my life. I had to discard the dry academic style in which I had been trained and find a truer, freer, more imaginative voice. The effort cost me blood, sweat, and tears; but I managed to send something off, and within ten days I received a letter from Longmans that they were commissioning the book.

But how did one write biography? I was going off to Spain for a summer holiday and I took with me a suitcase filled with biographies to discover what I liked in biography. I lay on the beach on the Costa Brava acquiring a tan (no-one talked about skin cancer in those days) while I carefully evaluated the sort of biography that appealed to me.

I remember being impressed by Geoffrey Faber's life of Jowett and, oddly, André Maurois's biography of Proust. I liked graphic detail, a sense of period, and an insight into the inner man.

But, back in London, I was faced with a blank sheet of foolscap paper. Curiously enough, it was not as difficult as I feared, since I wrote the book for myself. But there were other problems I had not foreseen – one of the executors of the estate, Dame Janet Vaughan, was opposed to the project; but her cousin, Katharine West, became my champion. Kitty was the daughter of Symonds's daughter Lotta, and a qualified editor for John Murray. I well remember her bringing Dame Janet to my house for lunch, and the highly charged tension in the air. Kitty eventually managed to soften her cousin's attitude. Kitty read the finished manuscript very carefully, and her suggestions were invaluable ('Don't you believe in the comma?', she asked at one point). She remained my close and steadfast friend until her death.

The British reaction to the book in 1964 was extraordinary. Would that such reviews could have continued throughout my life! One must remember that the Wolfenden Report recommending the decriminalization of sex between two consenting adults had not yet been implemented; and the distinguished actor, Sir John Gielgud, was arrested for an incident in a tube station. That pubic opinion was changing was apparent when he next appeared on the stage and was given a rousing round of applause by the audience. Yet I do not think my book would have had the impact it had if it had not been written without any overt polemical intention. I believe it was also important that it had been written by an unknown Canadian woman. I might add that, once Dame Janet read the book and was aware of the critical reaction, her attitude changed to friendliness.

For me personally the book was very important because it was the beginning of my career as a biographer. But all the consequences were not altogether pleasant. I learnt that there were English departments in universities which refused to consider hiring me because of the subject matter of the book. (Today numerous universities offer courses in gay studies.) Worse than anything else was a letter I received from my father telling me in no uncertain terms that I was a disgrace to the family. I assure you that it was the most devastating letter I have ever received.

It was, as I said initially, a very strange experience to re-read this book. At one crucial period in my life I was steeped in the personalities and the events, yet now it was as though I were reading a book written by someone else, although occasionally I recognized certain familiar stylistic mannerisms. But – apart altogether from my personal reaction –

would I write it differently, would I see Symonds in a new light, were I to write it now?

The answer, in the main, is no. My memory of it was that it was perhaps a rather sentimental book, a memory possibly coloured by the fact that I was a good deal younger and more sentimental at the time. To my surprise and delight, it was not sentimental, although I had tried to see Symonds's life through his own eyes, and at times he tended to self-pity. But my sense of relief came to an end when I reached the chapter entitled 'The Problem'.

This was the chapter dealing with Symonds's homosexuality and its aetiology. In the second paragraph I write: 'To attempt to probe into the psychological depths of his neuroses would be beyond the scope of this book. Symonds himself believed that his condition was congenital; modern psychiatrists in the wake of Freud attribute inversion to some early conditioning, usually a fixation on a female (in most cases of course the child's mother).' That statement is a period-piece. At the time I knew so little about Freud that I was naïve enough to believe that he was the final authority. Then two pages on I read the following passage:

> While it is true, as Freud pointed out, that the sexual drive is initially undifferentiated, it does not follow that those who persist in a preference for their own sex therefore prove the existence of an inborn bias, as Symonds claimed . . . What Symonds failed to realize was that his own bias might have been formed irrevocably by some trauma predating . . . early intimacies.

Opposite this I have recently placed a large exclamation mark – how quaint all that sounds now!

Two visible minorities have made immense strides since 1964 – women and homosexuals. It was brave and reckless for a man to come out of the closet in 1964 – think of the present, when vast numbers now celebrate Gay Pride Day. And consider how much the mood has changed since Symonds undertook to write his memoirs under the impression that he was a mutation, an isolated being. His revelations were so incendiary that as late as 1926 a group of so-called civilized men demanded that the memoirs be placed under a 50-year embargo.

What has caused this remarkable change? Undoubtedly, the shift in attitude is linked to the radical change that took place within the sexual landscape, particularly in America in the 1960s and 1970s. Sex became a national obsession, fuelled by the culture of the hippies and the flower children. Demythologized and stripped of its puritanical coat, the new mores spawned a vocabulary of its own – 'one-night stands', 'wife-swapping' and 'cruising'. This outpouring of sexual libido emerged from the widespread use of the Pill, the legalization of abortion, and cures for gonorrhoea and syphilis.

Such general attitudes were bound to affect the homosexual community. A crucial event occurred in the early morning hours of Saturday, 28 June 1969, in New York City, when the police raided the Stonewall Inn, a gay bar in Greenwich Village. This incident rallied gays for two days of violent protests, resulting in the formation of local and national coalitions to work towards destroying homophobic prejudice. But the most hopeful sign of change came in 1973 when, after years of debate, the American Psychiatric Association's Board of Trustees voted to remove homosexuality as a mental disorder from the Diagnostic and Statistical Manual of Mental Disorders (known commonly as DSM). In 1952, DSM-I listed homosexuality and nymphomania as forms of mental illness. In 1980 it contained admission of something called 'egodystonic homosexuality'. In 1987 the word 'homosexuality' appears in the index but there is nothing in the text. By 1994 (100 years after Symonds's death) in DSM-IV homosexuality has disappeared completely and, indeed, there is a gay branch of the American Psychoanalytic Association, once the most homophobic of organizations.

What would Symonds have thought of all this? Would he have been a different man if he lived today? I was extremely annoyed when the American publishers of my book entitled it *The Woeful Victorian*, despite my indignant protests. The key question for us to ponder is this: Would his life have been significantly different? Would he have been happier? I have attempted to avoid using psychoanalytic terminology, but it is difficult to avoid describing Dr Symonds as his son's super-ego, his introjected conscience or punitive object. I quote a revealing dream Symonds recorded while on a continental tour with his father in 1862. He sees himself in a looking-glass as a terrifying image. He stumbles towards his father's room:

> ...he turned round and looked intently at me and inquiringly. I shrieked, 'Papa, don't you know me?' but even while I cried the vision of my own distorted features came across me, and filled me with utter loneliness. At last he cried, 'My son,' and, burying his face in his hands, he added, 'All in one night.' In an ecstasy of deliverance I clasped his neck, and felt that now I need not go back into that twilight room with its bed and the mystery behind the curtains. But he went on in a hesitating voice, 'My poor boy! what fiend – or

demon?' I stopped the question with a yell. Something seemed to tear me, and I awoke struggling. Such was my dream – more horrible than it seems, for the terror of dreams bears no relation to the hideousness of their incidents, but to some hidden emotion.

This is a revealing and horrifying dream. Symonds is tormented by guilt and by anxiety about causing pain to his beloved father, longing to confess his true nature and to receive absolution. He truly believed he was evil; and in a letter to Graham Dakyns after meeting Tennyson's sons he wrote:

> You say they have 'la maladie du siècle' already. But Good God! do you know what form this will take with one or both of them? I see it. In this I am not apt to be mistaken. But the bitterest cup may be kept from them. Would I could die for you, my brothers . . . There is such waste of sorrow in the world. A worm like me lives through one misery; and after he is safe he sees angels beginning the same life & cannot save them . . .

This letter was written only a fortnight after his marriage.

Certainly, in today's climate, he would never have married Catherine North. It is painful to read of the years of tension and resentment in which they lived. On the other hand, his four daughters were a source of great joy to him; and I found myself taken aback by the frankness of his attitude about his proclivities to his daughter Madge. The turning-point in his life, of course, occurred with his self-exile to Switzerland. Far from the censorious eyes of his countrymen he was free to behave openly with Swiss peasants or, during his frequent visits to Venice, with Italian gondoliers. Yet his Puritan upbringing had bitten so deeply into him that he could speak guiltily about 'this dreadful Italian pathology'. Nevertheless, in these years we do encounter a man with a capacious appetite for living. Think of his love of flowers, of good conversation, of warm friendships like that with Margot Tennant. Think, too, of his enormous capacity for work.

Let us consider the productivity. Why would a man undertake a huge project like the history of the Italian Renaissance? He was bitter because his poetry was not more warmly received. He believed that the reason for its dismissal was because he could write only allusively about his passions, but the truth of the matter was that he had no gift for poetry. *Renaissance in Italy* raises more interesting questions. Like almost everything Symonds wrote, the work was shot through with a polemical intention. It was, as I have argued in the book, a form of legitimization, proof to his father that he was no febrile weakling, but a man capable of monumental endeavour. Conceived of as part of an even more impressive undertaking, a complete history of Italy, it remains the first full-scale history of the period in English. But these seven volumes were not written only for his father. Anyone who would undertake such a work was not seeking simply parental approval, but fame itself. When he talks of *l'amour de l'impossible* he is perhaps partly referring to the sort of recognition that was beyond his talents.

And did he really know what he meant by that rather sentimental phrase *l'amour de l'impossible*? He believed he glimpsed it in elusive images of idealized beauty. But the idea of a fulfilled emotional relationship with a partner of his own sex never seemed to occur to him, because that indeed was truly impossible. The general view today would support Symonds's contention that genetics plays a strong role in determining everyone's sexuality. It is doubtful that if he lived today he would forever be on the alert, hiding his true nature in a cloak of invincibility, hypocrisy, and self-hatred. Nevertheless, I would question whether, if Symonds lived today, unafraid of public opinion, he would inevitably be a contented man. There was a strong streak of melancholia in his nature – which of course he attributed to his frustration – but I am convinced that his depression was not by any means simply the result of his particular condition. His story is sad – but not tragic in the sense that Oscar Wilde's was. He was not self-destructive, he was not flamboyant, he wisely refrained from *épater le bourgeois*.

Symonds was the first of a number of depressive exiles I have found myself writing about during the course of my biographical career. Apart from his considerable achievements, part of his attraction lies for us in his struggle with his demons. That he managed to accommodate them as effectively as he did is a triumph of a kind.

Appendix: Symonds's Peccant Poetry

Ian Venables

Out of the estimated 1,000 poems that Symonds wrote during his short life, 776 have survived. These include 232 poems that appear in 15 privately typeset booklets, referred to by Symonds as the 'Peccant Pamphlets'. Symonds's own bound volumes of his homosexual verse, preserved in Bristol University Library, present us with an opportunity to review this poetry, which remained largely unpublished. An attempt was made by Percy L. Babington in 1925 to catalogue the contents of seven of these pamphlets, and Timothy D'Arch Smith recorded a further seven in his book *Love In Earnest* (1970). However, their contents remained unlisted, and he did not mention a fifteenth pamphlet entitled *Crocuses and Soldanellas*. The majority of these pamphlets were produced during the late 1870s in a print run of 10 or less for distribution to friends.

The complete listing of Symonds's 'Peccant Pamphlets' follows, with the date of the last-dated poem in each.

Principal Poems

1.	*Dead Love* (1860)	
2.	*Fragilia Labilia* (1862)	
3.	*Old and New* First Series (1863)	
4.	*Tales of Ancient Greece* No. 1 (1868)	'Eudiades' and 'A Cretan Idyll'
5.	*Tales of Ancient Greece* No. 2 (1867)	'Lysis'
6.	*Genius Amoris Amari Visio* (1869)	
7.	*The Lotus Garland of Antinous* (1869)	
8.	*Crocuses and Soldanellas* (1870)	
9.	*Lyra Viginti Chordarum* (1871)	'Three Visions Of Imperial Rome' 'The Upas Tree'
10.	*Studies in Terza Rima* (1871)	'Love and Death: A Symphony'
11.	*Liber Temporis Perditi* (1871)	'Callicrates and Bianca'
12.	*The Love Tale of Odatis* (1871)	
13.	*Pantarkes* (1872)	
14.	*Old and New* Second Series (1875)	
15.	*Rhaetica* (1878)	'A Vista'

In his memoirs, Symonds recorded that Shakespeare's 'Venus and Adonis', read at about the age of 10, 'gave form, ideality and beauty to my previous erotic visions . . . It etherealised my inborn craving after persons of my own sex.' These adolescent experiences correspond to the stage identified as 'pre-emergence' in the model of homosexual development presented by Siegel and Lowe.[1] They culminated in 1857 after Symonds read Plato's Dialogues, *Phaedrus* and the *Symposium*. This was a moment of intense self-realization: 'I had touched solid ground. I had obtained the sanction of the love which had been ruling me from childhood. Here was the poetry, the philosophy of my own enthusiasm for male beauty, expressed with all the magic of unrivalled style.'[2]

Symonds's relationships with two Bristol Cathedral choristers, Willie Dyer and Alfred Brooke, marked a progression towards the self-acknowledgement stage of the Siegel and Lowe model. His idealized love for Willie Dyer brought into focus his emerging sexual identity and unleashed a torrent of creative writing. All of Symonds's early love poems are to be found in the first three 'Peccant Pamphlets'. They are romantic in style and are clearly indebted to the lyrics of Heine and Tennyson. In the poem 'In Dreamland', from *Crocuses and Soldanellas*, Symonds draws inspiration from Plato's *Symposium* to vocalize his feelings of isolation as a result of not being able to express his love openly:

> On a bank above the river
> Lie two lovers in the fern,
> And they see the starlight shiver
> And the beacon feebly burn.
>
> Stately ships like swans are gliding
> Seaward 'twixt the leafy shores,
> While a song the dusk dividing
> Times the boatmen at their oars.
>
> Still the lovers wait and listen,
> Two fair youths, hand locked in hand;
> Caring not though dewdrops glisten
> On the pages their eyes have scanned –
>
> Plato open lies before them –
> Caring not though one by one
> Heaven's pale lamps are lighted o'er them,
> Sinking westward to the sun.
>
> For they read the fate of spirits
> Born to wander mid the spheres,
> And the prize that Love inherits
> When this mortal disappears.

In his love for Alfred Brooke, Symonds attests to a different kind of passion: 'It was more intense, unreasonable, poignant – at one and the same time more sensual and beautiful and more ideal.'[3] Symonds turned this experience into the poem 'What Cannot Be'. Although written as early as 1861, it was published only in 1884, in his last volume of verse. Comparing the published poem with the original, we find that the pronouns have been changed from the masculine of the original to feminine in the published version:

> 'What cannot Be' (original 1861 version)
>
> My heart was hot and answered: 'What might be!
> Love, peace, content, the brotherhood of strength;
> He offers it of all convention free:
> Will thou not take and eat and rest at length?

> His brow is framed of beauty, and his soul
> Sits throned within his eyelids orbed in light;
> And from his parted lips harmonious roll
> Full floods of music, rivers of delight!'
> Oh, heart! false heart! why tear'st thou me again?
> To touch, to handle stretching forth thy palm;
> To sleep forgetful of sharp self-disdain;
> It were so easy, and so sweet the calm
> Calm as the dead sea; easy as sin;
> Sweet as love apples hiding dust within.

In the change of gender to feminine in the third line the whole dramatic force of these lines was lost, and replaced with a meaning that is obscure. Many of Symonds's published poems suffered this fate, and it must certainly be one of the reasons why they sounded a hollow note to his Victorian readers.

These early poems reflect Symonds's growing awareness of his sexual identity. However, he is unable to make the full transition to the self-acknowledgement stage, since he cannot escape the grasp of Platonic Idealism, and denies to himself the sexual basis of his feelings. This exacerbated an already heightened sense of alienation. Symonds expressed this in the deeply confessional poem 'The Tale of Theodore', printed in *Dead Love*.

These events led to Symonds's first mental breakdown, in 1862. Faced with intolerable inner emotional conflicts, and with outside pressures to conform, he sought a 'cure' for his homosexuality; but his marriage to Catherine North proved an unsuccessful exercise in self-deception. It combined with a chance meeting with a male prostitute in Hyde Park in 1865 to accentuate the transition towards self-acknowledgement. A naïve and somewhat shocked Symonds refused the youth's services, broke away 'with a passionate mixture of repulsion and fascination', and sought relief in literary expression: 'I began to make verse the vehicle and safety valve for my tormenting preoccupations.'[4] He embarked upon a series of long narrative poems which he collected together under the title 'The John Mordan Cycle', and in which he moved away from his earlier self-centred expression of homosexual love to embrace the 'Love of Men' as a universal theme. This poetic conceptualization of his homosexual nature is an important indication that he had successfully managed the self-acknowledgement stage of his sexual development. The most important of these 'John Mordan' poems were 'The Cretan Idyll' and 'Eudiades'. Here Symonds explores the ritual of Greek courtship between an older and a younger man, and in the 'Cretan Idyll' he recreates the Doric myth of Ithocles and Lysander. In the following extract, the lover Ithocles has found his beloved sleeping in a cave. Ithocles is overcome by Lysander's beauty, but his sexual advances are repulsed:

> Panting, I asked the unutterable thing;
> But he, sad, solemn, with dishonoured eyes,
> And altered aspect, bent stern brows on me,
> And well I knew that dread doom had come.
> 'Weak reed,' I cried, 'child in a strong man's arms!
> Be bruised and broken if thou wilt not yield!'
> But he, robed in invincible innocence,
> Rose with strange sorrow in his gaze, and bound

His sandals to his feet, and left the cave,
And journeyed to the city and his home.

By the middle of 1867, Symonds had completed over half of the John Mordan cycle. This new surge of creativity was in part due to his discovery of the poetry of Walt Whitman. 'This man has said what I have burned to say; what I should have done if opinion and authority and the contamination of vile lewdness had not ended in sophisticating my moral sense and muddling my brain.'[5] It was a discovery that would sharpen his poetic vision, and bridge the gap between the youthful idealism of his dreams and the reality of existence.

Despite Symonds's success in achieving self-acknowledgement, events of 1867 were to show that he had not yet matured sufficiently to reach the next stage identified by Siegel and Lowe, that of self-identification. His psychological development was hindered by his inability to discard the teachings of a conventional Christian morality and its rejection of homosexuality. This is clear from a letter written to W. J. Courthope: 'The forms of Greek life and art haunt me. They wait at my bedside and follow me about my walks , and seem to say: "Make marble for us out of words the world shall read, that we may live once more." Then a great storm sweeps through my mind, and I see Christ crowned with thorns and robed in purple, the blood-dew on His forehead.'[6] The crisis came at Cannes in December 1867, and as it subsided Symonds replaced the conventional Christian paradigm with a uniquely personal philosophy that he described as 'The religion of Cosmic Enthusiasm', a combination of scientific pantheism and Stoicism. Symonds's physical and mental health improved rapidly as he began to resolve his religious difficulties and realigned his concept of self to include his own homosexual identity. In taking this important step Symonds had opened the door upon the self-identification stage in his psychological development. It cleared the way for him to satisfy his emotional needs through the defining power of sexual intimacy with another man.

In December 1868 Symonds was introduced by Henry Graham Dakyns to a sixth-form student at Clifton College, Norman Moor. A passionate and tempestuous relationship ensued, and for the first time in his life Symonds experienced love that was both erotically charged and rich in sensuality. The whirlwind affair with Moor inspired Symonds to finish his series of Greek poems with 'Eudiades'. It was the crowning achievement to the first set of epic poems that make up the 'John Mordan Cycle'. In basing his verse upon actual experience, Symonds was at last able to transcend the world of dreams. To Henry Sidgwick he wrote: 'The poem was written with an attempt to realise an historical situation. You ask me what I meant by the temptation of the lovers. I chose to depict one of those young men of Plato's *Phaedrus* who recoil from acts which were permissible in Hellas.'[7] The overriding problem for Symonds, as with the ancient Greeks, was whether this love should remain asexual. It was a problem he evaded by killing off the lovers before they had become tainted by physicality. For Symonds love and death were inseparable.

Although this affair was short-lived, it was a psychological milestone in Symonds's life, as it marked a further progression towards his self-identification as a homosexual. He no longer needed external validation, and he had broken loose from many of society's conventional supports, such as religion. He was now able to recognize his emotional needs.

After Norman, Symonds began to explore the sexual side of his nature: 'With [Roden] Noel and with [Claude] Cobham, when they came to stay with me, I now and then gave way to lust – and always suffered from intense reactions.'[8] Despite his feelings of shame, Symonds was at least anchored to reality, and a whole new world of sensations, impressions, and desires was opened up. This brought about a striking change in his poetry. In October 1870 he wrote his 'Three Visions Of Imperial Rome'. He explained that the first of the visions, entitled 'Midnight At Baiaie', was conceived in a dream and written up later as a prose-poem. This evocative and voyeuristic piece portrays a scene in Caligula's palace in the hours following a night of debauchery and violent carnal excess. Symonds leads his readers through a labyrinth of sensuous description and decadent imagery and at the climax of the poem shocks them by making them accomplices in sadistic pleasure:

> Thereon I saw a naked form supine.
> It was a youth from foot to forehead laid
> In slumber. Very white and smooth and fine
> Were all his limbs; and on his breast there played
> The lambent smiles of lamplight. But a pool
> Of blood beneath upon the pavement stayed.
> There, where blue cups of lotos-lilies cool
> With reeds into mosaic-wreaths were blent,
> The black blood grew and curdled; and the wool
> Whereon his cloudy curls were pillowed, sent
> Thick drops slow-soaking down o'er gold and gem.
> Spell-bound I crept, and closer gazed at him:
> And lo! from side to side his throat was gashed
> With some keen blade; and every goodly limb,
> With marks of crisped fingers marred and lashed,
> Told the fierce strain of tyrannous lust that here
> Life's crystal vase of youth divine had dashed.

The death of his father, in February 1871, had a liberating effect. Symonds could now freely indulge his passions and pursue his ambitions of a literary career. A group of comrades that included T. E. Brown, Roden Noel, F. W. H. Myers, C. D. Cobham, and Edward Clifford encouraged and nurtured his poetic vocation and Symonds believed that through his poetry he could promote an atmosphere of acceptance and tolerance, thus bringing to his Victorian readers the kind of invigorating ideas and beliefs that Walt Whitman was propagating in America: 'My Prophecy of Love of Comrades as a future institution of Democracy came upon me; and I began to believe more in my own poetic vision.'[9] Symonds had found his artistic voice. He wished to become the Walt Whitman of England. He believed it was possible to breathe new life into the ancient Greek ideals, combining them with the Whitmanesque concepts of comradeship and adhesiveness, and thus create a new form of democracy. These ideas were expressed in a long prose poem called 'Love And Death: A Symphony'.

In October 1871 occurred an incident that had a profound effect upon him. It involved an assignation with a young soldier whom he had met in Hyde Park. He described the revulsion he felt as he 'touched the man immodestly'. 'This yielding to abnormal impulses pained [my] conscience with a terrible sense of danger and impending ruin.'[10] Symonds translated this experience into the poem 'The Upas Tree', later retitled 'The Valley of Vain Desires' for publication. In a letter to Mrs Arthur H. Clough, Symonds explained the poem: 'The Upas Tree is an allegory of the attractions which some forms of vice have for even the most beautiful natures, when they are tainted with morbidity and madness.' This is nowhere more starkly uttered than in the following passage, where thrill and revulsion coalesce in one intoxicating moment:

> . . . keen fever burned
> Yet in his veins: then he would crawl and lean
> Weak limbs against the trunk: – at times he spurned,
>
> At times he clutched the mellow fruit that green
> And rank bent downward to his panting lip . . .

It is clear that Symonds's psychological development was being arrested by the internalization of shame and guilt. This impasse was partly resolved while he was lecturing in London in 1877. His visit to a male brothel marked a momentously important milestone in his life and revealed yet another layer of truth about himself: 'For the first time in my experience I shared a bed with one so different from myself, so ardently desired by me, so supremely beautiful in my eyes, so attractive to my senses.'[11] For once, Symonds found sexual experience enjoyable. Here was a young soldier who offered him something that was both 'comradely and natural', and aroused in him passions that he had not conceived of before: 'I learned from it , that the physical appetite of one male for another may be made the foundation of a solid friendship.'[12]

In 1877 Symonds left England with his family and settled permanently in Davos. It was here that he finished *Rhaetica*, the last of the 'Peccant Pamphlets'. In Davos, he found a society uncluttered by the moral and cultural values that he believed were in part responsible for his psychological difficulties. He found a liberating environment in which he could assume a homosexual identity. His vision of a 'New Democracy' was brought sharply into focus by his friendship with a young Swiss peasant named Christian Buol, who was 'so dignified, so courteous, so comradely, realising at one and the same time for me all that I had dreamed of the democratic ideal and all that I desired in radiant manhood'. Symonds brought these Whitmanesque themes to fruition in his visionary poem, 'A Vista', which uses dream-vision to describe a utopia in which all mankind is ennobled by a democratic spirit and a deep sense of comradeship.

With Christian, Symonds found a comfortable and emotionally rewarding bond of friendship. He did not, however, have a sexual relationship with him. 'Absorbed in love, which was itself so spiritually sensual that the needs of the body disappeared and were forgotten . . . , I asked nothing except his proximity.'[13] Symonds closed the chapter on Christian in his memoirs with a poem that was omitted from the published edition. It recalls the memory of one perfect moment spent with him, and it is a meditation on the transience of beauty:

> Half-light of dawn in the hushed upper room
> Where all night long two comrades, side by side,

Have slumbered in the summer-scented gloom,
Fanned by the faint breezes from a window wide.

He sleeps, and stirs not. He meanwhile awake,
Steadfastly gazing and with mind intent
To drink soul-deep of beauty, dares not break
By breath or sigh his own heart's ravishment.

Bare arms light folded on the broad bare chest;
Dark curls crisp clustering round the athlete's head;
Shoulder and throat heroic; all is rest,
Marble with loveliest hues of life o'erspread.

Life in the glowing cheeks, the hands sun-brown,
The warm blood tingling to each finger tip;
Life in youth's earliest bloom of tender down,
Tawny on chin and strong upper lip:

Life in the cool white, flushed with faintest rose,
Of flank and heaving bosom, where each vein,
Half seen, a thread of softest violet, flows,
Like streaks that some full-throated lily stain.

Deep rest, and draught of slumber. Not one dream
Ruffles the mirror of that sentient sea,
Whereon the world and all its pride will gleam,
When the soul starts from sleep, so royally.

Hush! 'Tis a bell of morning. Far and near,
From sea-set tower and island chimes reply:
Thrills the still air with sound divinely clear;
And the stirred sleeper wakens with a sigh.[14]

In 1881, while Symonds was staying with Horatio Brown, he was introduced to a gondolier (and gigolo) called Angelo Fusato. Entranced, Symonds engaged him as a servant. This affair marks his transition to Siegel's and Lowe's second phase – accepting a homosexual identity. Symonds saw the possibility of lasting companionship, if only he could restore his damaged self-esteem and remove the concomitant feelings of shame and remorse that accompanied his sexual relationships. To accomplish such a change, he would need to integrate his homosexuality into the wider concept of self, and so redefine himself as normal and restore his sense of integrity. This process of self-examination found its cathartic relief in a series of sonnets entitled 'Stella Maris', or 'The Sea Calls'. Symonds wrote: 'I do not suppose I have ever expressed my deepest self so nakedly before as I have here.'[15]

Within a sequential narrative of 67 sonnets he described the emotional and spiritual journey that he had taken with Angelo. Symonds was at last able to overcome his feelings of shame and guilt. This healing process helped him to rebuild his damaged self-esteem and achieve a fuller acceptance of his homosexual identity. It also gave him the inner strength to face up to the tragic reality of his life, so powerfully stated in the closing lines of his memoirs: 'While he obeys the flesh, he is conscious of no wrong doing. When he awakes from the hypnotism of the flesh, he sees his own misdoing not in the glass of truth to his nature, but in the mirror of convention.'

By 1884, Symonds had entered the final phase of self-expression. As his confidence and his ability to celebrate his true sexual nature grew, he no longer needed therapeutic and cathartic release of poetry. He also realized that, if he was to effect a change in the understanding of and attitudes about homosexuality, he would have to engage the medico-legal profession directly. He therefore started work on his *Memoirs* (1889), on *A Problem in Modern Ethics* (1891), and on his collaborative work with Havelock Ellis, *Sexual Inversion* (1897).

Notes

1   Stanley Siegel and Edward Lowe Jr, *Unchartered Lives* (New York, 1994). See also Vivienne Cass, 'Homosexual Identity Formation: A Theoretical Model', *Journal of Homosexuality*, iv, 3 (Spring 1979).
2   J. A. Symonds, *The Memoirs of John Addington Symonds*, ed. Phyllis Grosskurth (New York, 1984), 99.
3   Ibid., 122.
4   Ibid., 189.
5   J. A. Symonds, *The Letters of John Addington Symonds*, ed. Herbert Schueller and Robert Peters (Detroit, 1967–9), i, 696.
6   Ibid., i, 783.
7   Symonds, *Memoirs*, 201.
8   London Library, Symonds's Memoirs (typescript), fol. 390.
9   Symonds, *Letters*, ii, 161.
10 London Library, Symonds's Memoirs, fol. 390.
11 Symonds, *Memoirs*, 253–4.
12 Ibid., 254.
13 Ibid., 266.
14 London Library, Symonds's Memoirs, fol. 408.
15 Symonds, *Letters*, ii, 708.

Index